DATE DUE

Opera Biographies

This is a volume in the
Arno Press collection

Opera Biographies

Advisory Editor
ANDREW FARKAS

Associate Editor
W.R. MORAN

See last pages of this volume
for complete list of titles

THE MEMOIRS OF

BENIAMINO GIGLI

TRANSLATED BY DARINA SILONE

ARNO PRESS

A New York Times Company

New York / 1977

Editorial Supervision: ANDREA HICKS

Reprint Edition 1977 by Arno Press Inc.

Reprinted from a copy in
The University of Michigan Library

OPERA BIOGRAPHIES
ISBN for complete set: 0-405-09666-6
See last pages of this volume for titles.

Manufactured in the United States of America

Library of Congress Cataloging in Publication Data

Gigli, Beniamino, 1890-1957.
The memoirs of Beniamino Gigli.

(Opera biographies)
Reprint of the 1957 ed. published by Cassell, London.
Discography:
1. Gigli, Beniamino, 1890-1957. 2. Singers--Biography. I. Title.
[ML420.G43A313 1977] 782.1'092'4 [B] 76-29937
ISBN 0-405-09679-8

BENIAMINO GIGLI

THE MEMOIRS OF
BENIAMINO GIGLI

TRANSLATED BY DARINA SILONE

With a frontispiece, 24 pages of half-tone illustrations and a discography

CASSELL & COMPANY LTD
LONDON

CASSELL & COMPANY LTD
37-38 St. Andrew's Hill, Queen Victoria Street
London, E.C.4

and at

31–34 George IV Bridge, Edinburgh
210 Queen Street, Melbourne
26–30 Clarence Street, Sydney
24 Wyndham Street, Auckland, New Zealand
1068 Broadview Avenue, Toronto 6
P.O. Box 275, Cape Town
P.O. Box 11190, Johannesburg
58 Pembroke Street, Port of Spain, Trinidad
Haroon Chambers, South Napier Road, Karachi
13–14 Ajmeri Gate Extension, New Delhi 1
15 Graham Road, Ballard Estate, Bombay 1
17 Chittaranjan Avenue, Calcutta 13
Macdonald House, Orchard Road, Singapore 9
P.O. Box 959, Accra, Ghana
Avenida 9 de Julho 1138, SaoPaulo
Galeria Guemes, Escritorio 454–59 Florida 165, Buenos Aires
Marne 5b, Mexico 5, D.F.
25 rue Henri Barbusse, Paris 5e
Bederstrasse 51, Zurich 2
25 Ny Strandvej, Espergaerde, Denmark
Kauwlaan 17, The Hague

First Published 1957

Set in 12pt. Bembo type and printed in Great Britain by Wyman and Sons, Ltd., London, Fakenham and Reading

F.257

TO THE

MEMORY OF MY MOTHER

and

TO ALL MY AUDIENCES

CONTENTS

ILLUSTRATIONS

CHAPTER I

HOW I BECAME A SINGER

I WAS born with a voice and very little else: no money, no influence, no other talents. Had it not been for the peculiar formation of my vocal cords, I should probably at this moment be planing tables or sewing trousers, or mending shoes as my father did, in the little Italian town of Recanati where I was born on March 20th, 1890. I should still be poor, as my father was. But God gave me a voice, and that changed everything. I was good at singing, and nothing else. I enjoyed singing, and nothing else. I *had* to sing: what else could I do?

This makes my life sound easy, and in a way it was: I never needed to doubt, hesitate, retrace my steps, begin again; I never needed to choose or decide. There was only one thing I could do, so I did it. But the old, dim church where I sang as a choir-boy was a long way off from the footlights of the Metropolitan. It took me many years of patience, rebuffs, hunger and hard work to get from the one to the other. Looking back now, I feel glad that my early years were years of hardship and struggle; had my career as a tenor required no more effort than the opening of my mouth to let the sound come forth, I could scarcely have a sense of achievement.

Perhaps it was from my mother that I inherited my voice; at any rate, she was the first person who taught me to sing. When I was little, she always sang me to sleep with old peasant lullabies, and gradually, as I emerged from babyhood, the lullaby became a duet. Every evening before I fell asleep she would sit with her arm round my shoulders, her cheek close to mine, and we would sing together. She encouraged me, flattered me, told me I already sang better than she did, which I would hotly deny; but she invariably added the warning that in order to sing well one had to be good and kind and feel love in one's heart.

One of the songs, I remember, was about a girl locked up in a convent and pining for her sweetheart; it contained the lines:

'My mother a countess
My father a knight . . .'

For a long time I assumed, in some childish way, that the words applied to me, that *my* mother was a countess, *my* father a knight. I admired my mother so much, and thought her so beautiful, that it all seemed perfectly natural to me; but in reality things were very different. My parents were poor artisans, and just about that time, when I was five or so, they lost what little they had.

My father, Domenico Gigli, 'il Roscio' (the Red-haired) as he was nicknamed, was a cobbler by trade; my mother, Ester, was the daughter of a country schoolmaster. My father could make shoes as well as mend them; at the end of the nineteenth century, factory-made shoes were only beginning to reach the smaller places of provincial Italy, and if you could afford boots or shoes at all you got them, directly or indirectly, from the cobbler who had made them, perhaps with the help of an assistant or apprentice, in his own little workshop.

The shoes my father made were not pretty or fashionable; he catered, not for the noble families living close by in their gloomy, stern old palaces, but for farmers, small tradespeople, artisans—the humble folk of Recanati. All the same, he took an honest pride in doing his work well, in making good strong boots that would stand up to wear. He never expected his customers to order a new pair every year. One pair was meant to last a lifetime, and, indeed, was sometimes handed down from father to son. Of course, such long-lived boots were not worn every day; for ordinary purposes people usually wore wooden clogs, and my father made these also.

As can easily be imagined, it was not the sort of work that brought in big profits; but living was cheap in those days, and we lived very modestly. My mother was an energetic woman, for in spite of having six children she generally found time, after getting through the housework, to help my father. She learned to sew the upper parts of a boot, first by hand and then by machine; indeed, I believe she was the first person in Recanati to learn how to use the sewing-machine for leather. She liked to improvise floral designs with a white thread on the black leather;

I suppose it gave her an outlet for some latent artistic impulse.

I was the youngest of six children, four boys and two girls. I was born into this atmosphere of quiet, laborious contentment, but I can barely remember it. When I was about five, there were puzzling changes. My father sent away most of his workmen, and my brothers left school and began working for him instead. Sometimes, when our supper was more meagre than usual, I would notice that my mother looked worried; but of course I had no notion of what was happening.

Later on, I found out that my father had been hit by the first competitive blows of mass-production. Some middlemen in neighbouring towns, who had always placed steady orders with him, went bankrupt; and he had no savings to fall back on, to tide him over the difficulty or enable him to experiment. Moreover, he was an old-fashioned man, a man of tradition, unable to comprehend the machinery that was slowly grinding him and his kind out of existence, leaving hand-made shoes as a luxury reserved for the rich.

I can only remember deriving enjoyment from the new situation. It meant that instead of clinging to my mother's skirts, I began to do things on my own. I had to; even I, the five-year-old, could help—I could run errands.

Often, for instance, I would be sent to Mastro Parò, the carpenter, to fetch a supply of wooden heels for the hobnailed peasant boots which my father made. Mastro Parò soon found out that I could sing; after my mother, he was my first audience. He would plant me on his bench, while I looked down in terror at the ground, too far below me to jump, and pleaded that my father wanted the heels in a hurry; but there was no escape for me until I sang. He would demand the latest song-hit; I already knew them all. When I had finished, there among the wood shavings, the chisels and the dust, I got my first applause.

I suppose he must have told the neighbours about me, for I soon found myself being waylaid by all sorts of people begging me for a song. I took longer and longer to do my errands, for no matter what time of day it was, as I trudged up or tottered down the precipitous narrow streets, there was always some old woman sitting lace-making in her doorway, ready with a sweet to bribe me; or if I went to play with other children around the fountain in the square, the old men chatting in the shade would call me over to them, and there was no getting on with the game until they were satisfied. Quite apart from the odd reward of sweets or pennies, whatever annoyance I might feel at the interruption was offset by a strange feeling of elation that, looking back, I can recognize clearly. Throughout my life I have felt it whenever an aria, a phrase, a single note well sung has moved my audience and made me one with them. It is the feeling that a deep-rooted need is being fulfilled—the singer's need for applause, for recognition, but also for communion. We singers are often accused of being vain, and, indeed, one comic episode before the footlights after another proves that many of us are so; but more often than not this vanity is only a distorted reflection of the urge we feel to be reassured that we are in contact, that through our singing (for we are sometimes so helpless in other ways) we can reach out, beyond the barrier of impresarios and camp-followers, to the hearts of our fellow-men. I need hardly say that these are afterthoughts, but they do have some bearing on the pleasure I felt increasingly, as a child, whenever I was asked for 'just one little song, Beniaminello'.

Singing was by no means my only pleasure, however. Indeed, had anyone asked me, when I was five or six, what I most enjoyed doing, I would probably have answered: 'Playing *piastrella*'—a game not unlike the English 'conkers', in which walnuts or peach-stones took the place of chestnuts. My passion for this game once led to a misadventure which my brothers have never allowed me to forget. It was in summer, and very hot; I had had a triumphant afternoon playing *piastrella* in the square, demolishing and confiscating the peach-stone 'castles' of the other boys. When the game was over I crept home, elated and awed by my new wealth; I had amassed a small fortune in peach-stones. Determined to be left in peace while counting them and gloating over them, I retired under the big bed in my sisters' room.

The hours passed, it was supper-time, and my place at table stayed empty. There was a hullabaloo; my brothers were sent out to search the town; my sisters, Ada and Ida, tried to comfort my mother, who was having the usual visions of disaster; my brothers returned empty-handed; my father declared there was nothing for it but to tell the police. Suddenly my mother stood up, as if on an inspiration, and seizing a broom, began poking into every corner and under every piece of furniture in the house, until she found me fast asleep on my hoard of peach-stones under my sisters' bed.

Meanwhile one after another of my father's few remaining wholesale customers had gone bankrupt or failed to renew their orders; apart from some farmer's daughter wanting a pair of boots for her trousseau, local custom had dwindled to repairing the solid footwear that people already possessed. By this time it was plain that shoemaking alone could no longer support the family. It was decided that of my three brothers, only Egidio should stay on to keep the workshop going; Abramo left it to study for the priesthood, and Catervo (later to become a sculptor) got himself apprenticed to a cabinet-maker. As for my father, to his sorrow he was forced to give up his only skill and look about him for odd jobs. He got a hawker's licence and a barrow, and went here and there to country fairs, selling ribbons, trinkets, bootlaces, gaudy scarves, whatever came to hand. I often went with him, and for me it was fun; but he had no heart in his shoddy wares, and it was a relief to my mother, who was fretting about him, when a steady and dignified job came his way at last.

The Cathedral bellringer died, my father applied for the post, and being honest, sober, a churchgoer and father of a large family, he was appointed. It meant a tiny but regular income, a few scraps of land from which rent might be collected, and free lodgings next to the Cathedral. We moved in at once, and at first my parents thought they had 'caught Saint Anthony by the beard', as the saying goes in our parts. It was splendid to live in the Cathedral square, thrilling to climb the steps of the bell tower and summon the citizens of Recanati to their prayers. Our family wore a new dignity in the town. But this very dignity meant that my father could no longer peddle haberdashery in his spare time; and if his bellringer's wages bought us bread, they did not allow of much soup and spaghetti. So our new life, as it turned out, was not much easier than the old one. To me, the six-year-old, however, it opened new horizons.

From the age of six I grew up in the shadow of the Cathedral; it formed me, taught me, gave me my first opportunities. For a poor boy, coming as I did from an unlettered family, its very stones were an education, far more of an education than I got in the primary school where I was now spending the first of the five obligatory years of resigned boredom, devoted to the three R's which were to be the sum total of my formal instruction.

No one ever seems to have heard of Recanati Cathedral; it is barely mentioned in the more detailed guide-books, and tourists anxiously looking for the birthplace of the poet Giacomo Leopardi give it at most a glance. Artistically speaking, I suppose it is inferior to some of the other churches in Recanati: it is a modest, homely little Cathedral, dating from the Middle Ages but re-fashioned and re-touched by many hands in the centuries between—the very place for a child to learn about the past. For years it seemed to me a kind of annexe to my own home. The services which took place there became as much a part of my daily routine as eating, sleeping or going to school, since for each one of them my father had to climb the bell tower and ring the bells; but at the same time the music, the chanting, the incense, the choir singing gave me my first encounter with mystery, my first poetic experience.

There, in the shadowy quiet lit only by candles and the solitary lamp burning before the tabernacle, my eyes opened on the world. I was not in the least precocious or imaginative; indeed, I was a very ordinary boy, but even so, with the sculptured and frescoed saints of long-dead artists for my familiars, I could scarcely help acquiring a sense of the past—the Italian past, at any rate. I have never been a student of art or history, or anything at all except singing; I know few names outside of opera, and no dates; but after a childhood spent running in and out of the Cathedral, I somehow come to find myself aware of all those bygone centuries, of all those artists, architects and artisans whose work was guided by a love of beauty so prodigal that it could spill out from Rome and Florence and Venice, to create marvels in an obscure place like Recanati.

I felt at home with these marvels, since they were literally on my doorstep, but I also felt reverence for them. At some stage it began to dawn on me that I too was an Italian, and I felt glad and proud. Later, whenever my singing was applauded in distant places such as Buenos Aires or San Francisco or Cape Town, I always felt that the applause was due more to Italy than to me personally, for without Italy I should have been nothing. The

(*Above*). A view of Recanati, the town of my birth

(*Right*). The interior of Recanati Cathedral, where I sang as a boy

(*Below*). The tablet on the wall tells visitors to Recanati that I was born in the room whose window is immediately beneath it

My first operatic rôle at fifteen — as a soprano! Angelica in the operetta 'La Fuga di Angelica' at the Teatro Lauri Rossi in Macerata

In more normal attire at the age of fourteen in Recanati

thought of Italy has always meant for me, first and foremost, the simple, beautiful, ancient buildings and landscape which surrounded me in childhood.

Sometimes my mother would take me with her to attend Benediction in some other church. I always wanted it to be Santa Maria sopra Mercanti, because I had discovered a picture there that I never tired of looking at. She had explained to me that it represented the Annunciation, but I liked it because of the cat. The cat made the Annunciation real for me. There it was, right in the middle of the Blessed Virgin's room, arching its back in resentful astonishment at the angel, this intruder with a lily in his hand. The angel's hair was windswept; he did look as if he might have flown straight down from heaven. In the left foreground, the young Virgin, beautiful and modest, had turned away from the book she was reading. She had obviously just heard the angel's words and was making a gesture of obedient acceptance. This was just how she really had looked, I felt; this was just how it really had happened. In the left background stood a washstand—hers, obviously—with a water-jug, and a towel folded over it—just like at home, only grander, of course. Beyond the balcony in the right background you could see a vine-trellised pergola, an umbrella-pine, and a cypress. The Holy Land was apparently just like Italy. Then my eyes would return to the cat. It was fascinating to think that Our Lady had had a cat. Did the angel allow her to keep it afterwards, I wondered?

Many years later, when I was at the Metropolitan, New York, I went back for a holiday to Recanati, and paid a visit to my childhood favourite in Santa Maria sopra Mercanti. My interest no longer centred on the cat, but I still thought the picture beautiful—the best picture of the Annunciation I had ever seen. It was painted, I discovered, by the great Renaissance Venetian, Lorenzo Lotto. As I looked again at the washstand and the trellised vine, I thought of how my two children, in New York, were being taught Art as a subject, and taken in groups to visit museums on Saturday mornings. Well, no doubt they already knew more about it than I would ever know.

Leaving the church, I decided to walk home. Recanati is built on a hill-top; the surrounding plain undulates softly from the foot of the serene Apennines to the shores of the Adriatic. The sea is only five miles away from the town, and I had recently built a house half-way between the two. As I walked along the cypress-bordered road, I saw farmers ploughing their fields with great white oxen, and a girl kneeling beside a stream, washing her long black hair. Then the fields gave way to olive groves, where vines had been trained to enlace the gnarled branches of the trees. It takes centuries of loving care to make a vineyard yield good wine, and Verdicchio, the pale green-gold wine of the countryside around Recanati, is very good indeed. The painter of the Annunciation had made the Holy Land look like Italy, but after all, I thought, maybe he was not so far wrong; what lay before my eyes at that very moment might well have been a landscape of the Old Testament. Again I felt grateful for having grown up in Recanati, where all I knew of heaven and all I knew of earth had touched and intermingled at every step. My children were growing up in New York; suddenly I felt anxious. With all their advantages, they were missing so much. Would all be well with them?

I have tried to give some idea of what the Cathedral taught me, but I have not yet spoken of the most important thing of all: it taught me singing. I was not quite seven when Maestro Quirino Lazzarini, the Cathedral organist, asked my parents to let me join the Schola Cantorum. This was a boys' choir which he had recently founded in the Cathedral, modelling it on that of the Basilica in the neighbouring town of Loreto. I owe a great deal to Maestro Lazzarini. He was a remarkable man, disinterestedly devoted to music, endlessly kind and patient with small boys who showed any signs of talent. He took pride in building up his choir, and it soon enjoyed quite a reputation in our part of the world. At that time Gregorian chant was not obligatory, and we had a varied repertory which included sacred music by Rossini and Gounod, pieces written specially for us by Maestro Lazzarini himself, and the works of the young Don Lorenzo Perosi, for whom our maestro had a kind of hero-worship. Don Perosi was already director of the Sistine Chapel choir, and an eminent composer of church music in the great Italian tradition that began with Palestrina. Throughout my life it has always given me great pleasure to interpret his music, and in later years, I am proud to say, he honoured me with his friendship.

There were about twenty of us in the Schola Cantorum. For some time I was the baby, and the maestro had to stand me on a stool so that my head might appear above the railing of the organ-loft. He treated me very affectionately and took great pains to teach me. I saw nothing out of the way in this—as the youngest in my family I was used to being petted—until finally it dawned on me that I was being trained to sing the solo parts.

Singing in the Cathedral choir now became my chief delight. This was something entirely different from amusing Mastro Parò. It was beautiful and thrilling; it gave me a sense of importance—I might almost say, a sense of purpose. At school I was more or less a dunce; in the choir, it seemed, I was the most promising of all. Maestro Lazzarini was leading me into a new world, and I felt able and eager to follow him. After singing solo at a Pontifical High Mass for the first time, I knew for certain that I wanted to be a singer.

That, of course, was still in the remote future, and I had no idea of how it could come about. I was still a very small boy, with only the vaguest notion of practical difficulties. Meanwhile our choir was beginning to be invited to give concerts here and there, mostly in the neighbouring towns and villages of our own province of Le Marche, although on one splendid occasion we travelled half-way across Italy, as far as Cortona, to sing at a special ceremony in honour of the city's patron, Saint Margaret. Sometimes we were paid a small fee, and I was very proud of my first professional earnings, as I handed them over to my mother.

I lost no time in learning that a singer's life has its ups and downs. One summer our choir made a trip to Ancona. We left Recanati at dawn; the train was very crowded and we had to stand in the corridor all the way; then we stood all through the sweltering heat of late morning at the Mass in Ancona Cathedral. Our maestro saw to it that we got a good meal afterwards, washed down, for a treat, with some Verdicchio. He gave us the afternoon off to explore Ancona; it was the biggest city I had ever seen, and my brother Catervo and I trudged all over it in wonderment. When the time came for us to board the slow train back to Recanati, we were worn out. Stumbling drowsily down the darkened corridor, we took possession of an empty compartment. The seats were hard boards, but we were soon stretched out full length on them, fast asleep.

That was all very well, but when trains actually condescend to stop at the station of Porto Recanati, they only stop for one minute. By the time Maestro Lazzarini had counted his sleepy charges on the platform and discovered that two were missing, the train was already puffing out of sight. My brother and I slept on until we were awakened, three hours later, by the strident voice of a vendor selling hot coffee in the station of San Benedetto del Tronto. We made a frenzied leap from the train just as it began to move. It was six in the morning, and we had only a few coppers between us, not nearly enough to buy tickets back to Recanati. There seemed to be nothing for it but to walk, so, averting our eyes from the temptation of the hot-coffee vendor (our pennies, we agreed, had to be saved for midday) we set out.

The July sun beat fiercely down on us as we plodded along the dusty road. Now and then we got a lift from some kindly peasant with a donkey and cart; the donkey's pace was not much faster than ours, but it was blissful to rest for a while, squeezed in between the scythes and the sacks of manure. Twice we stopped at wayside taverns, feeling rather grown-up as we ordered a slice of bread and a glass of wine apiece; unfortunately we rather spoiled the effect by carefully inquiring beforehand how much it would cost, and doing hasty mental arithmetic.

At six o'clock in the evening we reached home, filthy, ravenous, with bleeding feet, and in a state of collapse. Never again, I sobbed, as I buried my face in my mother's apron, never again would I leave home to go and sing in strange places. Never again!

I was growing up. People no longer offered me peppermints when they wanted to hear me sing. The fact was, I no longer waited to be asked. Singing had become so necessary and so delightful to me that I could scarcely bear to stop. I am afraid that this may sound like a Hollywood script-writer's notion of the Singer's Boyhood, but it happens to be true. I sang at home, I sang in the streets; and best of all I loved to climb the steps of the bell tower and sing out at the top of my voice, far above the roofs, into the clear air. This earned me the nickname of '*il canarino del campanile*', the bell-tower canary; and as long as I remained in Recanati, I never lived it down.

Apart, however, from Maestro Lazzarini's patient training in the Cathedral choir, no particular fuss was made by anyone about my voice. The choir, after all, was a side-line; there was no talk of singing as a career, though somewhere inside me hope lingered obstinately. In due course I would get my primary school certificate and learn a trade, and that would be that. So far as my family and the neighbours were concerned, singing was my accomplishment, my recreation, my mania; it kept me out of mischief; above all, it gave me a '*sfogo*'.

This, of course, they considered important. To have a *sfogo* —an outlet—is one of the prime necessities of life for an Italian. '*Beniamino si sta sfogando,*' they would say in tones of indulgent approval, when they heard me warbling *Tantum ergo* on my way home from school. 'Beniamino is letting off steam.' Italian children are not trained to be shy or reticent, to imprison their feelings or curb their impulses; on the contrary, long before the days of 'permissiveness', even by parents who never laid eyes on a manual of child psychology, children were always encouraged to let whatever was inside them—good or bad—come out into the fresh air. If it is good, why suppress it? If it is bad, better get rid of it; it might be poisonous, like pus. Either way, a *sfogo* is healthy, a safety valve for the nervous system. This capacity for *sfogo*, acquired in childhood, becomes second nature to us Italians. We explode with anger, excitement, joy, we shout or sing: at once we feel better. I know that strangers to Italy find it somewhat disconcerting, but I think it helps to keep us sane, or at any rate cheerful.

Singing was to become my career, my whole life; but the neighbours were not far wrong in deciding that it was my *sfogo*. Basically it was just that. Even now, no matter how angry I may feel about something, I have only to open my mouth and let out a few bars of, say, '*Questa o quella per me pari sono . . .*' I am amazed to find how quickly my anger subsides, unspoken. When the day is fine, or I start winning the family game of poker, my gaiety almost invariably bubbles over into a snatch of '*La donna è mobile*' or whatever tune comes to my mind. As I write, it comes back to me how I once got stuck for three-quarters of an hour by myself, between two floors, in the lift of an English hotel, just as I was leaving it to give my concert. Down below me on the next landing, the organizers of the concert were terrified. They expected me to be 'temperamental', to get into a fury or a frantic state of nerves and sing badly, or perhaps refuse to sing at all. They were rather surprised by the sounds they heard coming from the prisoner in the lift. I felt I had either to scream with exasperation (which would have been bad for my voice anyway) or to sing. So I sang. I rehearsed my concert. It was rather like playing a record in one of those little booths in a gramophone shop, only this time I was the record. I went right through the numbers on my programme. I had just got to the end, and was about to give an (unsolicited) encore, when the lift started working again. I emerged in high feather, feeling secretly rather pleased with myself, and hastily assured the bewildered people that their concert would be all right, thanks to my *sfogo*.

There is one time of day, I must admit, at which I have never felt any inclination to sing, and that is the early morning. Physically speaking, it has always been very difficult for me to do so: many singers, of whom I am one, seem to wake up with a kind of catarrh which produces hoarseness for several hours, until it has all been got rid of. But quite apart from this, I would rather sleep late than sing early. There is nothing of the lark about me, and my boyhood memories become painful when they begin to dwell on icy winter mornings before dawn.

I had taken over new duties at the Cathedral. I was altar-boy now, as well as choir-boy. A French priest, Don Romano Dupanchel, had asked me to be his acolyte. For my services, such as they were, he paid me two *soldi* a day. I have since heard that it is very unusual for acolytes to be paid anything, so I am afraid it was pure charity on the good Father's part, though I was unaware of it at the time. In order to earn—as I thought—these two *soldi*, I had to get up at half-past six and serve seven o'clock Mass for him before going out to school. My mother, poor woman, needed all her energy to wake me. She had to pummel me and roll me over on the bed, and even then I often fell asleep again. Don Romano was a saintly old man, and never scolded me for arriving late and sleepy-eyed, nor even for getting the Latin responses mixed up.

The tortures of early rising were mitigated only by the proud thought that they were helping to support my family. Two *soldi* a day did not amount to much, even then, but it was better than nothing. Our budget remained chronically unbalanced, despite the fact that my mother also had become an employee of the Cathedral: she swept, scrubbed, dusted and polished it for eleven *soldi* a day. She was always intending to put my two *soldi* into a clothing fund for me, but somehow there was usually a more pressing need to be met, such as the family supper. Without my humble 'earnings', this would often have consisted of nothing but dry bread and a slice of raw onion or a green pepper apiece; and the thick bean and macaroni soup—*pasta e fagioli*—on the occasions when it was provided by me, tasted more delicious than anything I have ever eaten since.

On summer evenings, after I had served Benediction or Vespers for Don Romano, he would sometimes take me for a walk to the Colle dell'Infinito. In his gentle voice, with the clipped French accent that had survived a lifetime in Italy, and had seemed so comical to me in the beginning—he was the first foreigner I had ever known—he would tell me that this 'Hill of the Infinite' was called after a famous poem by Leopardi, that Leopardi was the greatest Italian poet, next to Dante, that he was born and grew up in Recanati, and that I must know what he looked like because his statue stood in the Piazza.

The hunchbacked poet's sad and lonely life brought tears of sympathy to my eyes, but on the whole I am afraid I disappointed Don Romano. The 'Infinite' was too much for me; I preferred his stories about old feuds and bygone battles. I marvelled that Recanati should still exist, comfortably and safely, so many centuries after the Ancient Romans, the Goths, the Lombards and a dozen others had done with wresting it from each other, burning it down and building it up again.

'Recanati people must have changed a lot,' I said to Don Romano once. 'They seem to have been quite fierce in those days.'

He smiled. 'Did you ever hear about Pope John XXII and the Devil? It was a long time ago, in the days when Christians thought nothing of leaving home for years on end, to go and fight the Turks and try to get the Holy Land back from them. The people of Recanati had been causing such trouble, picking quarrels and provoking wars with all their neighbours, that the Pope came to the conclusion they must be possessed by the Devil.'

'And were they really, Father?' I wanted to know.

'Well, my child, it was never actually an article of Faith. At any rate, the Pope proclaimed a Crusade against them, just as if they had been Turks. To everyone taking part in it he granted the same indulgences as they would have gained by fighting the Turks. The enemies of Recanati—there were quite a few of them, naturally—jumped at the opportunity. They saved their souls without any of the trouble or expense of an expedition to the Holy Land, and they got their revenge into the bargain. They certainly must have chased the Devil away; I don't see any sign of him here now, do you, Beniamino?'

I was very fond of Don Romano, but you never quite knew when he was joking. This kind of talk puzzled me: it was altogether different from what I had learned in the catechism class. Our own Italian priests took the Devil very seriously.

'But, Father,' I protested, 'isn't the Devil beside us all the time, tempting us to be wicked?'

Don Romano only laughed. 'Oh, don't worry too much about the poor old Devil, Beniamino,' he said. 'He's kept so busy in the big cities, I doubt if he has any time left now to bother about Recanati.'

Those were glorious days, when Recanati could arouse a Pope to wrath. But now it was true what Don Romano said; the Devil seemed to have lost interest in this peaceful backwater. It was an innocent sort of place. No one had ever explained to its inhabitants how affairs were conducted in the great world that lay beyond the Apennines. To them, Rome and Milan were remote, frightening Babylons—even more remote and frightening, somehow, than New York or Philadelphia, where at least one knew that one would find Antonio the baker's nephew and Gigetto the saddler's first cousin. Whenever my father announced at supper: 'Annamaria So-and-so has had a letter,' we all knew what he meant: a registered letter, containing dollars, from her son in Newark, New Jersey. In almost every Recanati family (ours was an exception) there was someone who had 'crossed the water'—driven by restlessness, hopeless poverty, or daydreams of American gold—and most of them had managed, God alone knew how, to dig their heels in on the other side and send home registered letters. A few would-be emigrants had returned, empty-handed and disillusioned, to bewilder an audience of loiterers in the Piazza with gibberish about '*il bosso*' (Italo-American for boss) and '*la giobba*' (job), and to be known for the rest of their lives as '*Americani*'. Life in Recanati, from the cradle to the grave, followed such time-honoured patterns and was set in such rigid grooves, that if anyone wanted to strike out for himself, America seemed to be the only place to do it in. Piazza Leopardi and Mulberry Street were the two poles of possible existence: in between, nobody knew of anywhere else to go.

This was the society to which my parents belonged; so perhaps it is understandable that, when I finally told them of my resolve to be a singer, they should have dismissed it with a fond smile. I found myself smiling in the same way recently at my youngest grandson, when he informed me of his plans for the future: to start a motor-car factory on the moon. My ambition, to my parents, can have sounded only a little less fantastic than this sounded to me. When I pleaded, they reasoned with me. *Where* could I be a singer? Not in Recanati: the only place to sing in Recanati was the Cathedral, and I was there already, and while the small sums I earned occasionally were very welcome, they would never amount to a livelihood. Not in America: people went to America to work as stonemasons or carpenters, not to sing. Where else was there to go? Grudgingly they admitted the existence of places in between—Rome, for instance. Maybe Rome was the place, all right, but once there, how did one become a singer? Nobody knew the answer.

'Besides,' my father would say, 'there's no money in it. Musicians starve, everyone knows that. Learn a good, honest trade, my son,' he would add, momentarily forgetting his own experiences, 'and you'll never regret it.'

"And you know, Beniamino,' my mother would chime in, 'I wouldn't like you to sing on the stage. I don't think it's quite right—not if you do it for money, anyway,' she once concluded cryptically.

If it was not one objection, it was another. Illogical, contradictory, what did it matter? The real difficulty lay deeper than words. Despite their poverty, my parents were quite unable to envisage me as a professional singer; or if they were, they shrank from the notion; it was abhorrent to them. It lay outside their range; it belonged to the cruel, baffling world beyond the Apennines, as did the shoe factories that had ruined my father's craft.

For the time being, it seemed, I might as well obey my parents: what else could I do? I was only eight when, in their anxiety that I should learn a trade, they had begun sending me to Mastro

Parò in the long summer holidays, to acquire the rudiments of carpentry. For two summers I was a carpenter's apprentice, but not, I think, a very apt one. When I was ten, they decided I might do better as a tailor; and the next two summers were spent grappling uneasily with thimble, needle and thread. That cannot have been much of a success either, for when I left school for good, at the age of twelve, no more was said about tailoring. Signor Verdecchia, the chemist, needed a boy to help in the shop: I got the job, and kept it for the five remaining years that I was to spend in Recanati. It was not at all a bad job, as jobs go; but all the time, as I stood behind the counter, a question kept throbbing in my head: 'How can I become a singer? How, without money, can I become a singer?'

CHAPTER II

THE CHEMIST'S ASSISTANT

EVERYONE thought I had settled down for life as the chemist's assistant who sang so nicely. Why should I ever give up such a pleasant, safe, easy job? Why should anyone help me to give it up? For five years, no one did. It was a long wait, and I was almost beginning to lose hope. Then, by one of those accidents on which life so often seems to hinge, I met the right person. This person understood my problem, which was always the same: how, without money, could I become a singer? He helped me; he encouraged me; he found the answer for me. Had it not been for him, I might never have got to Rome, never had my voice trained properly. More than to any other single individual, I owe my career to him. He was not important or influential or rich; he was not even very intelligent. He was not an impresario or a bishop or a member of parliament. He was a cook.

Later in this chapter I shall tell the story of how I came to meet him, but meanwhile there were still five years to be lived through in Recanati; five years in which I could make only crablike, sideways approaches to the fulfilment of my ambition—five dusty, drowsy, provincial years of rattling the Venetian blinds up and down in the Farmacia on sunbaked afternoons, of half-heartedly swatting flies, of sticking labels on bottles. A waste of time, years lost to my career? I used to think so; but it seems increasingly clear to me, as I grow older, that nothing in life is useless or unimportant. Those slow, dreamy years were fruitful in their own way.

Now that I have retired, the thing I most enjoy doing is sitting quietly in my garden, with my Alsatian bitch Zara for company, and looking back at the past. I settle myself in the cane armchair and throw a ball for Zara to fetch. She loves that. What a commotion she makes, kicking up the gravel as she tears after it down the path! I never really had time to play with Zara before, but now I have all the time in the world—no journalist for an interview at two-thirty, no train to be caught at five-forty-seven, no curtain going up at eight. At last I have time to think—or, if thinking is too big a word, time to dream the hours away. When did I ever have it before? Memory, like a spool of film unwinding backwards, shows me a series of glimpses—now blurred, now distinct: batons raised for the overture, glasses raised for the after-dinner toast in some language I cannot speak, audiences clapping, wheels whirring to carry me elsewhere. The images recur, overlap, recede, are crowded out by others: myself, anywhere, got up in velvet doublet or leather jerkin, singing some operatic rôle—any one of sixty; myself in Rome, summoned in the interval to the royal box; playing Father Christmas to the orphans of New York firemen; in Detroit, guarded by detectives because mysterious enemies have threatened to assassinate me; in Venice, hurrying at midnight from a glittering benefit concert at Verdi's Fenice opera-house, to repeat my programme for an audience of gondoliers, scullery-boys and impecunious honeymoon couples, under the stars in the Piazza San Marco; on the Piave, in 1917, singing for the troops; in the wings of the Teatro Sociale at Rovigo, in 1914, gulping black coffee to brace myself for my début. What a fantastic kind of life it was, for a humble Recanati boy! I enjoyed it all, of course—all forty-one years of my life as a singer; but where was the time to sit and think, to sit and dream? Well, earlier, perhaps—student days? The film of memory unwinds again to show a garret in Rome, a footman's livery flung aside for an hour as I rush to a singing lesson. . . .

No, there seems nowhere to pause, nowhere to be quiet, until I find myself back in the Farmacia Verdecchia with the cough syrup, the magnesia powder and the flies. That is why I have come to the conclusion that the years I spent there were not wasted. They gave me time: time to develop will-power and faith in myself; time to dream, and to let my dreams solidify into resolution.

Time to spare: for anyone leading a public life, what a luxury it is. I had it then, when I was looking forward; now that the time has come for looking back, I have it again, at last. As for the headlong pace of the years between—well, it is only fair that success should have to be paid for somehow. If, as I hope, I have managed to remain sane and simple in spite of it all—if I have not changed too unrecognizably from what I was before I crossed the Apennines—I think it is largely due to the five years in which, before becoming a singer, I had time to become myself.

But I am growing too solemn and straying too far from the twelve-year-old boy behind the counter. It may seem in contrast with what I have just written to add that I worked an eleven-hour day in the Farmacia; but in reality there were long periods of doing nothing, no one was in a hurry, and I could always get time off if I asked for it. Being rather shy, docile and 'soft'—not the lively, mischievous type of Italian ragamuffin—I didn't ask very often; it was my first real, grown-up job and I was very proud of it, but also scared of doing it badly. Of course the work was easy enough and I became quite good at it in the end. In fact, I grew so fond of the Farmacia that, had it not been for wanting to sing, I could have stayed there, quite contentedly, for the rest of my life.

The Cathedral had opened my eyes to the past: the Farmacia gave me my first insight into the everyday world of grown-ups. In the small towns of Central and Southern Italy the chemist's shop has always been something more than just a shop; it is also a place for conversation, a clearing-house for local gossip—a sort of club, in fact, at once democratic and genteel: democratic because access is free to all, genteel because there is a vague atmosphere of culture (all those Latin names on the little drawers and on the big, coloured jars) and no tavern rowdiness. (Of course, Recanati was equipped with a proper club, the Circolo dei Signori, a sanctum reserved for members of the local gentry: but that was another matter.) I overheard far more than was good for me in the way of gossip between Signor Verdecchia and his customers about the private lives of everyone in town; and not being over-busy, I had plenty of time to puzzle things out for myself. Old ladies regaled me with gruesome details of their ailments, and the ailments of their relatives; I soon became a repository of curious information, and went through a phase of seeing people, not as themselves but as their perambulating intrigues or afflictions.

Another discovery I made was about educated persons. Except for Maestro Lazzarini, the schoolmaster (if one could count him), and the Cathedral priests, I had never met any. Now I saw them every evening—two lawyers, a doctor, a notary, a magistrate. Sometimes there were other faces, but these were the regulars. They came to talk with Signor Verdecchia as friends, not as customers. A bit like conspirators they were, I always thought, as one after another of them would poke his head through the tinkling beaded curtain in the doorway and look searchingly around the shop, then step inside and walk straight through to the little back room where the chemist made up prescriptions. But it was no conspiracy, only a few men trying to while away their boredom. Signor Verdecchia himself had plenty of book-learning. He knew Greek and Latin, would spend hours reading poetry when business was slack, and subscribed to a number of journals that were not on sale in Recanati but came to him by post from Rome and Milan. He was a kind man, but he had a shrewish wife, and I think he was terrified of going home in the evenings.

When his friends arrived, he would offer them a glass of aniseed liqueur, or they would take it in turns to order strong black coffee, sending me out to the nearest café to fetch it. Then they would sit for hours in front of the empty cups or glasses, smoking cheroots and talking. I was on duty in the shop and could rarely hear more than snatches of the conversation, except when it developed into a loud argument; in any case, it was above my head. I knew that to be educated was a great advantage, but as it had not been granted to me, I could only wonder curiously what they found to talk and argue about, evening after evening. It was then that I came to know of the existence of something mysterious called politics. It has remained mysterious to me ever since.

In America, people often asked me: 'What sort of work did you do in the drug-store? What kind of sandwiches did you make? Do you still remember how to mix ice-cream sodas?' I always had to explain that an Italian *farmacia* is quite unlike an American drug-store, that there are no sandwiches or ice-cream sodas in it; but as a matter of fact the Farmacia Verdecchia did stock fizzy lemonade as a side-line, and it gave me one of the worst humiliations of my life. Even now I feel uncomfortable at the memory of it.

Signor Verdecchia prepared the lemonade himself, from a

secret formula, and it went very well, especially in summer; but as the shop was small, he had evolved a method of arranging the bottles in elaborate pyramids, to save floor space. Building up these precarious pyramids—thirty, forty, fifty bottles at a time—was by far the most difficult task required of me, one that called for much more skill than the mere measuring-out of powders into transparent envelopes or sealing of pills into their little boxes. I never completed the pyramid without a shudder of triumphant relief. I was constantly visited by a nightmare in which the whole thing kept toppling over and crashing about my ears. One day I made a clumsy move, and the nightmare came true. The result was every bit as dreadful as I had always feared it would be—the shattering noise, the floor a sea of lemonade and broken glass, Signor Verdecchia rushing out in despair from the little back room where he had been sitting peacefully with his friends. It was horrible, every moment of it. I fully expected to be given the sack, but the old apothecary, as I have said, was a kind man: at the sight of my misery he silenced his own feelings, merely remarking that he didn't suppose I would let it happen a second time, and now I had better try to clean up the mess. Of course, the whole town got to know about it, and I was covered with shame for weeks afterwards; but, strangely enough, the nightmare never came back.

A few doors down the street from the Farmacia, there was a little school of music. It was a one-man enterprise, run by Maestro Silvano Battelli, an occasional member of Signor Verdecchia's coterie. He knew me from having heard me sing in the Cathedral. One evening, when he was sitting there with the others, he called me into the back room and asked me if I would like to play the saxophone.

I blushed with embarrassment. What was a saxophone? I had never as much as seen any musical instrument at close quarters, except the Cathedral organ; I had often listened to the concerts given by the municipal brass band in the Piazza on Sunday afternoons, but I was quite unable to tell one instrument from another. Moreover, I had never even learned to read a note of music. How could I play the saxophone—whatever it was?

'Don't be shy, Beniamino,' said Maestro Battelli. 'I'll teach you. We need a saxophonist in the junior band. Won't you help us?'

Would I help him! I was overcome with pride and gratitude.

Under Maestro Battelli's guidance, I developed a passion for the saxophone. I found it comical and merry, a fascinating contrast to the organ, on which I had been, one might say, brought up. In the band I played, if not with artistry, at least with enthusiasm. Our programme consisted almost entirely of operatic overtures and arias—my first real introduction to operatic music. Some of them were from operas that I later came to know by heart, such as Meyerbeer's 'L'Africana'. Of course, opera is a part of Italian folk culture, and I had never been entirely unaware of it; all the same, before joining the band I knew scarcely anything but sacred music and popular song-hits, so it was a new departure for me.

Soon I was to find myself approaching opera by another path. My eldest brother Abramo, who was studying for the priesthood, began devoting his Sunday afternoons to a group of teenage boys, including myself. With the idea, no doubt, of keeping us out of mischief, he coached us to perform little musical plays and sketches. We met in the newly-opened Ricreatorio, or parish recreation centre; it had a tiny stage, and we actually did give some performances, to an audience of about a hundred, all parents, relatives and friends. Abramo himself concocted wigs and beards for us out of maize floss, and gave us burnt-cork moustaches. At first I was very reluctant to get out on the stage and make a fool of myself; to my amazement I found the experience not only enjoyable, but strangely exhilarating.

The fact that these performances had the sanction of the Church, as personified by my brother Abramo, probably did something to undermine my mother's opposition to the stage; otherwise I cannot imagine how she would ever have agreed to what happened next.

I was fifteen, but my voice had not yet broken. One evening I locked up the Farmacia as usual at ten o'clock and got home to find my family in a state of mingled terror and excitement. Three young gentlemen had called. Three students. They had come all the way from Macerata, the capital of the province, just because of me. And what did they want? They wanted me to dress up as a girl and sing the soprano rôle in an operetta! Such a thing was out of the question, said my mother. She had refused point-blank to tell them where to find me, and forbidden them to search; it was a pity that they should have had the long journey

With my parents (my Mother in the centre, Father on the right at the back) brothers and sisters in 1905, when I was fifteen

On military service in Rome, 1910

With the choir of the Recanati Seminary—a photograph taken when I was on holiday from my studies in Rome

for nothing, but it was their own fault for entertaining such an outrageous idea. She had given them black coffee and some of the home-made macaroons that she kept in a tin for feast-days and visitors; then, politely but firmly, she had sent them away.

I felt rather let down. I wished my mother had not been quite so firm, or so precipitate. She might at least have allowed me to hear their proposals myself. Of course it would be horrifying to dress up as a girl—but still, it was flattering too. Fancy their knowing about me in Macerata, and wanting me all that badly! Didn't they have any soprano voices there? And how did they get to know about me in the first place?

Bit by bit, I learned the story. A group of university students had decided to stage an operetta: they would have some fun, and by giving public performances, they hoped to earn some money for themselves as well. It seemed they had set their hearts on one particular operetta, 'La Fuga di Angelica' (Angelica's Elopement), but no young lady could be found in Macerata to take the part of an eloping heroine; or at any rate, no respectable parents would allow their daughter to appear in public in such an equivocal rôle. The students had been on the point, they said, of regretfully abandoning the whole idea, when one of them suddenly remembered having been in Recanati a few Sundays previously and hearing a certain boy soloist at High Mass in the Cathedral of San Flaviano. 'Dress him up, whoever he is,' the student had said, 'and he'll make a perfect Angelica.'

So a deputation set out for Recanati, inquired at the Cathedral, and found its way to my home, only to be palmed off with my mother's macaroons.

They were evidently determined to get me, however, for the following Sunday the same three students were back on our door-step, begging, laughing, imploring, explaining, insisting. I would have, they said, a share of the proceeds. This cut no ice with my mother; to take money for my performance would only make it, in her eyes, all the more reprehensible. But I think it influenced my father, who began to murmur, 'Well, after all, perhaps there's no great harm in it'. It certainly attracted me. This time the students managed, before departing, to extract from my parents a grudging promise that they would think it over.

Then consultations began. My mother had expected to find an ally in my brother Abramo, and she was greatly taken aback when, after reading the text of the operetta, he declared that he could see nothing in it to frown on. Admittedly there was the elopement, but it amounted to no more than a farce, and everything turned out to be quite proper in the end. In his considered opinion the operetta presented no danger to faith or morals, and if Beniamino would enjoy taking part in it, why stop him?

Maestro Lazzarini, on the other hand, was horrified at the idea—not on any moral grounds, but because he thought the operetta, musically speaking, beneath the dignity of a member of his choir. This argument shook me, but only for a while. He then tried to dissuade the students by telling them that my voice, being contralto, was unsuitable for a soprano part; but they brushed the objection aside. (It is a curious fact that tenors almost always have contralto voices in boyhood, while boy sopranos tend to become baritones.) The maestro finally softened, however, when he saw that my heart was set on Macerata; and after some severe remarks on the subject of light music in general, he gave me his permission.

Hoping for an authoritative verdict against which there could be no appeal, my mother then put the case before Don Romano, the old French priest at the Cathedral. But he only gave her one of his slow smiles and said, 'Beniamino is a good boy, and he has few enough amusements. It is for you, his mother, to decide; but I see no harm in letting him go."

My mother could be very stubborn when she felt she was in the right, and even now she held out long after everybody else had come round. There was a great deal of toing and froing and the students were frantic; but in the end, she gave in.

The next few weeks were full of excitement. I had to make several trips to Macerata for rehearsals, and began to feel quite a globe-trotter. Incidentally, I discovered why the students had been so anxious to perform this particular operetta, when there were so many to choose from. It had already been performed in Siena a few years previously. The composer, Maestro Alessandro Billi, lived in Florence, but his brother was the town clerk of Macerata. There are quite a lot of ways in which a town clerk can help—or hinder—a group of students who want to stage an operetta and get the public to come and see it. In this case, the town clerk was anxious to help as much as possible—provided the operetta was his brother's masterpiece, 'Angelica's Elopement'. For example, instead of some grim little hall, we were to be given the municipal theatre. It had boxes and a dress circle, it was all gilt and red plush, and it inspired me with as much awe as if it had been the Scala.

A tenor cannot seriously claim to have made his operatic début in a soprano rôle; but I sometimes allow myself a joke about it. I tease people by inviting them to guess what was my very first appearance. If they ask me for a clue, I describe the costume I wore: a long white dress with leg-of-mutton sleeves, a black velvet bonnet with two big white flowers, and a parasol of sky-blue silk. Then I sit back to enjoy their bewilderment.

I was bewildered enough myself, however, that first evening in the dressing-room of the Teatro Lauri Rossi, when I saw Angelica in the looking-glass. My cheeks were pink, plump and smooth beneath the silky brown curls of my wig; I was a really convincing girl, and I found this rather upsetting. I felt a wave of adolescent shyness, and then a vague sense of panic. Out there in the audience were all the fine ladies of Macerata; worse still, out there was my father. How could I face them? I was only too painfully aware that this was not the parish hall in Recanati. I didn't hear my name being called, and someone had to grab me and push me towards the stage.

Then, suddenly, everything was all right. Twirling my parasol, as I had been taught to do at rehearsals, I sauntered back and forth singing '*Passeggiando un anno fa*'. This song had been written specially for my voice and inserted into the opera by Maestro Billi, so I suppose it gave me a chance to show off. At any rate, it seemed to win my audience: I could scarcely believe that all the applause and cries of '*Bis!*' were really for me. It was overwhelming. I felt like the girl I was supposed to be—I wanted to cry.

But I swallowed back the tears. After all, I was *not* a girl. I tried instead to exchange a glance with my father, whom I had spotted a few rows back in the stalls. He was sitting quite unmoved in the middle of all the cheering and clapping, and was not looking in my direction at all. I felt very disappointed. Later I discovered that he had simply failed to recognize me in my bonnet, my frills and flounces, and was still waiting impatiently for me to appear!

After the success of '*Passeggiando un anno fa*', I got an ovation from the audience every time I came on the stage. Indeed, I felt ashamed at getting so much more than my share of the applause: I thought the others sang very well, especially the baritone, Armando Santolini, and the tenor, a student called Manlio Urbani, who had the part of my fiancé.

This Urbani was a gentle boy with a slight limp. I remember liking him very well at the time. Many, many years later, on tour in South America, I sang in Buenos Aires at a benefit concert organized by a local Italian newspaper *L'Italia del Popolo*. There was a banquet afterwards, and I found myself sitting next to the editor of the newspaper, who was also president of the concert committee. We talked about all the usual things—Italy, music, the Italian colony in Buenos Aires, and so forth; then he began to ask me about my career, where I had studied and how I had begun. To make him laugh, I told him about my début in Macerata, in a student operetta, dressed as a girl. Then I stopped dead: my neighbour was staring at me with a most peculiar expression on his face. Had I made some dreadful *gaffe*? He burst out laughing, rocking with incredulous delight.

'My Angelica!' he shrieked, and threw his arms round my neck. It was Manlio Urbani, my old fiancé.

The first night of 'Angelica's Elopement' was a triumph, and people said it was because of me. The theatre was immediately sold out for all the remaining performances, and we had to give a few extra ones to meet the demand. Then I came back to Recanati, and everything was the same as before: the beaded curtains tinkling in the doorway of the Farmacia, the saxophone in the junior band, Palestrina motets in the Cathedral organ-loft, burnt-cork moustaches in the parish hall on Sunday afternoons. Everything was the same as before, and yet not quite the same. I had filled a theatre with my voice, held an audience and brought it to its feet. I could do it again. I *would* do it again.

Two years passed. I was seventeen. That summer I often played bowls in a little vine-roofed yard beside a tavern on the outskirts of Recanati. There I met a man named Giovanni Zerri. He worked as a cook at the Portuguese theological seminary in Rome; the students were spending the summer months in a house by the sea at Porto Recanati. We would play a game or two of bowls, and afterwards, over a glass of wine, would find ourselves talking about music. He was from the Romagna district, where even cooks are opera-fanciers; moreover, having been employed for some years by the celebrated tenor Alessandro Bonci, he had picked up a miscellaneous assortment of notions about voice-training, and of gossipy anecdotes about opera singers. No doubt he enjoyed showing off his knowledge to such an eager and admiring listener as I was; but underneath his bluff and vanity, he had a genuine love of operatic music. After hearing me sing in the Cathedral he predicted a great future for me, if only I would come to Rome. Every time we met he repeated, 'You must come to Rome'—the very words I had been longing to hear. Lack of money need be no obstacle, he assured me. He would look after me. He would find me a job as a music-hall ventriloquist. He knew an usher at the Teatro Olimpia. 'And, by the way, haven't you got a brother in Rome?' he asked. It was true; my brother Catervo had recently won a scholarship and was studying sculpture at the Academy of Fine Arts. 'Well, can't you stay with him? I'll smuggle food to you from the seminary kitchen; and with the money you earn as a ventriloquist, you can take singing lessons. I know all the best teachers. Then some day, when you're famous, you'll remember me and send me two tickets for the stalls. What will it be? "Bohème"? "Rigoletto"?' And off he would go into day-dreams of future glory and riches.

All summer Giovanni Zerri talked, urged, promised, enticed. It was now or never, he told me; and I knew he was right. Maestro Lazzarini and my brother Abramo, now a priest, were on my side, and helped me to persuade my father and mother. By the time September came, I had convinced them that I must go. Catervo wrote from Rome to say that he would be glad of my company in his attic, and that he had found me a job as assistant to a chemist in Via Cavour. (This was more reassuring, somehow, than the prospect of becoming a ventriloquist.) It all happened quickly in the end. I saved up the money for my railway ticket and Abramo borrowed sixty lire extra for me. With this sum in my pocket and with the protection of a cook, I said good-bye to the Farmacia Verdecchia, to the Cathedral, to my parents and to Recanati, and set out for Rome and the world beyond the Apennines.

Of course my friend the cook, carried away by his enthusiasm, had been exaggerating. This became clear to me after a month or so in Rome. He had not introduced me to any singing teachers, let alone to the best ones, and I began to be sceptical of his boast that he knew them all. I was often very hungry, but that was my own fault. I could scarcely explain that I had been counting quite literally on his promises to smuggle me food from the seminary kitchen. Whenever I paid him a visit there, he would welcome me with formal ceremony; then, suddenly conspiratorial, as though about to overwhelm me with some delectable treat, he would draw up two chairs to the kitchen table, pour out two glasses of Frascati wine, and plunge all over again into his reminiscences of opera singers. This would go on for an hour or two, depending on how busy he was; to interrupt him with hints about the real object of my visit would have been unthinkable. Before I left he often did give me some titbit, which generally served to stimulate my appetite rather than appease it. Perhaps it was all a misunderstanding; perhaps he was elaborately trying to save my face and hesitated to offer me food when I gave no indication of wanting it; perhaps he had forgotten the extent to which, in Recanati, he had pledged himself as my protector. At any rate, I decided that it was useless to count on him for everyday support; but I still felt, and in this I was right, that he would help me in emergencies. Moreover his friendship, however erratic, was still something to be grateful for, since it had spurred me to come to Rome.

No hunger or disappointment could take that from me—I really was in Rome at last. Indeed, I was in the very heart of it; my brother's garret was in the Passeggiata di Ripetta, a quiet, tree-lined street between the Academy of Fine Arts and the Tiber. A few minutes brought me to the Corso, where my provincial eyes were dazzled by carriage-drawn Roman society parading in the late afternoon; to the Piazza del Popolo, with its five churches, its fountains and its Egyptian obelisk; and to the Pincio Gardens, where I stared in mesmerized puritanical horror at soldiers flirting brazenly with nursemaids, and stood for hours in rapture at the Punch and Judy show.

I have never been able to sing 'La Bohème' without recalling those first months in Rome, and the garret shared with my brother. It was 'La Bohème' without Mimi or Musetta; all the same, we had fun as well as hardship. Catervo looked the part of an art student, with his haggard face, wide-brimmed hat and black floppy tie. Sometimes his friends from the Academy would come to see us, and having no concrete hospitality to offer them, we would keep them amused by singing, or by our private game of imitating the street-criers, a skill we had perfected during our solitary evenings by candlelight. I really had talent as a ventriloquist. From behind the shutters of our window we would fill the street with the cries of the umbrella-mender, the knife-grinder or the water-vendor. The neighbours used to be baffled, until they found out.

We always ate the same supper: a few penceworth of *pezzetti* (literally: scraps), which I suppose might be described as a Roman equivalent of fish and chips. It consisted of tiny red mullet, bits of salted cod, and slices of polenta—a kind of hard maize porridge—all fried in oil. I developed an uncanny sense of timing, which enabled me to descend on the little *rosticceria* round the corner at the exact moment when a fresh batch of *pezzetti* was being lifted from the pan. Then, clutching them tightly to keep them hot, I would rush back to our garret. We had neither plates, forks nor tablecloth, but Catervo always had a clean sheet of paper spread on the table in readiness. Swiftly and silently, like bank clerks, we would count out the fried 'scraps' into meticulously equal shares; then, as swiftly and as silently, fall to and devour them.

We got rather tired of always eating the same thing, and were often homesick for my mother's soups; still, *pezzetti* were better than nothing. One evening I came back to find Catervo with a solemn face: he had just paid the rent, he told me, and there was no money left over at all. We would have to go supperless, unless I could enlist the help of my friend the cook, Giovanni Zerri. I reminded him of what had happened on previous occasions. 'Well,' said Catervo, 'why don't you try asking him straight out this time?'

My ravenous hunger gave me courage. I ran as fast as I could to the Portuguese seminary—it was not very far—and knocked breathlessly on the kitchen door. It opened only a few inches, to show me part of Zerri's red floury face. 'We've nothing to eat,' I told him point-blank. 'Ssh . . . the Father Bursar is in the kitchen just now; I'll get you something in a moment, but wait at the bottom of the stairs, and try not to let anyone see you.' Ten minutes later he appeared on the landing, finger on lips. 'Catch!' he whispered, throwing me down a parcel; then he vanished.

Clumsily, I missed it; it fell to the ground at my feet. A soggy, spattered mess was all that remained of what had obviously been a beautiful golden omelette. There were tears in my eyes as I stumbled home; but somehow I had overcome my shyness with Giovanni Zerri, and afterwards I never hesitated to tell him frankly when we were really hungry.

My job in the Farmacia Felleroni was monotonous and impersonal, quite unlike the homely, gossipy atmosphere of the Farmacia Verdecchia in Recanati. But there were compensations. To get from the Passeggiata di Ripetta to the Via Cavour, I had to walk the full length of the Corso. All the wonders of the universe, it seemed to me, were gathered and displayed in the shop windows that lay along my daily route. I felt no covetousness, only curiosity. For whom were they intended, these silks, these furs, these fragile tapestried chairs, these tiny gold watches, these marvellously-wrought silver cups, these jewels? To find my answer, I had only to glance at the passing crowd. Never had I seen women of such surpassing beauty and elegance: at the very least, I thought, they must all be duchesses.

When, emerging from the Corso, I crossed the Piazza Venezia into the maze of narrow streets and lanes that has since been pulled down to make way for the broad avenue now leading to the Colosseum, I found myself in another world, reminiscent of Recanati in its humble simplicity but quite foreign to me in its teeming exuberance. Here cobblers, tailors, cabinet-makers by the dozen plied their trade on their doorsteps; goats were milked as required into the jugs of waiting housewives; balls of flavoured rice were fried, over braziers, in great cauldrons of sizzling oil, and sold to passers-by. In the morning, of course, I was always in a hurry, but in the evening I could linger, warming my hands on a halfpennyworth of roast chestnuts, or cooling my lips with a slice of water-melon, according to season; and as I sauntered along I kept reminding myself joyfully that this air I was breathing, this freedom I was savouring, were the air of Rome, the freedom of Rome.

Rome, Rome—suddenly it would come back to me—why was I there? Why was I letting the days, weeks, months slip by, wasting my time, no nearer than ever to becoming a singer? With a sense of panic I would rush back to Catervo and beg him to think of something.

In our ignorance we made silly mistakes. The first of these cost us a great deal of time and trouble. For years, ever since Maestro Lazzarini first told me about Don Lorenzo Perosi, I had dreamed of singing in the Sistine Chapel choir. Now more than ever I felt convinced that this would be a way of breaking into the charmed circle; and surely, I thought, after all my years in the Cathedral, I had a chance of being admitted. I wrote to my priest-brother Abramo in Recanati and begged him to get me some kind of introduction. At Abramo's request, the Archbishop of Recanati wrote to Prince Antici Mattei, a member of the old Recanati family to which the *palazzo* where Leopardi was born now belongs, and an officer of the Pope's Noble Guard. The Prince received me in his magnificent Roman apartments; it was all very awe-inspiring. However, he put me at my ease by chatting in Recanati dialect, and gave me a letter of introduction, not to Don Perosi himself, but to his deputy, the vice-director of the Sistine Chapel choir, Maestro Boezi.

Success, I now felt, was assured: how could the maestro refuse anyone introduced by so exalted a personage as Prince Antici Mattei? (I had not yet learned that in Italy letters of introduction are a sadly depreciated currency. It is always easier to write one than to tell someone an unpleasant or disappointing truth. Americans, I have since discovered, call this 'passing the buck'.) Joyfully I fetched Catervo, and we set out together to visit Maestro Boezi. He lived on the fourth floor, and my excitement mounted with each step we climbed.

The maestro opened the door himself; he was just on the point of going out, he explained. We stood in trepidation on the landing while he opened the precious letter. He barely glanced at it; then handing it back to me, he said, 'I'm sorry, my boy, but you've passed the age limit for the choir. Don Perosi won't accept anyone who's a day over sixteen, and in any case your voice has broken. I'm afraid there's nothing I can do for you."

I stood there stupidly, uncomprehendingly, while Catervo thanked him, and he shut the door. Then Catervo tugged at my hand, and we went slowly down the stairs, not saying a word to each other. There was nothing to say. I walked with him as far as the Academy. There we parted, and my feet began automatically to carry me towards the Farmacia and my job. I felt a surge of despair. Everything was turning out so differently from what I had hoped. Perhaps I ought never to have left Recanati. I had been a fool to think I could make my way in this big city. So far no one in Rome except Catervo's artist friends, who didn't count, had heard me sing; if anyone did, they would probably laugh at me and say, 'You want to be a singer? Well, that's a good joke! Don't you realize that this is Rome, and not the provinces?' My mother was lonely for me; Abramo had said so in his letter. If I was going to have to spend my life as a chemist's assistant, I might as well go back to Recanati, I told myself, where at least I had friends, and a proper bed with clean sheets, and hot bean soup in the evenings; and my mother.

This time I was unable to choke back the tears. My eyes kept filling as I hurried along the hard pavement of the Via Cavour. The rays of the afternoon sun, refracted by the windows of the great barrack-like houses, dazzled and almost blinded me. I could scarcely see where I was going, and collided with several people. They must have thought I was drunk. What did it matter? After all, they didn't know me. They were all strangers.

I returned that evening, still brooding over my disappointment, to find my brother in high spirits. All things considered, I thought it very unsympathetic of him to be so jolly. From his mysterious hints and smiles I gathered, moreover, that he had some secret; but he was a tease. I was in no mood to play this game, and in the end I said, 'Well, keep your old secret.'

'All right,' retorted Catervo, 'then I'll have to tell Professor De Stefani that you don't want the audition.'

'What audition?' I shrieked.

'Sunday afternoon, at his house,' said Catervo, complacently triumphant. 'He's expecting us—I talked to him about you today at the Academy—Pietro De Stefani; you know he just does sculpture as a hobby, but he's quite a well-known professional singing teacher. I'm kicking myself for not having asked him sooner. Well, he's so much older than me, and all that. But today I felt I had to do something to cheer you up. He said he's looking forward to hearing your voice. Now do you feel better?'

I thought it would be undignified to discard my mood of despair too rapidly, but I allowed Catervo to spend the rest of the evening consoling me.

The following Sunday we rang the bell of Professor De Stefani's flat in Via Cicerone. (In Italy, anyone who teaches anything is called Professor.) He received us with a great show of fussy friendliness, but to my dismay we had to spend well over an hour admiring his sculptures, in which I was not at all interested, while no reference whatsoever was made to the audition. I was beginning to feel miserably certain that he had forgotten all about it, when he suddenly replaced the dust-sheet on a massive marble group representing four of the Nine Muses (the other five, he had explained, would be added as soon as he could move to a bigger flat) and uttered the alarming words: 'Now, boys, we must forsake one Muse, but only to embrace another.' More reassuringly, he added, 'Come to the piano.'

First he made me sing the scale, then any notes I felt like; then he asked me to go through my whole repertory. I said jokingly, how many different Masses did he want to hear? At any rate, he listened to me for two hours, making no comment except for any occasional muttered '*Bravo*!' At the end, ignoring me, he turned to Catervo, and said with what seemed like genuine emotion 'My dear Catervo, I never expected anything like this. Your brother has an extraordinarily beautiful lyric tenor voice. It's a crime not to have it trained.'

'We know that,' said Catervo quietly. 'That's why we've come to you. The trouble is, we're very poor.'

The Professor found it necessary to clear his throat a few times before replying. Then, suddenly brisk and business-like (I found his lightning changes of manner somewhat disconcerting) he said, 'Yes, yes, I understand perfectly. Well, as he's your brother, I could make special terms—twenty lire a month instead of thirty. Thirty's my usual fee, but I'm an idealist, you know, and I like helping people.' He paused to let this sink in, then added, 'Besides, it would be an honour to train such a voice.'

Not knowing what to make of all this, I let Catervo do the talking. I didn't see how I could pay twenty lire a month for lessons out of the sixty on which I was already half-starving, but Catervo agreed to the Professor's terms. Afterwards he said to me, 'I know we can't afford the lessons, but you must begin your training now. We'll find a way out.'

The Professor's peculiar behaviour had made me somewhat sceptical of him, but Catervo assured me that he was highly esteemed professionally, and would never have praised my voice unless he really meant it. I think he was a good teacher, but I have only the haziest recollections of what he taught me in the two months during which I was his pupil. I had lessons three times a week, at nine o'clock in the evening, as I was not free during the day. In order to pay him, I had to give up altogether my evening meal of *pezzetti*. Catervo was no better off than I was: I refused to let him share his already meagre portion with me. On my four free evenings I used to call on my friend the cook; but on the other three evenings I went hungry.

It strikes me that the reader may be shocked by the frequent references to food in these early pages. It may seem an unromantic preoccupation for a budding singer. But I cannot convey a truthful impression of my early years if the word hunger is left out. I wanted to sing, but I needed to eat. There was no escaping that.

From my job in the Farmacia I would rush, empty-stomached, to the Professor's flat, to be greeted at the door by an intoxicating aroma of stew or tomato sauce. The Professor and his family would be just finishing supper; sometimes they would offer me a cup of black coffee. The Professor generally greeted me with a hearty thump on the back, and even before the lesson began I was already dizzy.

I am no hero, I suppose; at any rate I felt I could make no progress with my lessons when I was always so tired and hungry, and the whole thing seemed to me, not only hopeless but also a waste of money. At the same time I felt I simply must not give up; so I began to look around for some other solution. I was beginning to learn the truth of the old adage that 'God helps those who help themselves'.

Then two things happened within a few days of each other. Feeling that I had had as much as I could take of genteel starvation, I left chemists' shops behind me for ever and went to work as a servant in the house of Countess Spannocchi, a noble lady from my own Marche province; and Catervo found me another singing teacher who was prepared to give me credit.

I suppose this is the point at which biographers say, 'From then on, he never looked back.' It would be more accurate to say, 'After that, he always managed to keep going somehow.' But in fact I was never again to feel the sort of discouragement I have been describing hitherto. I was now eighteen, and in one way or another I contrived to support myself, studying all the time, until I made my début at the age of twenty-four.

To some young singers of the present day six years of study may seem a long time, but I think they were necessary. I still feel the utmost gratitude for the various teachers who not only trained my voice but also taught me patience. At first I had imagined that two or three years would be enough; but as soon as I got properly started I began to feel that even in a lifetime I could never learn all there was to know. Now that I have retired, I am often asked what I think of the future of *bel canto*. I have only one answer: it depends on hard work. Every generation will have its share of outstanding voices: but unless young singers are prepared to face six or seven years of training, *bel canto* will decline.

Countess Spannocchi lived in the Piazza delle Tartarughe—the Square of the Tortoises, so called because in the middle of the little square there is a fountain, and if you look closely you can see that the whole weight of the fountain rests on the backs of four small stone tortoises. The Countess called me a *tartaruga* myself because I was slow at my work. I slept in a sort of dark cupboard under the stairs, but I could eat all I wanted. There were five other servants, and I was the lowest of all. I cleaned boots, ran errands, and helped the butler to wait at table. It was not a very strenuous life. I have grateful memories of the Countess. She never got angry; she was the sort of woman who is amused by everything. Several times she caught me serving guests with the fingers of my white gloves all stained and greasy; on my way from the kitchen with some mouth-watering dish, I had been unable to resist sampling it in the corridor. Of course I always felt very ashamed at being found out, but the Countess would only laugh.

So far as I was concerned, the arrangement worked very well, in spite of the fact that my wages were almost nil. The Countess took a great interest in my singing, and gave me two hours off every afternoon, for lessons or practice. I had no worries, since she fed, housed and even clothed me; all I needed was pocket-money, and this my wages provided. As I have said, Catervo had found me a singing teacher who had such faith in my future that she was willing to wait indefinitely for payment. At last I was able to write to my parents that I had settled down in Rome and was making progress; and although Catervo politely pretended to regret our lost *vie de bohème*, I could see that he was getting far more work done, now that he no longer needed to look after me.

The teacher's name was Agnese Bonucci. Her husband was a clerk at the Law Courts, so she was not entirely dependent on her own earnings; nevertheless, it was extraordinarily generous of her to give her time so freely to an unknown boy. For two years I had a lesson with her almost daily. She loved music, with discernment, and her belief in me gave me once and for all the self-confidence essential to a singer. She inspired me with such a feeling of security that I never panicked, never lost heart again. Moreover, her method of voice-training suited me exactly—for she had none. Or rather, having grasped the fact that every voice is different and has different needs, she never tried to impose any set rules or discipline. She taught me the fundamentals of voice production, and after that I never felt that I was being taught at all. She guided me, she accompanied me; at times she even seemed to follow me. I felt that I was obeying my instincts, my voice, rather than any teacher. Of course I realized afterwards that this was simply teaching of the highest quality.

CHAPTER III

THE ARMY—AND IDA

LOOKING back over my life, I have difficulty in remembering the episodes of spitefulness and jealousy which singers are liable to encounter even more frequently than other people. They are part of the price one pays for success, and one might as well forget them. The memories that linger, I find, are almost always grateful ones—memories of people who helped me when I was poor and unknown. Perhaps human beings are mostly kind when they get the chance, or perhaps I was just lucky. I was certainly lucky in meeting Colonel Delfino.

I must explain that after a peaceful year spent working for Countess Spannocchi and making daily progress in singing under Signora Bonucci's guidance, I was alarmed and horrified to find myself suddenly called up for two years' military service. Of course it was the normal thing that happens to every able-bodied young Italian, but I had never let my thoughts dwell on it because I dreaded so much having to interrupt my studies. I suppose I had vaguely hoped that there might be some oversight, and that the attention of the War Ministry would never fall on my humble person. Instead, here was this sinister piece of grey paper demanding that I present myself on such-and-such a day at such-and-such a barracks. Then I would be sent to Sicily, no doubt, or to the French frontier, or to any one of a thousand places where singing lessons would be out of the question. And I had wasted so much time already. In despair I begged the Countess to help me. She sent me, with a little note, to Colonel Delfino at the Territorial Command in Via Paolina.

'Well,' said the Colonel, when he had read the note, 'sing me something.' I was astonished, but reassured. Singing was easier than talking. I sang '*La donna è mobile*', an *aria* which, however hackneyed it may have become, is one of the most beautiful Verdi ever wrote, and also one of the richest in scope for a tenor voice.

'Good,' said the Colonel, in a matter-of-fact tone, when I had finished. 'Now, I have a proposal to make to you. You may do your military service right here in Rome, on one condition: you must promise me a box in the dress circle the first time you sing at the Costanzi.'

The Teatro Costanzi, which later changed its name to Teatro Reale dell'Opera, was and still is the Opera House of Rome. For a few moments I was too puzzled to say anything. Then the Colonel laughed, and I laughed.

'At your orders, *Signor Colonello,*' I said joyfully, making my first attempt at a military salute.

Six years later, when I was twenty-five, I sang for the first time at the Costanzi—as Faust in Boito's 'Mefistofele'. The day before the performance, I went to the Territorial Command and handed Colonel Delfino the key of a box in the dress circle. 'I always try to pay my debts,' I told him.

Meanwhile, the good Colonel did nothing by halves. Not only did he grant me an envied privilege by assigning me to a Roman regiment, the 82nd Infantry; he rescued me from the normal routine of barracks life by appointing me telephone operator at the Territorial Command. This delighted me for three reasons. It meant that I was more or less directly under the wing of the Colonel himself. It meant—to my relief, for I have never been an athlete—escaping the strenuous marches and fatigues that are generally the lot of an infantryman. Best of all, it meant an elastic time-table into which my daily singing lessons fitted very neatly.

It happens so often that life turns out differently from what one had hoped; fortunately, it can also be different from what one had feared. I had dreaded military service; but, looking back, I can truthfully say that the two years during which I wore the clumsy ill-fitting grey-green uniform of a private in the Italian infantry were the happiest years of my youth. Materially speaking, barracks life was austere enough, but at least I had no worries about food or lodging; moreover, for the first and perhaps the last time in my life, I had real comradeship. There was no feeling of stagnation, no waste of time; my whole existence was geared to my singing lessons. And my duties as a telephone operator were so light that I had plenty of time in which to remember that I was twenty years old, plenty of time to be gay.

The telephone itself was a new and wonderful instrument to

As Enzo in 'La Gioconda', the performance in which I made my début as a tenor, at Rovigo on 15th October, 1914

Myself in 1916

Faust in Boito's 'Mefistofele'

me, a toy that I never tired of playing with. Somehow or other, the girls at the central exchange came to know about my singing, and when work was slack they got into the habit of asking me for a song over the telephone. I was always ready to oblige. It was all practice. The Toselli Serenade and '*Torna a Surriento*' were their favourites, I remember.

One of these girls—her name was Ida—had a beautiful speaking voice. I felt drawn to her even without having seen her face. She asked me for songs more often than any of the other girls, yet she seemed shyer than they were, never telephoning without some pretext such as, 'I would like some information, I have a brother in the army.'

'Why don't you come over here yourself?' I asked her one day. 'I can't give you any information, but I'll take you to an officer who can.'

She came that very afternoon. I was dazzled. Normally I would never have dared to approach such a beauty; but after all, we were already acquainted—by telephone. I summoned my courage and asked her if we might go for a walk together when I came off duty at six o'clock.

The simplicity with which she answered 'Yes' gave me an extraordinary sense of relief and achievement. It was the first time I had ever taken a girl out. Not knowing what to talk about, and not caring, I walked blissfully at her side through the jostling crowds of the Via Nazionale. The passers-by no longer seemed strange or hostile or indifferent. In any case, I had as much right to be there as they had. Rome—as personified by Ida—had accepted me.

We reached the Trinità dei Monti and stood for a while looking down at the great sweep of the Spanish Steps, at the children playing and the beggars begging, the English ladies reading poetry and the lovely peasant girls, who worked as artists' models, waiting to be chosen. The great avenue leading to the Pincio was ablaze with flowering oleanders, then cool and shady with acacia and ilex. As we strolled along we could see, as from a balcony, the city spread out before us, its ochre domes, spires and roofs incandescent in the late afternoon sunlight. In the Pincio I bought two ice-cream cones, feeling every bit as much in command of the situation as if I had ordered champagne. Then a sudden fit of shyness descended on us, and we drifted over to the Punch and

Judy show, where we laughed heartily at the silliest jokes until our shyness was forgotten. Afterwards we sat on the parapet of the terrace overlooking the Piazza del Popolo, watching the sunset fade, until at last it was time to go back. Happiness welled up in me and overflowed. I felt half-strangled by the impulse to sing; it was the only way I could express myself. But Ida gave my arm a little squeeze and said: 'Not now, people would stare.'

All through that autumn and winter my friendship with Ida ripened, and by the time summer came round again I had had a suit of civilian clothes made with the express purpose of paying a solemn call on her parents and formally requesting her hand in marriage. But the suit of clothes had to be laid away in moth balls, unworn. The very Sunday that had been fixed for my state visit to Ida's family saw me instead at the railway station, one of a thousand recruits, bidding my first love a sad farewell as I set off for the wars. It was 1911. Italy had embarked on the conquest of Libya.

The crowded train pulled out of the station and Ida's fluttering handkerchief dissolved into the distance. I eased my heavy knapsack off my shoulders into a corner of the corridor, sat down on it, and sighed. It was a sigh of melancholy, but also of relief. I was upset at the interruption of my studies, sad at being parted from Ida, and frankly terrified at the thought of fighting the Arabs, with whom I personally had no quarrel whatsoever; at the same time, there were other reasons which made me not altogether sorry to be extricated from Rome at this particular juncture.

To begin with, there were the practical problems of my relationship with Ida. I was heading straight for marriage with her. It seemed a blissful prospect, and yet I had misgivings. Her parents had endured with reluctance the course of our romance. Humble folk themselves, they felt nevertheless that their pretty daughter could do better elsewhere; and as things stood, I could hardly blame them. They would certainly not tolerate a long engagement based on vague hopes. They would insist that I give up my studies the moment my military service ended, and either find a steady job of some kind, or else plunge immediately into seeking work as a professional singer. I was not prepared to do either of these things. Yet I loved Ida and did not want to lose her.

Had I stayed in Rome just then, I might have ended by yielding to pressure. Instead, here I was, already speeding through the

Pontine Marshes, at a safe distance from matrimony, if not from guns. I looked out of the window at the melancholy landscape, and found it almost reassuring. Soon I would be in Naples, soon I would be in Tripoli. There was, of course, a chance that I might never return; but if I did (and at this point I allowed myself some vainglorious daydreaming about the prestige of a seasoned warrior), surely Ida's parents would no longer dare to disapprove of me. For the moment I need make no decisions, I told myself comfortably; Fate had taken my existence into its hands

But further reflection proved less comfortable, or comforting. The Ida situation could scarcely be helped; but I had been making some stupid mistakes elsewhere and was not feeling at all proud of myself.

Just then the train emerged from a tunnel, rounded a corner, and the blue bay of Formia lay glittering before my eyes. For the first time in my life, I saw oranges growing on a tree.

Did war make one wiser? I wondered. I certainly hoped so. I felt the need of a little wisdom. It was no good laying the blame for what had happened on my old friend, the cook Giovanni Zerri. It was all my own fault, my own responsibility.

The trouble had started a few months previously, when Zerri began taking a renewed interest in my voice. I had paid him a visit one evening, for old times' sake, and had sung for him in his kitchen. He professed himself amazed at my progress, but deeply concerned that my training should be in the hands of a 'mere woman'. Only the best and most famous teachers—men, of course—could now, he said, do justice to my voice. I ought to have answered that my progress was due in no small measure to the splendid teaching and to the generosity of Signora Bonucci, this 'mere woman'. Alas, I allowed myself to be impressed by his arguments.

Shortly afterwards, Zerri took me to meet his former employer, the renowned tenor Alessandro Bonci, who was in Rome at the time, singing in 'Elisir d'Amore' at the Teatro Costanzi. Bonci was staying in a luxurious apartment on the top floor of the Hotel Excelsior; when we called, he was wearing a magnificent silk dressing-gown. What would my father think? I wondered. I could still hear his words of warning, 'There's no money in singing, my boy: stick to a good, honest trade.'

I sang a few pieces for the great man, and he complimented me, adding that if I liked, he would introduce me to Professor Martino, 'perhaps the greatest singing teacher alive today'. Then, turning to Zerri, as though resuming the thread of a previous conversation, he murmured, 'Put your money on that voice; it will pay dividends.'

The implication of this remark did not dawn on me until a few days later, when Zerri came to see me at the Territorial Command.

'It's all settled,' he told me gleefully. 'Bonci has talked about you to Martino. You're to start lessons with him next Monday.'

'Why the hurry?' I asked. 'What am I to do about Signora Bonucci? I haven't said anything to her yet. I wanted to consult her. After all, I've been with her two years, and she's never taken a penny. I can't just leave her overnight. And how am I to pay Martino, anyway?'

'Don't worry,' said Zerri lightly. 'I'll take care of that. He's expensive, all right. You can't expect to get the best without paying for it, of course. But I'm going to do the paying, for the present. You can pay me back later. I've prepared a little agreement for you to sign. Here, have a look at it. And as for that woman, don't be absurd. You've got to think of your career. Martino is doing you a great favour by accepting you as his pupil; he'd be furious if you backed out now. Don't let this chance slip; your future depends on it.'

I felt guilty, but at this stage there seemed to be no way of escape. I glanced at the agreement which Zerri had drawn up; it looked an impressively legal document. Zerri undertook to pay for my lessons with Professor Martino, and in exchange I was to hand him over thirty per cent of my earnings for the first two years after my début, and forty per cent for the following three years. I felt a pang of remorse, remembering how Signora Bonucci had never asked me for a single scrap of paper; but I followed Zerri obediently to a notary's office, and signed. My début! It all seemed so remote.

Then I went to Signora Bonucci and told her I had been advised to study under Professor Martino.

Many years later, I learned the English saying, 'Hell hath no fury like a woman scorned.' I realize that it is generally applied to situations altogether different from the one I am describing; but in this case it is apt. All her sweetness vanished; she shrieked, she heaped insults on my head, she accused me of base ingratitude, she slammed doors, she told me to get out of her house at once and never let her see me again. I was terrified, aghast, overcome with shame; it was one of the most agonizing experiences of my life, much worse than upsetting the mountain of bottles in the Farmacia Verdecchia; but of course it was all very Italian, and perfectly comprehensible to me. Signora Bonucci was having a *sfogo*. She was an impulsive, warm-hearted woman. In giving me free tuition, she had done something exceptional. There was a vague understanding that one day I would repay her; but had I remained with her, she would probably never have referred to it. She believed in my voice, she took a pride in it—a proprietary pride, no doubt. I was her star pupil, and it was quite natural that she should look forward, not only to my future triumphs, in which she so confidently believed, but also to her own share of credit for them; or at least, to her own private feelings of satisfaction. She had laid the foundations of my art as a singer; now I was turning my back on her, telling her, in effect, that she was not good enough to accompany me through the final, more rewarding stages of my training. I had wounded her pride; she had every right to be angry.

In her anger, she brought a lawsuit against me. I had to appear in court. The judge asked me if it were true that Signora Bonucci had given me singing lessons almost every day for two years. Yes, I replied, it was perfectly true. I felt very sad that things should have come to such a pass, but I had only myself to blame. I was sentenced to pay for the lessons—two thousand five hundred *lire* altogether, a reasonable charge when spread over two years, but in those days a vast sum when you said it all at once, especially for a twenty-year-old soldier earning ten centimes a day. I was frightened and miserable.

'Your Lordship,' I told the judge humbly, 'I'll set aside all my pay, and refund half a lira every five days; but I'm afraid it will take a long time.'

The Signora did not press for payment, however; obviously she had only wanted to make a gesture, and I heard no more of the matter, from her or anyone else.

Twelve years later, when I was at the Metropolitan, I wrote to my old teacher. I had some trouble in finding her address; she was no longer in Rome, her husband having been transferred to the island of Rhodes in the Dodecanese Archipelago, which at that time belonged to Italy. I begged her forgiveness and asked for her friendship. She answered my letter very cordially, and I felt with joy that our old relationship had been restored. But many more years were to pass before we finally met again. During the summer of 1939, in my villa at Recanati, I got a telegram from Rome; 'Am here on holiday. Let me know if you want to see me.' Of course I telegraphed back inviting her to Recanati. She came at once, but insisted on staying at a hotel; some lingering relic of wounded pride prevented her—or so I guessed—from accepting my hospitality. At any rate, we made a pilgrimage together to the nearby Basilica of the Madonna of Loreto, and offered thanks for our happy reunion; then, before we parted, I was able to make amends by repaying the good Signora at last, and adding to the original sum a bonus commensurate with the gratitude I felt.

But that was in the future, and to the recruit Beniamino Gigli, private in the 82nd Infantry, sitting on his knapsack in the corridor of the troop train to Naples, blushing at the thought of his past misdeeds, it was still an unknown quantity.

Professor Martino was undoubtedly a great teacher, but I was his pupil only for a few months, up to the time of my departure for Libya. In this same period Giovanni Zerri, having reorganized my studies, proceeded to busy himself with my education in other departments also. He introduced me to a world I had never known before—the world of low, rowdy taverns and loose women. I suppose it is a phase that many young men feel they have to pass through, in one way or another; it certainly held a morbid fascination for me, and I cannot pretend that I put up much resistance to following Zerri's lead. I did think remorsefully, from time to time, of my mother, and even more, perhaps, of Ida, who suspected nothing, and merely thought that I was having to devote more time than usual to my singing lessons.

I soon began, however, to find myself out of my depth, involved with Zerri in all sorts of jealous intrigues with which I was quite unable to cope. Some gossip reached the ears of Zerri's wife, Cecilia (incidentally a woman who, although completely blind, was renowned for her beauty). The gossip must have been somewhat distorted, because she decided on the basis of it that I was having a bad influence on her husband. She told him that I was a good-for-nothing, and that he was wasting his money on me. Zerri naturally knew the truth of the matter, but he was scarcely in a position to explain it to his wife. All the same, he managed to hold out against her scenes and scoldings. Then came the news that I was ordered to Libya. The day before I left, he came to see me, bringing the contract we had both signed.

'Look,' he said, 'I know you'll understand. I can't have peace under my own roof until I tear this up. You're not going to need singing lessons for the present, anyway. Here goes.' And he tore the contract to pieces before my eyes.

That was the last I saw of Giovanni Zerri for a very long time. He left Italy shortly afterwards, taking his family with him, and all I heard was that he had settled down in California.

In November 1920 I made my North American début at the Metropolitan, New York, as Faust in Boito's 'Mefistofele'. The papers next day devoted a good deal of space to it, and congratulatory telegrams began to pour in. I was going through them with some self-complacency, when I got a sudden jolt. The telegram I had just opened was from San Francisco. 'IF YOU REMEMBER ME,' it said, 'WELL AND GOOD STOP IF YOU DON'T YOU MAY GO TO THE DEVIL FOR ALL I CARE.' It was signed, of course, by Giovanni Zerri. I was not sure whether the 'devil' was meant to refer to 'Mefistofele', or whether it was just a coincidence; at any rate I telegraphed back at once, reassuring my old friend that I looked forward to seeing him again.

In the early autumn of 1923, I went to San Francisco. The civic authorities were excited about the first full-scale season of Italian opera ever to be held in the city, and I was given almost royal honours. A police motor-cycle escort, complete with sirens, accompanied me from the railway station to my hotel; and there, in the hall, I found Giovanni Zerri.

So it all came true in the end, his talk in the vine-trellised yard of the little wineshop in Recanati where we had played bowls together. 'You'll give me two tickets, won't you? Which will it be? "Bohème"? "Rigoletto"?' It was both 'Bohème' and 'Rigoletto'; indeed, as long as the season lasted, he never missed a performance. I was really overjoyed by this 'happy ending'. Our friendship had had its ups and downs, but I could never forget that, without Zerri's encouragement, I might have spent my life behind a counter in Recanati, wrapping pills.

Whenever I could, I would escape from officialdom and high San Francisco society, and steal away after the performance to join Zerri and Signora Cecilia (who seemed to have changed her mind about my being a good-for-nothing) over a midnight plate of spaghetti in the little restaurant with which they had 'made good' in the New World.

'Can't I help you?' I asked him one evening. 'It's my turn to help you now.'

'No, thanks,' he said gruffly. He had always treated me as an equal, and I could see that he intended to go on doing so.

'Are you sure?' I insisted.

'Well,' he said hesitantly, at last, 'perhaps there is just one thing you could do for me. Will you let me call this place the Beniamino Gigli Restaurant? It would be good for business, you know.'

As the train approached Naples, that Sunday afternoon in 1911, I was far from imagining that one day there would be a Beniamino Gigli Restaurant in San Francisco, owned by Giovanni Zerri. I was still thinking back on the three-and-a-half years I had spent in Rome. Life in a big city had not proved to be quite as terrible as my mother and father thought it was; still, it was undeniably more complicated than life in Recanati. Next time, I told myself, as I heaved my knapsack on to my shoulders—next time, if ever there was a next time, I would manage things better.

Meanwhile, I found myself already beginning to look forward to the sea journey, to the date palms, the camels and the desert. I was only twenty, and I had had quite a hard life so far. War, after all, might turn out to be a pleasant change.

I was quite right, in a way. Being ordered to Libya proved a pleasant change; but I never reached Libya. I lost my one chance of becoming a war hero, covered with medals. I saw no camels, no Arabs, no desert. Instead I found myself serving Mass and singing motets, being pampered by nuns and given plump legs of chicken to eat.

On reaching Naples we were piled into a vast barracks. From all over Italy troops were arriving daily, to await embarkation for Tripoli. One week passed, then a second, and a third. For the moment, nothing seemed to be happening. Discipline was relaxed, and to relieve the general monotony, and keep myself in practice, I sang almost continually from morning to night. One day, when I was washing my underwear, and at the same time singing '*Questa o quella*' at the top of my voice, a Neapolitan sergeant from the Medical Corps happened to be within earshot. On his own initiative, and without a word to me, he spoke about me (as I afterwards learned) to one of his superior officers. The upshot of this was that I found myself transferred to the military hospital at Caserta, outside Naples.

'Just keep pretending you've got a pain,' the sergeant told me.

'But why?' I protested. The whole thing seemed too idiotic, even for the Army.

'I can't explain, but don't worry,' said the sergeant mysteriously. 'It's for your own good.'

On arriving at the hospital, I was assigned a bed in one of the wards, and there I had to stay, as though I were really sick. For a few days I faithfully endeavoured to obey the sergeant's instructions, and kept complaining of my pains; but towards the end of the first week I could see that the doctor—a certain Major Mattioli—was not taking my invalid status very seriously.

'Well, Mr. Tenor,' he inquired breezily, 'and where is your pain this morning?'

'I can't move my left arm, *Signor Maggiore*,' I murmured feebly.

'Too bad,' said the Major, winking at me. 'Still, I think that perhaps you could manage to walk, if you really tried—eh? How about getting up and helping me with a few odd jobs?'

Before another week passed, I had abandoned all pretence of pains, and was unofficially installed as Major Mattioli's assistant. I followed him on his rounds, making notes of the instructions he gave for each patient, copying them out clearly afterwards, and keeping a record of each case. And when the Major discovered that I had once worked in a chemist's shop, he handed me the key of his little pharmacy and told me to keep it in order.

It was all quite pleasant, but I was still puzzled. What had become of my orders for Libya? Finally I asked the Major straight out.

'*Signor Maggiore*,' I said, 'I don't mean to be impertinent; but can you tell me why I'm here?'

He grinned. 'You can thank that precious voice of yours,' he said. 'Some people apparently think it so very precious that they decided not to let it go to Libya. The desert sand might irritate your throat, I suppose.'

'But what about my regiment?'

'Your regiment? Oh, it sailed three days ago.'

I had made quite a big effort in screwing my courage to the sticking-point; and now there was to be no war for me after all. It did not take me very long to get used to the idea; my new existence was comfortable, and getting adjusted to comfort is never very difficult. I had no immediate worries or responsibilities. Everything was delightfully vague. I decided to enjoy myself.

In this I was encouraged by the good nuns who ran the hospital. No one had enlightened them as to the real reason for my being there, and they presumed that I was suffering from some invisible malady. As I was, nevertheless, well enough to serve Mass and sing in the chapel, I soon became their special favourite. They mothered me, spoiled me, and showered me with delicacies. They were greatly impressed by my 'goodness' because, my own singing lessons being out of the question for the moment, I had started a singing class for convalescent patients. In actual fact, I had discovered teaching to be a useful exercise that helped me to get my ideas clear.

Ever since leaving Rome I had been writing constantly to Ida. At first she answered me promptly and lovingly. Then her letters dwindled; but the few that came were still unfailingly affectionate. Finally, without explanation, she stopped writing altogether. I had been away for three months. I knew her too well to believe that her feelings for me could have changed in so short a time. Something peculiar, I felt, was happening. Suddenly I became impatient of my dallying in Caserta, anxious to be in Rome again.

'How much longer do I have to stay here?' I asked Major Mattioli ungraciously.

'I thought you were having a good time.'

'So I was, but now there are reasons why I'd like to go.'

'If I discharge you from here, someone else may send you off to Libya by mistake, and I've undertaken to see that that doesn't happen,' he said. 'However, perhaps I could send you home to Recanati on a month's convalescent leave. Would that solve your problems?'

'I'm very grateful to you, sir,' I stammered, 'but couldn't I go to Rome instead?'

'I'm sorry,' said the Major, 'but it's Recanati or nothing, I'm afraid. Think it over.'

At any other time I would have jumped at the opportunity of seeing my mother again; but now I was obsessed with the thought of Ida, and for the moment nothing else mattered. Even a day in Rome, even an hour, would be enough: I only wanted to see her once, find out what was happening, be reassured. If only I had some money, I might contrive to get my railway ticket to Recanati re-routed via Rome; but it would be a big detour, and would certainly cost more than I could possibly scrape together.

The following morning, I got a letter from my mother. As I opened the envelope, something fluttered out. It was a five-lire note. Five lire was the equivalent of fifty days' pay, and naturally represented a small fortune for me; but I was well aware that it would not be enough for the railway company. I had calculated that I would need almost fifteen lire to make the detour by way of Rome. The five-lire note was providential, yet not providential enough. For a long time I sat contemplating it. Then despair inspired me. I went out to a tobacco shop and spent the entire sum on cigarettes, cheroots and plain tobacco.

Smoking was officially forbidden in the hospital wards. The regulation was not very strictly enforced, but it did mean that for patients confined to their beds, tobacco was extremely difficult to get hold of. I knew that, with nothing else to spend their money on, they would be quite prepared to pay a little extra for it, and I decided to take advantage of this situation. It was not very noble of me, but my frenzy about Ida had swept me beyond such niceties.

For three nights in succession, at a time when everyone was supposed to be asleep, I made the round of the wards, hawking my wares. On the third night I sold my last cigarette, and the five lire had become fifteen: just what I needed.

'I've thought it over, sir,' I told Major Mattioli next day. 'I'd like to go to Recanati after all.'

My ticket was valid only for slow trains. I travelled all night from Naples, and reached Rome in the early morning. Long before eight o'clock I was pacing up and down before the telephone exchange, waiting for Ida to arrive. At nine o'clock there was still no sign of her. I went inside and made inquiries.

'She hasn't been at work for weeks,' one of the girls told me. 'We don't know what's happened to her, but she was rather strange lately.'

Terrified, I ran to her house. Her mother received me very coldly.

'Ida is not here,' she said. 'Please go away.'

'Tell me where to find her,' I begged.

'I am afraid you cannot see her.'

'But I must, I must. I've come to Rome on purpose. Please, let me see her, just once.'

'Ida is in hospital. She has had a nervous breakdown, and we are very worried about her. The doctor has strictly forbidden her to have visitors. Excitement of any kind is very bad for her. Now will you please go away?'

Tears rolled down my cheeks. I made no effort to repress them. I wanted to touch this woman's heart.

'Very well,' I said, 'but at least tell me where she is, so that I can send her flowers.'

The tears had worked. Grudgingly, she gave me the address. It was a small private hospital on the Janiculum.

I put the bunch of flowers down on the bed and waited for Ida to laugh, cry, open her arms. But she only turned her head away.

'Ida,' I said. 'Ida, darling, it's me.'

'Why did you come?' she said at last. Her voice sounded tired, faint, distant. It scarcely seemed a voice at all, only the echo of a voice.

'When you stopped writing,' I said, 'I had to come.'

'Didn't you understand?' she asked wearily. 'It's no good. It's all over. I gave in.'

'What do you mean?'

'Oh, I fought them. I held out for ages. But they said it would kill them. So I gave in, in the end.'

'Who are *they*?'

'My parents, of course. A girl can't fight her parents. It isn't right. So I gave in. Then I was very sick. I kept fainting all the time. Now it's all over. I'm getting better. But I've promised them. So please go away, Beniamino.'

'Promised them *what*?'

'Not to see you. Not to write to you. Not to marry you.'

'But why? What have I done?'

'Oh, nothing. You're poor. They say you'll end up singing in the streets. They say I might as well marry a beggar and be done with it. Oh, I know it isn't true. But if only you did have some proper job, then I could have argued with them. Anyway, I tell you, it's all over now. I'm sorry, Beniamino. Don't make things worse than they are. Please go away, and forget me.'

'But, Ida,' I began.

She turned her head on the pillow and looked me straight in the eyes.

I trembled.

'Don't insist,' she said slowly. 'It's no use. You see, I've changed. I don't love you any more.'

I looked at her incredulously for a long moment. Then I rushed from the room.

I never saw Ida again.

CHAPTER IV

THE ACADEMY OF SANTA CECILIA

THE month in Recanati did me a lot of good. After the break with Ida, my mother's love was a healing balm. I felt a child again, cared for and protected.

It was something of a shock to open the grey envelope and find that at the end of the month I was to return to Rome, to my old post as telephone operator at the Territorial Command. How was I going to face Rome without Ida, within reach of Ida but forbidden her sight?

Never had I felt so lonely. The one consolation I had was Colonel Delfino's kindly, familiar face. But all my old comrades were gone from the barracks—gone to Libya; my brother Catervo was studying sculpture in Carrara; Giovanni Zerri had disappeared; Signora Bonucci was angry with me; I had no money to resume my singing lessons with Professor Martino.

When I was off duty, I often found myself with nothing better to do than wander aimlessly up and down the Via Paolina, outside the Territorial Command. I could scarcely help noticing a certain fair-haired girl who passed down the street at the same time every evening, and entered one of the houses. I began to wonder who she was.

Some weeks went by; we found ourselves saying 'Good evening' to each other. One day we walked the length of the street together. She told me her name; it was Costanza Cerroni. Her father was a *sensale*, a kind of broker who made cash advances to farmers in return for the promise of their crops. He conducted his business in the traditional way, on the steps of the fountain in the Piazza del Pantheon. She herself worked in the office of the daily newspaper *La Tribuna*, addressing the copies of the newspaper that were to be sent out to postal subscribers.

I had not forgotten Ida, but she had wounded my pride. Costanza banished my loneliness. Soon after our first conversation, I asked her to marry me, explaining that it would mean a long wait. She accepted, although I could only offer her my poverty and my hopes.

Meanwhile I was without a singing teacher. What was more, my military service was due to end in a few months' time, and I would have to find a job. Life seemed to be a series of beginnings.

I entered my name as a candidate for one of the clerical posts that had fallen vacant in the municipal administration. I was painfully aware of the inadequacy of my schooling, but felt, optimistically, that I had learned something in the Army. On the day of the examination I sat for an hour staring in bewilderment at the arithmetic paper. It cannot have been so very difficult, but as far as I was concerned, it might have been Chinese. Finally I drew a note of music on the blank page where I should have written the answers, and followed it up with a slightly modified version of Cavaradossi's famous line in 'Tosca':

'*Svanì per sempre il sogno mio . . . d'impiego!*'

('My dream of . . . employment vanished for ever!' Of course the original is '*il sogno mio d'amore*', 'my dream of love'.) Then I handed in the sheet of paper, and walked out of the examination hall.

Once again I found myself appealing for help to Colonel Delfino. He promised to keep a look-out for a job for me, and told me not to worry.

'By the way,' he said, 'what's happening to your music? Don't forget you promised me that box at the Opera.'

I explained that for the moment I was unable to afford a singing teacher.

'Well, now,' he said, 'they should be able to do something for you at the Academy of Santa Cecilia. Why don't you go along and have a talk with them?'

The Academy of Santa Cecilia is Rome's august and renowned school of music. I had really never dared to think of it in connexion with myself. However, I followed the Colonel's advice, and discovered that there would shortly be a scholarship examination. I decided to enter for it.

There were seventeen of us competing. As my test pieces I sang arias from Flotow's 'Marta' and from 'Luisa Miller', ending with '*Giunto sul passo estremo*' from 'Mefistofele'. I felt confident enough; but then came something I had not expected—the examination in pianoforte playing. There was no bluffing my way out of that predicament. I told the examiner frankly that the only instrument I had ever learned to play was the saxophone.

I felt so mortified that I would rather not have waited to hear the results announced, but all the other candidates stayed on, and I decided that by leaving I would only disgrace myself still more. We had to wait a long time, while the examiners conducted their post-mortem. Finally Professor Stanislao Falchi, the director of the Academy, mounted the podium. He went through all the other candidates, one by one; my heart sank with a final thud when I realized that I was being dealt with last.

'The candidate Beniamino Gigli,' began the Professor in a solemn voice, 'has presented himself for the entrance examination without even the most elementary knowledge of the piano. We are all aware that without some knowledge of the piano, no student can be admitted to the Academy.'

He paused, glanced at me severely, and proceeded: 'Notwithstanding, the board of examiners has been so deeply impressed by the vocal ability and artistry of the said candidate, that it has decided to make an exception in his favour.'

The Professor paused again, this time to smile at me.

'I have pleasure in announcing,' he concluded, 'that Beniamino Gigli has been awarded first place in the examination, and a scholarship of sixty lire a month.'

The term at Santa Cecilia would not begin until the autumn, and my military service was already ending. Colonel Delfino advised me to go home to Recanati for the summer.

'Your parents are not getting any younger,' he said. 'Let them have you for a little while. You'll be away from them long enough. Get your mother to cook those good soups for you, and take plenty of fresh air. Don't forget you still have a long pull ahead of you.'

He promised to write to me as soon as he heard of a suitable part-time job that would supplement my scholarship.

It was a golden, carefree summer. On my previous visit to Recanati I had been in mourning, so to speak, for Ida, and had rarely left the house. But now I found delight in revisiting the scenes of my childhood: climbing with my father to the top of the belfry tower and helping him to ring the bells; walking with

Enzo, Costanza, Rina and myself—New York, December, 1921

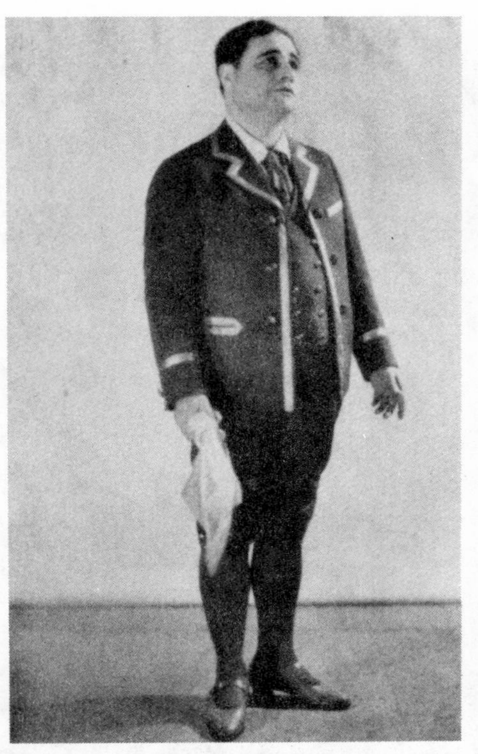

Three rôles: *Above, left,* Nemorino in Donizetti's 'L'Elisir d'Amore'. *Above, right,* Osaka in Mascagni's 'Iris'. *Left,* Elvino in Bellini's 'La Sonnambula'.

Don Romano to the 'Hill of the Infinite'; practising motets with Maestro Lazzarini in the organ-loft of the Cathedral, or chatting with Mastro Parò in his carpenter's workshop; playing the saxophone in Maestro Battelli's band, and being honoured by Signor Verdecchia, my old employer, with a glass of his aniseed liqueur. I felt as though I were once again being rocked in a cradle. To the eyes of the city-dweller that I had become, the old provincial life appeared soft, sweet and dreamy. I was loath to leave it, when the time came. I had to remind myself that in Rome Costanza was waiting for me, and that I was already more than half-way to becoming a singer.

My brother Catervo was back in Rome, married and living in a flat in Via dei Pontefici. Once again he offered to share his roof with me; but this time it was no longer the *vie de bohème*. We were both growing into staid, respectable citizens. Catervo had been commissioned by Angelo Zanelli to help cast some of the statues for the Altare della Patria, the vast white marble monument to King Victor Emmanuel II that is now a landmark of Rome. As for me, Colonel Delfino had kept his promise, and found me a job for the afternoons—'technical assistant' in the photography department of the Ministry of Education, at a salary of sixty lire a month. With my scholarship, this made a hundred and twenty lire altogether. I had never been so rich.

The mornings were devoted to study at the Academy. My first professor was the great baritone Antonio Cotogni. He had been on the board of examiners at the entrance examination, and had chosen me then and there to be one of his students. I consider it a privilege to have known Cotogni. He was not only a great artist, but also an exceptionally good and generous man who took a personal interest, not only in the musical progress of his students, but also in their material welfare, going so far as to send anonymous gifts of shoes, an overcoat or even money, when he thought they were needed.

He was completely free from the pettiness and envy that are common to so many singers. After having spent almost thirty years as 'the Tsar's baritone' at the Moscow Imperial Theatre, he was still at the height of his fame when another Italian baritone, Battistini, appeared on the Moscow scene. Cotogni immediately decided that his own innings had lasted long enough, and he set about training the younger man as his successor.

He called on Battistini, unannounced, one morning at eight o'clock. Battistini was somewhat taken aback.

'Young man,' said Cotogni without preamble, 'you must lose no time in preparing yourself to take over the rôle of Don Giovanni. Now, there are certain traditions attached to this rôle as sung at the Imperial Theatre; let me explain them to you.'

The night Battistini made his Moscow début in 'Don Giovanni', Cotogni embraced him in full view of the audience, and then spoke a few words of farewell. He left for Rome the following day, and never sang in opera again. So great was his prestige that the Academy of Santa Cecilia promptly offered him a professorship. When I arrived, he had been teaching there for twenty years or more.

I had never known anyone like Cotogni. It thrilled me to sit in his class and think that here I was, being taught by someone who had himself been one of the greatest singers in Europe. Moreover, one felt somehow ennobled by his very presence. It was natural, therefore, that I should have felt indignant when Falchi, the director of the Academy, told me that I was wasting my time in Cotogni's class. Where, I demanded, outraged, could one find a greater, more eminent teacher? But Falchi insisted. The training of my voice, he said, was now his responsibility. Cotogni was over eighty years of age, and his energy was failing. If I wanted to make progress, I should enrol as a student of Maestro Enrico Rosati.

I held out stubbornly as long as I could, but Falchi was, after all, the director of the Academy, and in the end I felt obliged to follow his advice. I hardly knew what explanation to give Cotogni, and as for Rosati, I entered his class unwillingly and with a very bad grace. Rosati was perfectly aware of this.

'You needn't stay if you don't want to,' he told me bluntly. 'Please yourself.'

However, I stayed. Maestro Rosati proved to be an ideal teacher. He could be stern and exacting, and he made his students work very hard. In this respect, no doubt, he was better for me than Cotogni would have been. Yet, like Agnese Bonucci at an earlier stage, he understood my voice completely, and led me forward with no sense of strain or effort. He remained my guide and mentor for the two years I spent at Santa Cecilia, and he prepared me for my début. I am happy to say that our association developed into a lifelong friendship, and I take this opportunity of recording my gratitude to him.

The foundations of my vocal training had of course by this time been laid, but my singing still had a number of faults, and these Rosati was determined to cure me of. For example, I had grown accustomed to singing at the top of my voice, with all the strength of my lungs; and the result was that high notes gave me some trouble. Rosati helped me to cultivate the finer shades of tone, and taught me a sense of proportion. He made me leave opera alone for a while, and concentrate on delicate seventeenth- and eighteenth-century songs. I remember in particular Mozart's '*Violets*'. After six months of hard work, both in his class at Santa Cecilia and in private lessons at his house, I was finally able to sing the extremely difficult '*Ingemisco*' from Verdi's 'Requiem Mass' to the maestro's satisfaction.

One Sunday towards the end of the first spring term, Maestro Rosati took his class for a traditional Roman *scampagnata,* or trip to the country. We went to Frascati, in the Alban Hills, and after a walk in the beautiful park of the Villa Aldobrandini, we sat down at a long trestle table in the garden of a little tavern, and ate raw broad beans with *pecorino,* a hard salty cheese made from ewe's milk, which naturally required to be washed down with draughts of amber Frascati wine. We were very gay, but there were some young ladies in the party, and in spite of the wine we all remained on our best behaviour.

A crisis arose, however, soon after we had squeezed into the crowded, bumbling old tram for the slow and uncomfortable journey back to Rome. A group of loutish youths, who had obviously had a great deal more Frascati wine to drink than was good for them, began to make coarse jokes at the expense of the girls in our party. At first we pretended to ignore them, but we were all packed so close together, and they were so obstreperous, that the situation soon became tense. It was the sort of situation that, in Italy at any rate, can easily lead to violence.

'For God's sake, sing something, Beniamino,' whispered Maestro Rosati in my ear.

The first thing that came to my mind was the '*Ingemisco*', and without stopping to think, I plunged straight into it. After a few notes I realized how madly unsuitable it was, but it was too late to stop. In the desperate effort of concentration to sing it well, I became oblivious of my surroundings.

When I finished, there was dead silence in the sweaty tram. I looked around me. The rowdy youths appeared to have been struck dumb. No applause could have given me such a feeling of triumph.

The end-of-term recitals at Santa Cecilia always drew a contingent of the music-loving members of Roman society. After performing in one or two of these recitals, I began to acquire a certain reputation, and was constantly invited to sing at the soirées of great Roman houses. This was strictly against the rules of Santa Cecilia; one was not allowed to sing professionally while a student of the Academy. But the money rewards were so temping that I decided to flout the regulations. In a single evening, I could earn two or even three times as much as in a whole month of afternoons spent at my job developing photographs in the dark-room of the Ministry of Education.

I gave up the job, and thenceforth devoted the afternoon to study, as well as the morning; while in the evening, under the pseudonym of Mino Rosa (a subterfuge to evade the ban of the Academy), I sang in the salons of the Marchese di Rudini, Signora Garroni, Count Blumenstiel, the Russian Ambassador Krupensky, and other society people. I even sang for my old employer, Countess Spannocchi; we had a good laugh together at my expense when she recalled how I used to serve at table with sauce all over the fingers of my white gloves.

I had to hire a dress suit for these occasions, but it sat so badly on my somewhat unorthodox figure that in the end I had one made to measure. With money, it seemed, everything became possible. I was already earning up to three thousand lire a month, a far cry from the sixty lire on which I had managed to exist in the old 'fried-scrap' days.

With the summer of 1914 came the last day of my last term at Santa Cecilia. The final examinations were over; I had won first place among the tenors. The great hall of the Academy was packed with the guests who had come to hear our recital, and with impresarios waiting, like wolves, to pounce on the lambs as they left the fold. Both Falchi and Rosati warned me to turn a deaf ear to their offers for the time being; feeling that their advice was sound, I followed it.

Somewhere in the chattering crowd of fashionable Roman ladies sat a silent old country woman, with a white kerchief knotted beneath her chin; it was my mother, who had made the long journey from Recanati quite alone. I sang '*O Paradiso*' from Meyerbeer's 'L'Africana', an opera that had been in the repertory of the little brass band for which I had played the saxophone in Piazza Leopardi on Sunday afternoons.

The explosion of applause at the end was all I could have hoped for, but I was rewarded with something else besides: the sight of the revered octogenarian Antonio Cotogni flinging his arms around my mother's neck, kissing her on both cheeks, and congratulating her on her son.

'And now,' said Maestro Rosati in a grave voice, 'you are ready to face the world.'

The long, hard climb was over. For the first time, I stood on a peak, and could survey the land. I had six years of training behind me; I had an unbroken record of first places at Santa Cecilia; I was twenty-four. As Maestro Rosati had said, now I was ready to face the world; or in other words, I was ready to face the impresarios, the critics and the public.

It was a formidable, and indeed a frightening prospect; but once again, I was lucky. Shortly after leaving Santa Cecilia I found myself, almost overnight, in a position to pick and choose among the proposals of impresarios.

Maestro Rosati had advised me to enter for an international singing contest that was to be held in Parma, in July, 1914. The aim of the contest was to discover and encourage new vocal talents; in order to qualify as a candidate, one had to be unknown. It was jointly sponsored by Maestro Cleofonte Campanini, an orchestra conductor and professor at the Parma Conservatorio, whose idea it was in the first place, and a generous American woman, Mrs. Elizabeth McCormick of Chicago, who was financing it. The winners were to be rewarded with engagements for an operatic season in Chicago. Maestro Campanini and Mrs. McCormick hoped to make the contest an annual event, thereby guaranteeing that every year a number of promising young singers would have a chance to prove themselves, without falling —as happened only too often—into the clutches of unscrupulous agents and impresarios.

The outbreak of the First World War not only prevented the

contest from being repeated in subsequent years; it even upset the plans for the operatic season that was to have been held in Chicago, with the winners taking part. As things turned out, almost the only person who benefited from this contest, in which so many hopes had been placed, and on which so much money had been spent, was myself.

There were a hundred and five of us gathered in Parma in that blazing July of 1914: thirty-two tenors, nineteen baritones, six bassos, forty sopranos, six mezzo-sopranos, and two contraltos. Italy was well represented, but the contest had received such wide advance publicity that there were candidates from all over Europe, from Moscow, New York, Chicago and Buenos Aires. Our return fares and our living expenses for the three weeks were paid by Mrs. McCormick.

The setting reassured me. I had never been so far north before, yet I felt at home in Parma; though built on a more princely scale than Recanati, it was provincial Italy. I knew, moreover, of its associations with Verdi, and of its reputation as a music-loving city, which I discovered for myself to be well founded; the ordinary citizens of Parma followed our contest with passionate interest, as though it were some kind of musical Olympic Games, and they treated us all with great kindness and hospitality.

Professor Italo Azzoni, vice-director of the Parma Conservatorio, presided over the examining board, which included two other Conservatorio professors, an orchestra conductor, a lawyer, and one old acquaintance, the tenor Alessandro Bonci, former employer of my friend the cook, Giovanni Zerri. Nine hours a day, for twenty consecutive days, the examiners sat in the concert hall of the Conservatorio; every candidate had to sing three pieces, and as there were a hundred and five of us, it took quite a long time. The heat was tropical, and in the intervals vast quantities of iced beer were consumed by examiners and candidates alike. I had never drunk so much beer in my life before, nor, I think, have I ever done so since.

My turn came at the beginning of the third week. I sang an aria from Reyer's 'Sigurd', the last scene of 'Traviata', and '*O Paradiso*' from Meyerbeer's 'L'Africana'.

Most of the candidates had some degree of talent, but a surprising number of them fell below the required standards because of faulty or insufficient training. A comical episode which I happened to witness on the last evening of the contest gave me some inkling of the ordeal to which the examiners had been subjected.

When the hundred and fifth candidate sang the last notes of his last piece, it was almost midnight. A few of us who had been lingering outside pounced on the weary examiners as they left the hall, and escorted them to Piazza Garibaldi for a farewell glass of beer. The beer revived everyone, and we were chattering merrily around a café table, when suddenly a sepulchral bass voice began to intone Cacico's aria from 'Guarany'—'*Giovinetta nello sguardo*'. The voice was cracked and hopelessly out of tune, but so loud that it filled the Piazza. It provoked the examiners to such a unanimous cry of exasperated protest that the carabinieri who had been lingering under the arcades began to move slowly in our direction. Still it persisted, louder and louder: 'To Love's paradise hast thou opened thy heart . . .' Finally a street singer emerged from the shadows and approached us, with outstretched hand, still singing.

It was too much for the examiners, and one of them, Maestro Silva, bounded to his feet. Pushing a five-lire note into the singer's hand, he shouted: 'Stop it at once and get out of here, or I'll *shoot*!' The line about 'thy sad and pallid countenance' died on the poor creature's lips; terrified into silence, he vanished from sight. Then we all collapsed into helpless laughter. Three weeks of tension had ended.

The results were announced the following day. I was proclaimed to have been the 'revelation' of the contest. At the bottom of my report, one of the examiners had written in block letters: 'AT LAST WE HAVE FOUND THE TENOR!' THE TENOR was underlined three times in red pencil.

So much publicity had been built up around the contest, that the news of the 'revelation' made headlines in the Italian press. I was snowed under with telegrams from agents, impresarios and theatres throughout Italy. This, I told myself firmly, was the point at which I must be careful not to lose my head. Back in Rome, I consulted Maestro Rosati. He put me in the hands of an excellent agent named Lusardi, and together they helped me to decide the question, so momentous for any young singer, of where to make my début.

It was plain that I could not afford to rest for very long on the laurels of the Parma contest. The problem was to find a reputable theatre having an opera with a good tenor part in its programme for the beginning of the autumn season. These requirements seemed to be met by the Teatro Sociale in Rovigo, which had offered me the rôle of Enzo Grimaldo in Amilcare Ponchielli's opera 'La Gioconda'.

Rovigo, like Recanati, lies just inland from the Adriatic, although much further north; this did something to predispose me in its favour. The opera season was scheduled to begin unusually early, in order to coincide with a big autumn fair that would be attracting visitors from all over Northern Italy. This was an advantage; the sooner I got started, the better. There would be a conductor of repute, Giuseppe Sturani, who had been on the board of examiners for the Parma contest. The other soloists, among them the soprano Tina Poli-Randaccio and the baritone Segura-Tallien, were all established singers. But what finally decided me to choose Rovigo was the fact, which I learned by chance in a conversation with Rosati, that Antonio Cotogni, the great baritone of former days, whom I had admired so much at Santa Cecilia, had made his début in the very same theatre. Somehow, I felt, this was a good omen.

CHAPTER V

DEBUT

AUGUST, 1914.

The words, I know, have a tragic ring. But singers are egoists, and my memories of that cataclysmic month are purely personal: long stifling days of standing by the piano in Maestro Rosati's darkened house, the windows tightly closed and shuttered in a vain attempt to keep out the heat, and the furniture shrouded in dust-sheets because the maestro's family had gone away for the holidays, leaving him behind to coach me for my début. We would pause to make coffee, or eat sardines out of a tin; then back to the piano again, hour after hour. Every day the strident 'Stop Press' cries of death in Flanders would penetrate to the shuttered room from the street below; I would wait till they had passed, then repeat my interrupted *pianissimo*. What else could I do? I had my own battle to fight.

When Nature gave me a voice, she was thoughtful enough to add the subsidiary gift of a good memory. I can scarcely imagine how, as an opera singer, I could have managed without it. Once, in four days, I had to learn Puccini's 'Rondine'; in a week, Mascagni's 'Lodoletta'. For my first rôle, however, I had six whole weeks in which to prepare, and the memorizing of my part took so little effort that I was able to concentrate on style and technique. Maestro Rosati was a perfectionist, and I think my début meant almost as much to him as it did to me; so he prepared me well, and I felt confident.

The rôle of Enzo I found almost ideal for a beginner. It made no excessive demands, yet it gave me a great deal of scope. However fundamentally undistinguished the music of 'La Gioconda' may be, it is decidedly a 'singers' opera', with splendid parts for six soloists: soprano, mezzo-soprano, contralto, baritone, bass and, above all, tenor. Performed for the first time in Milan in 1876, it belongs to the old-fashioned school of opera which aimed chiefly at providing plenty of good tunes, and a chance for singers to sing. Ponchielli was no revolutionary.

Nevertheless, 'La Gioconda' is something of a landmark in Italian opera. The pace is faster than was common at the time, the orchestration more incisive and theatrically more effective. The old forms of recitative and aria breathe with a new vigour. The libretto does not, perhaps, bear close inspection. It is a story of Renaissance intrigue, derived by that many-sided genius, Arrigo Boito, from a forgotten play of Victor Hugo's, *Angelo, Tyran de Padoue*. There are two unhappy love affairs, a foiled elopement, a fake poisoning, bartered virtue, and a suicide; there are statesmen and outlaws, beggars and spies, and fair damsels in distress. It may not be art; but I think it is excellent entertainment. The action may be involved and improbable, but it is vivid; it moves with a swing against a background of colourful pageantry. There is some scintillating ballet music, including the well-known '*Dance of the Hours*'. Looking back on the many occasions when I have sung 'La Gioconda' since that first time in Rovigo, I can say that both singers and audience have always seemed to enjoy it.

There was to be a fortnight of rehearsal with the rest of the cast. I arrived in Rovigo at the beginning of October, and found lodgings in the house of two elderly sisters, both of them midwives by profession. They treated me with almost as much care and solicitude as if I had been a new-born baby; as a background to the ordeal I was about to face, I found this extremely comforting.

The celebrated aria '*Cielo e mar*', which comes midway in Act 2, has always been the test and, when successful, the triumph of the tenor in 'La Gioconda'. It ends with the words, '*Ah, vien! Ah, vien!*' The final note, as Ponchielli wrote it, is G; but in the course of years the opera-going public had shown itself dissatisfied with this somewhat muted climax, and it had become traditional for the tenor, in defiance of the original score, to let his voice soar up to a final B flat.

I had sailed through the early rehearsals on a wave of self-confidence; but at the dress rehearsal I had a set back. The closed vowel sound in '*vien!*' seemed to get in my way, and I muffed the final B flat. For the first time, I began to feel nervous.

'Don't let the B flat worry you,' said the conductor, Maestro

Sturani. 'The rest of it went splendidly; why don't you stick to the score and sing G at the end instead?'

'But the audience want the B flat,' I objected.

'They won't expect it of you,' he said. 'After all, you're a beginner.'

The night of my début came at last; it was October 15th, 1914. I was well aware that for the crowd facing me in the Teatro Sociale, my presence on the stage was purely incidental; at most, it might arouse a certain mild curiosity. 'There's a new tenor; wonder what he's like?' They had come to hear Tina Poli-Randaccio in the title-rôle, Segura-Tallien as Barnaba, Ida Zizolfi as Laura. Despite Maestro Sturani's reassurances about my being a beginner, I knew I could hope for no indulgence. Whether I succeeded or failed, I was going to be judged by the highest standards; and I was glad of it.

Before the performance, I let my thoughts dwell on my mother, and I kissed her photograph. I prayed to the Blessed Virgin. I drank endless cups of very strong black coffee. Probably it all helped; I did sing well. But when I came to '*Cielo e mar*', I was in terror from the very first note. How would the finale go? I had not yet made up my mind about whether to attempt the B flat. As I sang, I searched the theatre with my eyes for my two midwife landladies. I had told them all about my problem. Now, if only our eyes could meet, perhaps some wave of maternal sympathy from them would carry me up to that B flat. But I had to give up the search; looking into the sea of faces was beginning to make me feel dizzy. I drew breath to sing the B flat; then, suddenly, I felt as though my throat were closing up. Instinctively I played safe and sang the G instead.

The audience clapped me enthusiastically enough, my colleagues were more than generous with their congratulations, my landladies embraced me and wept for joy, and I myself knew that, apart from funking the B flat, I had acquitted myself well. The Press next morning endorsed the opinion of the Parma judges. I was a 'revelation', a 'fully-developed and already mature artist'; the critics were unanimous in prophesying a great future for me. I heaved an immense sigh of relief, and decided to stop worrying about the B flat.

That same afternoon I overheard a conversation between a member of the orchestra and a member of the chorus.

'Gigli's range is a bit limited,' said one.

'Yes, did you notice he couldn't manage the B flat?' said the other.

Somewhat piqued, I marched straight over and confronted them. 'What do you mean?' I demanded. 'I sing B flat a dozen times elsewhere in the opera; I just don't like that particular one, that's all.'

By now I felt positively self-righteous about the whole thing. That evening, at the second performance, I sang '*Cielo e mar*' without a trace of nervousness, having settled in advance for the final G. But this time the audience responded coldly, and gave me no more than the most perfunctory applause. It was plain that they really did want the B flat; but I intended to stand my ground. After all, the critics had not reproached me. The audience should be cured of its whims, and taught to respect the score.

Or so I told myself; but in my heart I knew that these arguments were only a camouflage for my dread of that horrible sensation when my throat had seemed to close.

On the third night, I still felt defiant. I intended to sing the G, whether they liked it or not. But as I approached the end of the aria, I felt a sudden infusion of courage—or maybe it was only bravado. 'I'll show them,' I thought recklessly; and I pitched not only my voice, but my whole being, on B flat.

It won me an ovation—the first of my career as a tenor. (I had already had one in the days when I sang soprano!) The audience was on its feet, clapping, cheering, throwing programmes in the air, demanding an encore. The conductor had to lay down his baton; the performance was interrupted. But I refused the encore; I had no intention of tempting Providence. I was overcome, not only with relief, but with amazement at myself. How had I done it? I scarcely knew.

Sleep evaded me that night. Tossing restlessly in bed, I noticed for the first time that the sheets were unbearably scratchy. In a frenzy of discomfort, I turned on the light to investigate, and saw that the entire top portion of the sheet was covered with intricate and what I can only describe as massive embroidery. Stiffly laundered, it had become a labyrinth of rough edges. It was not the sort of sheet one would ever find in a shop. I realized that one of my maiden ladies, in her remote girlhood days, must have embroidered it for her bottom drawer.

That was life, I thought; plans go astray, hopes are cheated, ambitions dwindle and dissolve. Yet the triumph I had experienced, earlier that same night, before the footlights—that, surely, was a part of life also? Or was it only a dream, from which I would awaken? No, I knew it was not a dream. Was the rest of my life going to be like that? It was an awe-inspiring, in some ways a terrifying prospect. Why should I have been singled out? Why should I have the power to bring an audience to its feet, when neither of my landladies, sweet, good creatures though they were, had been able to find a husband? It was true that I had worked hard; but there were others whom no amount of hard work could save from disappointment.

I was no theologian. It was a mystery to me why God should have shown me such favour. I felt humble and unworthy; also, suddenly, I felt impelled to thank Him.

I got out of bed and went down on my knees.

I had learned an important lesson in Rovigo. The singer is dependent on his audience. The audience pays to hear him; it gives him his livelihood. Within the limits of his own artistic integrity, he must, in fair exchange, give it what it wants. He can propose, but he cannot dictate to it. He must please it, he must conquer its sympathies, or else he might as well get off the stage. The audience is his judge, his jury, his court of appeal.

The critics, too, fulfil a necessary function. But from the singer's point of view, they are of secondary importance. He could manage without them. Indeed, he sometimes thinks he could manage very nicely without them! One cannot, however, imagine a singer without an audience; they complement each other.

No singer, however well-established, should be too proud to learn from an informed, unbiased and constructive critic; but many criticisms amount to no more than a comparison of one's own performance last night with the way So-and-so sang the same rôle last year, or five, ten or fifteen years ago. Criticisms of this kind have never meant anything to me. The one question that always mattered to me was: How did *I* sing on that particular evening? Did my performance ring true to my listeners? Did I touch their hearts? Did I succeed in giving them a deep emotional and artistic experience?

No critic has ever had the power to wound or worry me as

long as my audience was satisfied. But no 'rave-notice' in the Press could console me if my audience withheld its applause, or if I knew in my heart that I had failed to reach it.

I am not complaining of my critics; throughout my career, they have almost always been more than generous in their praise of my singing. Occasionally, however—especially in England and America—they were inclined to deplore my 'playing to the gallery', as they called it. From a purist point of view, no doubt they were quite right. But singing differs from other forms of music in that inspiration comes to life, not through an instrument of wood or brass, but through the highly subjective medium of the human voice. I have already spoken earlier in these pages of the singer's need for communion. As he sings, it is vital for him to feel that he is evoking an immediate response, otherwise his performance remains a matter of technique; he cannot give of his best, he cannot put his heart into it. Sometimes, perhaps, in the emotion of the moment, I made the mistake of being too eager to elicit this response. But the critics must understand that a singer cannot sing without applause.

For the remaining eleven performances that we gave in Rovigo, I clung somewhat precariously to the conquered pinnacle of the B flat in '*Cielo e mar*'. At the end of October we had ten days' respite before transferring to the Teatro Verdi in Ferrara. I hurried back to Rome.

'I can't go on like this,' I told Maestro Rosati. 'I'm still terrified of that B flat. Sometimes I bring it off and sometimes I feel I don't. The Rovigo audience was on my side after the third night, but now I have to start all over again in Ferrara.'

'You'll be all right for Ferrara, I promise,' he reassured me. 'We'll do some intensive practising.'

And practise we did.

'Well,' inquired the Maestro, a week later, 'how do you feel now about your B flat?'

'I think I'm pretty confident of it at last, thanks to you,' I said.

He smiled. 'Yes,' he said. 'From now on I think you can be confident, not only of B flat, but of B natural and high C as well.'

'What do you mean?' I asked.

'A week ago, before we started practising, I had the piano retuned a whole tone higher,' he said mischievously. 'So every time you thought you were singing B flat, in reality it was a beautiful high C. Congratulations!'

One evening in Ferrara I was introduced to the great conductor Maestro Tullio Serafin.

'I heard you sing tonight,' he said. 'I have a proposal to make to you. The season at the Carlo Felice in Genoa will be opening on December 26th with Massenet's "Manon". Will you sing Des Grieux?'

The Carlo Felice is one of the half-dozen great Italian opera houses. There were about three hundred tenors available in Italy at the time. Yet only a month after my début, in the teeth of all this competition, I was being picked to open the season at the Carlo Felice, and by no less a conductor than Serafin.

'So that,' I said to myself, 'is what they think of me.'

To Maestro Serafin I only said, 'Thank you for asking me, Maestro. I'll try.'

In Genoa I began to feel that I was out in the wide world. Life there was lived at a faster pace than I had ever known. I was not at all surprised to learn that it was the birthplace of Christopher Columbus. The people spoke a dialect that I had difficulty in following. They were a race of mariners and traders to whom money was a commonplace, to whom the remotest point on the atlas meant no more than a market to be won or expanded. It was all very different from what now seemed to me by contrast the leisurely, homely rhythm of life further to the South. Throughout the centuries, when Rome and Recanati were ruled by the Popes, Genoa was an independent maritime republic. One could feel the difference. I, who knew nothing of history, found as I travelled in Italy that, all around me, history was coming alive.

In 'Manon', as in 'La Gioconda', I was to sing opposite an already famous soprano. This time it was Rosina Storchio. Unlike Tina Poli-Randaccio, she showed pique about being partnered with a beginner, and in fact complained about it to Serafin.

'Wait and see,' he told her.

'Oh, yes, I can imagine,' she said. 'Another of your infant prodigies. Don't you think I deserve something better?'

During the rehearsals she lost no opportunity of making me feel, in one way or another, that I was an upstart and had no right to be there. This attitude made it somewhat difficult for me to languish convincingly as her unhappy lover, but I was determined not to let it interfere with my performance on the opening night. There would always, I decided, be some obstacle to overcome. Now it was the prima donna's dislike of me, just as in Rovigo it had been the B flat.

I read the heart-breaking novel by the Abbé Prévost on which the *libretto* of 'Manon' is based. Then I read it again, and then again. Finally I succeeded in forming my own idea of what Manon was like, and holding it before me, in my mind's eye, even on the stage.

The expedient worked. When I sang the '*Dream Song*' on the opening night, Madame Storchio might have been a thousand miles away. I was thinking only of that heartless wanton, Manon Lescaut.

The rich Genoese were enthusiastic patrons of opera. Not having sung in such a large theatre before, I was genuinely amazed to discover that applause can really sound like a storm. Of course in Rome I had often sat in the gallery at the Costanzi, clapping my own hands off for Lazzaro or Bonci or Battistini; but somehow it sounded different when one was away from it, on the stage. Was this for me? It was almost terrifying. '*Bis! Bis!*' they were shouting now, stamping their feet. I looked helplessly at Serafin standing on the podium. He nodded to me. I clutched at my private image of Manon, and sang the '*Dream Song*' again.

If Rosina Storchio was a thousand miles away from me while all this was going on, she was right back at less than arm's length the moment the curtain fell.

'I must say you've lost no time in hiring your *claque*,' she lashed out at me.

'What do you think I pay them with, dear lady?' I retorted. 'Coppers?'

This was an allusion to the fact that although I was now getting double the amount I had been paid in Rovigo and Ferrara, it was still only a hundred lire a night—scarcely enough to pay for hired applause, even had I thought of such a thing.

While still in Genoa I got an invitation to Sicily for the end of February 1915. Maestro Gaetano Bavagnoli wrote from Palermo asking me to sing in 'Tosca' at the Teatro Massimo. My market value appeared to be soaring: the Palermo offer carried with it three times the figure I was earning in Genoa. At this stage the building up of my reputation was more important to me than money, but since it was a privilege to sing at the Massimo, and under Maestro Bavagnoli's direction, I did not hesitate to accept.

'Tosca' was my first public encounter with the music of Puccini. Later on I came to be considered primarily an exponent of this composer, and it is true that I found his works peculiarly suited to my voice. The rôle of Mario Cavaradossi, however, is wooden and insipid; fortunately for the tenor, it is redeemed by the beautiful aria of the third act, '*E lucevan le stelle*'.

The very fact that the rôle was lacking in characterization presented me with a challenge. I was determined to do something original with it; and in part, at least, I think I succeeded. I had never been able to understand why it should be common practice among tenors to sing most of the third act of 'Tosca' in tones of joy and hope. It had always seemed to me that the music was meant to convey sorrow and melancholy. After studying the rôle carefully, I decided to break with tradition and interpret the music in what I felt must surely be the way that Puccini had intended.

Floria brings Mario the safe conduct and tells him he is free to leave the prison; but—this is where my interpretation began to diverge—Mario is unconvinced. He cannot bring himself to believe that happiness is within reach at last. Floria, he thinks, must be the victim of a cruel deception. He humours her lovingly with words of hope, but all the time, up to the very end, he is certain that these are their last moments together on earth, and that he is about to die. At no time can he bring himself to smile.

To me this interpretation seemed completely logical; at the very least, I felt, it was permissible. I decided to submit it to the audience at Palermo.

In the train from Genoa to Palermo, I began to feel somewhat apprehensive. It was the longest journey I had ever undertaken. I had always vaguely imagined Sicily as being overrun with bandits. How, I asked myself, could bandits possibly be interested in my interpretation of 'Tosca'?

At first sight I found Palermo reassuring. There were plenty of beggars at the railway station, but not a single bandit identifiable as such. Nor did I meet any in the days that followed; but

I did see a number of other things that to me were strange and new. There was, for instance, a curious pink building which reminded me forcibly of some paintings of Morocco in Countess Spannocchi's drawing-room. I was amazed to discover that it was a church.

'A church?' I said. 'It looks more like a mosque to me.'

Then I was told that it had in fact been built as a mosque, a thousand years before, when the Arabs ruled Palermo.

Another time I commented to Maestro Bavagnoli on the number of fair-haired, blue-eyed giants—I presumed they were Scandinavian tourists—who spoke Sicilian dialect with such apparent ease. The Maestro was highly amused at my ignorance.

'They did come from the North originally,' he said, 'though not exactly as tourists. They were called Normans in those days —oh, seven or eight centuries ago—but I think their descendants consider themselves good Sicilians.'

I remembered how, as a child, I had listened in wonder to the old French priest Don Romano, when he told me tales of the history of Recanati, of battles lost and won. It had all seemed very impressive and exciting to me then, but now I was beginning to feel that it was not history at all. History, I thought, was what had happened in Palermo, in Genoa, in Rome; Recanati, hidden by the Apennines, cradled on its hill-top, had had no Arabs, no Normans, only puny squabbles with its next-door neighbours. My travels, I felt, were beginning to teach me a sense of proportion.

One episode in Palermo I have never been able to forget. After explaining to me about the Normans, Maestro Bavagnoli took me to see the great cathedral their kings had built on a hill above Palermo, at Monreale. The dazzling golden mosaics, the multicoloured pillars of the cloister, each carved and wrought in a different design—I had never seen anything like it before, and it seemed to me a dream of beauty. I wanted to linger, but the maestro reminded me that we had to get back for a rehearsal. As we stepped outside into the early spring sunlight, my attention was caught by a group of ragged children huddled over something in the gutter. I approached them, curious to see whether Sicilian children played the same games as we had played in Recanati. Perhaps they do; but I did not find out on that occasion. The object around which these children were gathered was a filthy piece of raw meat, covered with dust and flies. One child was dividing it up into portions, which they then proceeded to devour. I looked closer, and horror piled on horror; several of the children appeared to be afflicted with some terrible eye disease. Flies clustered on their raw, suppurating eyelids; they made no attempt to brush them away.

I thought I had known poverty and hunger in my own childhood; but neither I nor anyone else in Recanati had ever been that poor, or that hungry. This terrible scene haunted me for many days. Was it not frivolous to the point of wickedness, I asked myself, to sing opera in gilded theatres for the benefit of bejewelled audiences, when such things existed close by? What did the third-act sorrows of Tosca and Cavaradossi matter, compared to the sorrows of those children? Such questions were new for me; until then, I had never known anyone poorer than myself. On the other hand, what could I do about it? I felt frustrated, helpless. All I knew how to do was sing.

I had mastered the technical difficulties of 'Tosca'. My colleagues, the soprano Bianca Lenzi and the baritone Giacomo Rimini, were both extremely charming. This time the only obstacle came from within myself. Tortured by the memory of the children in the gutter at Monreale, I went through the rehearsals listlessly, mechanically, unable to identify myself with problems that now appeared meaningless, in the light of what I had seen.

One afternoon, on an impulse, I entered a church and sat down in the semi-darkness. I tried to think, but no thoughts came. Of course, I knew I had to go on singing, since there was nothing else I could do; but as long as I felt that it was frivolous and useless, I would never again be able to sing well.

A door in the wall opened and shut; an old Franciscan friar moved through the shadows and disappeared behind the curtains of a confessional. I went over and knelt down on the other side of the partition.

'Father,' I said, 'I need your help.'

No doubt I was incoherent, but he listened patiently. When I had finished, he murmured in tones of gentle reproof: 'Are you so ungrateful to God, my son? He has given you a great gift; do not offend Him by despising it. Remember how lovingly He spoke of the lilies of the field, that toil not, neither do they spin.

God gave you your voice for the consolation of your fellow-beings. It is your duty to cherish it. He wants you to sing. Do not try to thwart His plan.'

'You think it is my duty to sing, Father?' I asked. A load rolled off my heart.

'Yes, indeed, it is your duty. And now, have no fear, my son. Go in peace.'

I went in peace.

They told me afterwards that when the curtain rang down on the first night of 'Tosca' at the Teatro Massimo, there was scarcely a dry eye in the audience. My own face was bathed in tears. For once, I was scarcely conscious of the applause. I felt transported beyond myself. In expressing with my voice the sorrows of Cavaradossi, I had not forgotten the children of Monreale; I had tried to express all human sorrow. Never before had I experienced so completely the longed-for sense of communion with my audience. I felt no vanity, no triumph, only joy and peace.

CHAPTER VI

THE NEW TENOR

In so far as it is a composite but constantly shifting pattern of the sublime, the banal, and the grotesque, a singer's life is like any other. On the first night of 'Tosca' in Palermo, I had experienced something not far removed from religious ecstasy. A few nights later I lost every penny I had in a game of poker with my colleagues.

They chaffed me into playing with them; I had been reluctant. I was saving up to be married, and had no desire to jeopardize my small hoard. But they gave me no peace. 'What kind of singer are you?' they teased. 'Don't you know that all singers play poker? It's a tradition. You might as well learn from us; we'll teach you the rules properly.'

I learned the rules well enough to lose two thousand lire with the rapidity of a hardened gambler. The following morning, I did some thinking. I was in no position to become a regular, or even an occasional poker player; but to judge by my colleagues, that was precisely what, as long as I remained an itinerant bachelor, I was destined to become. Domesticity, I concluded, was the only way of escape. Already I could hear myself refusing the poker invitations: 'So sorry, old boy, but I've got to get back to my wife, you know.' I decided to marry as soon as possible. My mother would probably be horrified. To her way of thinking, no matter how poor one was, marriage was impossible until one had acquired a bed, a table, a couple of chairs, and some kind of a roof over one's head. However, it couldn't be helped; later on I would try to explain things to her, without mentioning my losses at poker, of course.

I went out to the post office and sent a telegram to Costanza. 'Prepare trousseau and have banns called,' I told her. 'We'll be married as soon as I can get back to Rome.'

Next morning I had Costanza's reply. 'Trousseau ready,' she telegraphed. 'It's what I'm wearing.'

Costanza and I were married in Rome on May 9th, 1915. I borrowed two thousand lire from my agent, and we had a little family party in a rustic inn near the Batteria Nomentana, on what were then the outskirts of the city. Our honeymoon consisted of a couple of days at Castel Gandolfo, overlooking the quiet lake and surrounded by the Alban Hills. Then I took Costanza home to Recanati, to introduce her to my parents.

It was so long since I had had a rest, I had almost forgotten how to be lazy. I was just beginning to fall back into the slow, gentle rhythm of Recanati life, playing bowls, chatting in the Farmacia, looking on in the kitchen while my mother taught Costanza to make our traditional festive dish of *lasagne*, when the news came: Italy was at war. It was May 23rd; I had been married a fortnight.

From that moment I lived in daily expectation of a summons to the front, but no grey postcard came. A month passed; the suspense was unbearable. I wrote to Colonel Delfino putting myself at his disposal for Army benefit concerts. He telegraphed back: 'Splendid, am arranging your first concert in Rome for next Monday.' I said good-bye to Costanza, and spent the rest of the summer travelling all over Italy in a kind of patriotic fever. At the end of August, finding myself still unclaimed by the Army, I accepted an invitation from Maestro Tullio Serafin to sing at the Teatro del Corso, in Bologna, the following October. The opera was to be Boito's 'Mefistofele'.

Looking back on the forty-one years of my career as a singer, I can truthfully say that no matter how many times I sang the same opera or the same concert programme, I never fell into a professional routine. Each performance was a challenge, a test, a fresh opportunity to prove myself, a fresh opportunity to conquer an audience. In this lifelong series of challenges, however, certain performances stand out as having been even more challenging than the rest. Such were my début at Rovigo, my début at the Scala with Toscanini, my début at the Metropolitan in the shadow of Caruso. Serafin's invitation to sing 'Mefistofele' in Bologna belonged to this category of super-challenge.

Bologna was entitled to take a proprietary interest in this complex, intelligent, daring opera, for it was in Bologna that it had come to life. Arrigo Boito was known chiefly as a poet and librettist; 'Mefistofele' was his first attempt to express his ideas in musical form. When presented to the public for the first time, in Milan, in 1868, with Boito himself conducting, it had been a sensational failure. The performance lasted from half-past seven in the evening until half-past two the following morning, and the singing was execrable. Half the exhausted audience walked out in disgust, leaving the other half in a seething uproar of protest. Boito, who had stood impassive on the podium throughout it all, found himself the following day challenged to several duels by outraged champions of conventional opera.

The clamour eventually subsided, and it looked as though 'Mefistofele' had fallen into oblivion, when suddenly, in 1875, it reappeared at the Teatro Comunale in Bologna—pruned, revised, reduced to normal proportions, and with first-class singers in the cast. The Bologna audience gave it an enthusiastic reception and adopted it, so to speak, as their own discovery. It remained from that day a traditional part of the Bologna operatic season.

The fact that I would have to face this demanding and knowledgeable audience was one aspect of the ordeal awaiting me in Bologna; but I was equally intimidated by the inherent difficulties of the opera itself. Boito was a thinker and a poet, and in 'Mefistofele' he had attempted to interpret Goethe's world-vision in musical terms. Gounod's 'Faust' is a more cohesive unit and has stood the test of time better; but 'Mefistofele' is undeniably on a more lofty intellectual pinnacle, closer to the spirit of Goethe, and much more difficult to sing.

It is, of course, the difficult rôles that, once mastered, give the greatest satisfaction. The more I studied the rôle of Faust, the more I found myself enthralled and stimulated by its dramatic possibilities. I worked particularly hard at rendering in three appropriately different voices the three periods of life—youth, maturity and old age—at which Faust is shown. Later on, at the Scala, this interpretation won me something that I still treasure—the praise of Toscanini; meanwhile, it helped me to pass the test of Bologna. There was, I think, good team-work, for the title-rôle was sung by the magnificent basso Angelo Masini-Pieralli, and Serafin conducted; but when I found myself being called on by the formidable Bologna audience to give encores of the two great tenor arias—'*Dai campi, dai prati*' and '*Giunto sul passo estremo*'

—I knew that my own ordeal was over, and another battle had been won.

The next invitation came from no less a person than the great composer Pietro Mascagni. I was still in Bologna when he wrote to say that he would be directing the opera season at the San Carlo in Naples that winter: would I sing in 'Mefistofele' and in his own 'Cavalleria Rusticana'?

To be asked to sing at the San Carlo was in itself quite an overwhelming honour; but to be asked by Mascagni! Of course I accepted. 'Cavalleria' was scheduled to open the season in December. It was already the end of October. As soon as I could leave Bologna, I hurried off to Rome, to study the score with Maestro Rosati.

Meanwhile there were family problems to be attended to. All this time, Costanza had been staying with my mother in Recanati. She was expecting a child, and now insisted on rejoining me for the final months. So at the beginning of December we set off for Naples together, and settled down for the winter in a furnished room at the Pension Bon Séjour. I found myself facing the San Carlo, Mascagni and fatherhood, all in one season. To tell the truth, I was rather overawed by the prospect.

One day, while waiting for the tram after a rehearsal at the San Carlo, I overheard a snatch of conversation between two Neapolitans.

'They say he's good,' said one, 'this new tenor Gigli.'

'I don't care how good he is,' retorted the other, 'he'll never be able to hold a candle to our Don Enrico.'

For a moment I was puzzled; then I realized that I was being compared—however unfavourably!—to the great Caruso, who of course was a Neapolitan and, even after so many years in America, still the idol of his fellow-citizens. It was a comparison that later on, in New York, was to pursue and torture me; but for the moment I felt only amused, a little flattered at hearing myself mentioned in the same breath with the famous 'golden voice', and more than a little defiant. 'So I can't hold a candle to their Don Enrico?' I thought. 'Well, probably not. But I won't have them pooh-poohing me either.'

I had been, as I said, somewhat apprehensive of meeting the great Pietro Mascagni. A year of success had given me new self-confidence, but otherwise it had not greatly changed me; I was still a bit of a rustic, unpractised in social intercourse, shy of meeting famous people. But it was part of Mascagni's greatness that he could and did instantly dispel one's shyness. My first encounter with him was the beginning of a friendship that lasted for thirty years and was ended only by his death.

'Cavalleria Rusticana' is, of course, his best-known opera, but it was not my personal favourite. 'L'Amico Fritz', which I was to sing many years later—in Rome in 1937—was much more suited to my voice. However, my relationship with Mascagni was at all times one of profound mutual understanding on the artistic plane, and I always found his operas interesting even when, from the tenor's point of view, they were unrewarding or difficult. In the end I had five of them in my repertory altogether—'Lodoletta,' 'Piccolo Marat' and 'Iris', besides the two already mentioned.

Although not in sympathy, musically speaking, with the dramatic violence of 'Cavalleria', I of course tried my hardest to interpret it well. In fact, at those first rehearsals with Mascagni himself at the San Carlo, I found him laughing at me for trying too hard. I remember in particular the exuberance with which I opened my lungs and poured my voice into the broad open vowel sounds of the Siciliana: '*O Lola ch'hai di latti la cammisa . . .*' When I got as far as '*E sidu moru*' I had no breath left.

'I'm not surprised,' said the Maestro. 'It was humanly impossible to finish it, at the rate you were going. Don't be such a spendthrift with your voice. You must learn to keep some of it in reserve.'

Under Mascagni's guidance, I did learn; and on the opening night of the San Carlo season, in December, 1915, my performance as Turiddu prompted one Neapolitan music critic to remark that 'we should all try to hear Gigli while we can; it will not be long before America claims him.'

America! It was still far from my thoughts.

In January 1916 our programme at the San Carlo was extended to include 'Mefistofele'. As a conductor, Mascagni was inclined to impose a rather slow tempo, and it was generally long after midnight before we finished. The performance of January 31st was no exception. By the time I had given an encore of '*Giunto sul passo estremo*', taken my curtain calls, stripped off the long white hair and beard of my octogenarian disguise, and jumped into a taxi, it was half-past two in the morning. I was rather tired, but one look at Costanza lying on the bed in our room at the Pension Bon Séjour was enough to tell me that sleep, for the time being, was out of the question. I ran down the stairs and out into the street again, looking frantically for a midwife.

The audience that had applauded the aged Faust would perhaps have been amused, could it have seen him, a few hours later, in the rôle of assistant midwife; but at least this active participation meant that I was spared the usual ordeal of pacing up and down outside. My daughter was born at eight o'clock in the morning. I had to give a concert that same afternoon. We called her Ester, after my mother; it soon became Esterina, 'little Ester', but that was too long a name for such a tiny creature, and so we shortened it, for the time being, to Rina. She has remained Rina ever since.

The San Carlo season came to an abrupt end shortly afterwards as the result of some crisis or other. I persuaded Costanza to go back with the baby to Recanati; then I rushed off to sing in a few performances of 'Mefistofele' at Modena, returning to Naples a fortnight later as Fernando in Donizetti's 'La Favorita' at the Teatro Bellini, where a continuation of the opera season had been hastily improvised under a different management. It was a hectic pace, but I realized that I would have to get used to it.

Haste, incidentally, was in the tradition of 'La Favorita'. Donizetti took only a week, while on a short visit to Paris, to compose the first three acts; as for the fourth act, he is reputed to have written it in less than three hours, to pass the time while waiting for the visit of a capricious Parisian lady. It is certainly not the best work of this prodigiously fertile composer; but an opera can be historically significant without being a masterpiece, and I think that 'La Favorita', together with Rossini's 'Guglielmo Tell', marks a turning-point in operatic history. Together these two form a bridge between the older concept of opera as primarily a vehicle of vocal virtuosity, and its subsequent development, through Verdi and Wagner, into an autonomous art form, a musical drama in which the music is completely integrated with the intellectual, emotional and spiritual content. This development has of course vastly increased the potentialities of opera (which some contemporary composers, I am baffled to observe, now seem inclined to throw away). By the same token it has led, sadly but perhaps inevitably, to the gradual decline of *bel canto*.

But to return to 'La Favorita'. When Donizetti came to Paris, Rossini's star was in the ascendant and his 'Guglielmo Tell' was the talk of the town. Nevertheless, the first performance of 'La Favorita'—on December 2nd, 1840, at the Opéra—was a sensation and a triumph. Donizetti knew well enough how to cater to fashionable taste, and there are evident signs of the prevailing French influence in the ballet music and elsewhere; but somehow I imagine that the enthusiasm of the Parisians was aroused less by these conventional *divertissements* than by the revolutionary undercurrents of the new opera, the insight it afforded into what must then have seemed the music of the future. Gone were the vocal acrobatics, leaving only a pure flow of melody, lyrical and dramatic by turns, according as the action demanded.

Finding Donizetti's music peculiarly suited to my voice, I had thrown myself with enthusiasm into the study of 'La Favorita'; but the performances at the Teatro Bellini were a disappointment. The cast had been too hurriedly and uncritically assembled, the rehearsals too slapdash and too few. I sighed with relief when the Neapolitan season was over and I could get back to Rome, to study and practise with my dear, conscientious Maestro Rosati. I had agreed to sing 'La Favorita' again, in Padua, at the end of April, but with a different conductor and a different cast. This time the conductor was to be Pietro Fabbroni, the soprano Luisa Garibaldi and the baritone Giuseppe Bellantoni—all famous names at the time. It was part of my good fortune that I so often found myself, even as a beginner, in the company of the foremost singers of the day. I learned a great deal from them.

The Padua season, which turned out to be as great a triumph as the second half of the Neapolitan season had been a failure, lasted well into May, and then it was good-bye to opera until the autumn; the summer open-air opera season had not yet been invented. I went back to Recanati for a fortnight, to see how baby Rina was growing; then I offered my services once again to Colonel Delfino.

This time he asked me to go to the front and sing for the troops. I accepted joyfully. Back and forth behind the Piave, and up to the Asiago Plateau, I jolted in Army lorries through the dust of that tragic summer of 1916. Often I gave three, sometimes even four concerts a day; yet I never felt I was doing enough. Never before had I known such wonderful, grateful, enthusiastic audiences. But the thing that impressed me most of all, in those boys who were facing death, was their gaiety. Often, as I sang for them, I myself would be moved to tears; but they were never satisfied until they had made me laugh.

On October 5th, 1916, at the Teatro Ristori in Verona, I added a seventh opera to my steadily-growing collection. It was Donizetti again, 'Lucia di Lammermoor'—the melodramatic story, borrowed from Sir Walter Scott, of a Scottish girl who is married to the wrong man, murders him on her wedding night, and goes mad. The part of Lucia was sung by Giuseppina Finzi Magrini and that of Lord Enrico by Mariano Stabile, while I, as the tenor, had of course the romantic rôle of Edgardo Ravenswood. The tenor's great moment in 'Lucia' is the beautiful aria in the last act, '*Tu che a Dio spiegasti le ali*'. (A typical Donizetti story is that he suddenly felt inspired to write this aria while playing cards with some friends. He rose abruptly from the gaming table, went into an adjoining room to note it down, and then came back to finish the game.)

Throughout the first night performance I had to keep reminding myself to save enough breath for '*Tu che a Dio*'. I had practised it very hard, but it was extremely difficult and demanding, and as usual I kept wondering anxiously how the audience would like it. No amount of self-confidence or strong black coffee could ever rid me of this inevitable first-night agony of suspense. Of course I had hoped for success, but I was not quite prepared for the twenty or more curtain calls, and still less for what the critics wrote the following day. One of them compared the occasion with the first performance of 'Lucia', at the San Carlo in Naples on September 26th, 1835, when the French tenor Duprez was greeted by 'a thunderous explosion of what seemed like the howls of madmen rather than applause, a kind of delirium impossible to describe'.

Donizetti is harder to sing than Puccini, and success in Donizetti is therefore, I think, a greater triumph for a singer than success in Puccini. A singer whose voice is mediocre, whose technique is far from flawless, will nevertheless often manage to bluff his way through a Puccini opera, and win applause into the bargain; singers of this kind would think twice, however, before attempting the mercilessly revealing music of Donizetti. It is not that the Donizetti rôles are in any way esoteric, or that they demand any special style such as is required for singing Mozart or Handel; they are, quite simply, lyric rôles, given over to melody, to the *cavatina,* the *cabaletta,* the leisurely *legato* aria. They require security of breath and security of tone; they require ease and poise of delivery—the bare fundamentals, it will be said, of vocal training. The fact remains that many singers nowadays embark on their careers while still a long way from having mastered these fundamentals. In some cases, of course, this may be due to the usual difficulties of financial pressure, but I think my own story suffices to prove that it need not be an insuperable obstacle. Or perhaps some teachers do not encourage their pupils to stay the long and arduous course of training, on the assumption that there is no need to prepare them for Donizetti and Bellini when they can so easily by-pass these stern taskmasters and achieve success in a comparatively vast range of less demanding rôles. Whatever the cause, one is inevitably forced to the melancholy conclusion that *bel canto* is in decline. Even though of course we have no direct means of comparison, I feel fairly certain that there is a good deal less of supreme singing nowdays than there was a century ago. I am prompted to this affirmation by the internal evidence of the operas of Donizetti and Bellini. Although, as I have already observed Donizetti bridged a transition period in 'La Favorita', in composing his operas he naturally had in mind the singers of his own day—singers such as Duprez, Rubini, Lablache, Persiani, Grisi and Pasta. To sing his operas well required, and still requires, vocal art in some measure comparable to theirs. I feel I must plead with all young singers: Be persevering in your studies. Have the courage and patience to postpone your début until you are really ready for it. Do not, I beg you, let the tradition of *bel canto* wither away.

From October to December, 1916, I was kept busy singing here and there in Northern Italy. After 'Lucia' in Verona there was 'Mefistofele' at the Teatro Donizetti in Bergamo and the Teatro Sociale in Brescia, and 'Gioconda' at the Chiarella in Turin. Finally, the day came that I had both longed for and dreaded; on December 26th, 1916, I faced a Roman audience for the first time from the stage of the Teatro Costanzi. It was the opening night of the season; the conductor was Edoardo Vitale; the opera 'Mefistofele'. Colonel Delfino had his promised box; Maestro Rosati was there with his family; Countess Spannocchi confessed that she was dying of curiosity to witness the Roman début of her former footman; and my brother Catervo sat in the stalls with his wife on one side and Costanza on the other. All three looked rather self-conscious; they were wearing evening dress for the first time in their lives.

To some extent, of course, the Roman public knew me already; not only from the time when, as a student at Santa Cecilia, I had sung in private houses under the pseudonym of Mino Rosa, but also from the Army benefit concerts which I had given the previous year. The Roman critics, however, had not yet had occasion to level their pens against me; it was their judgement that I awaited with some apprehension. In an ungrateful moment I felt that the critics of Rovigo, Ferrara, Genoa, Palermo, Bologna, Naples and so forth were provincial scribes whose benevolent verdict could not be considered decisive. What would they think of me in Rome? That was the question. As always, of course, it was the audience that mattered most to me; but on this particular occasion I did feel vulnerable to the opinion of the critics too.

Costanza and I were staying with Catervo. After the performance, I lingered with them into the small hours over a little celebration supper; then, when the rest of the family went to bed, I slipped out of the house. Sleep was impossible. I was in a strange mood, at once restless and nostalgic. I found myself wandering aimlessly through the frosty, deserted streets. In Piazza Navona the booths of the Christmas fair were boarded up, the ground littered with lollipop-sticks and the discarded wrappings of toys, the churches monumental in the moonlight. From there it was not far, along the river, to the Passeggiata di Ripetta, where in the old days I had shared a garret with Catervo and dined off 'fried scraps' by candlelight. I stood for some time looking up at the window from which we had played our ventriloquist tricks. After that my feet carried me of their own accord along familiar routes, across the Corso, past the Academy of Santa Cecilia where I had studied, up the Spanish Steps to the Trinità dei Monti where I had lingered with Ida, my first love, on my first rapturous walk with her; and from there to the Territorial Command where I had spent two years in my clumsy grey-green uniform, and outside which I had met Costanza for the first time. I had had no intention, when I started, of making this sentimental pilgrimage; but now that it was made, I felt better. It was not often that I found the opportunity to take a long look at myself.

By this time it was almost morning. I went to the railway station and sat on a bench, waiting for the newspapers.

The Roman critics proved, as I had expected, more severe than their provincial colleagues; but on the whole they let me off rather lightly. They all complained of my bad make-up; the *Messaggero* said I showed signs of nervousness; the *Tribuna* said I sang better in the first acts than in the last; the *Corriere d'Italia* said I was not yet a finished artist, but the raw material was good! The rest was praise: praise in measured terms, but praise nevertheless. I decided it was worth having. Feeling immensely relieved and also, suddenly, very tired, I stuffed the newspapers in the pocket of my greatcoat and took a taxi home.

'Where on earth have you been?' asked Costanza.

'Just for a walk,' I said. 'I couldn't sleep until I had read those newspapers. But I'm going to have a good sleep now.'

I stayed in Rome for two months, singing at the Costanzi. The beginning of March, 1917, brought a new adventure: my first trip abroad—to Spain. Maestro Tullio Serafin had been invited to direct a short season of Italian opera in Madrid and Barcelona, and for this purpose he had formed a small company, consisting of the tenor Aureliano Pertile, the baritone Segura-Tallien, the bass Angelo Masini-Pieralli, and myself. The female rôles were to be sung by Spaniards: I remember in particular the name of a soprano, Carmen Bonaplata.

Travelling, for a singer, is not really much fun. On this, the first of a long series of journeys in four continents, I discovered once and for all that the only three places a singer on tour can really get to know in a foreign town are the railway station, the hotel where he stays, and the opera house. He generally has a crowded schedule of performances, and even when he is not actually singing, he is practising or spraying his throat or signing autographs or meeting compatriots or giving an interview to a reporter from a local newspaper; he rarely has the time, and never the peace of mind, to sightsee, absorb atmosphere or otherwise get to know the country he is visiting. So my travels, although far-ranging, have left me ignorant. In any case, I have a suspicion that, although trains and boats have at times been as much a part of my daily routine as breakfast, I am not really a traveller at heart. If I had not had a voice, I am sure I should have been content to live quietly in Recanati. Whenever, in the course of my career, I could manage to snatch a holiday, Recanati invariably seemed to be the only place in which I felt inclined to spend it.

I did, however, learn enough about Spain on this occasion to make one astonishing discovery—the fanatical enthusiasm of the Spaniards for opera, far surpassing anything I had seen in Italy. I have never witnessed a bull-fight; but I think the passionate partisanship and, at times, what I can only call the collective hysteria of the Spanish opera-going public must be closely related to the emotions of the bull-fight crowd. Certain scenes in Madrid and Barcelona have remained unique in my experience. They were not usually, I may say, scenes of enthusiasm for me; far from it. They were demonstrations of loyalty to two other tenors, Gayarre and Masini, each of whom was considered by his own faction of devotees to be the sole worthy exponent of the rôle of Faust in 'Mefistofele', which I, an upstart—they implied—had no business to usurp.

The Spanish critics seemed to share, if on a more dignified level, the attitude of the public. They were, at best, condescending to me.

'He has a good technique and sings fairly well,' said *El Liberal*. 'If he works hard he can hope for a successful career.'

'A small but agreeable voice,' said *España Nueva*. 'He should, however, have known better than to appear before a Spanish audience in an opera as familiar to us as 'Mefistofele'. His rendering of the last act is not to be compared to that of Gayarre, and in the opening scenes he is decidedly inferior to Masini. . . ."

Better luck, however, awaited me in Barcelona, where I sang 'Gioconda' as well as 'Mefistofele'. I had not, it appeared, so many formidable rivals in the rôle of Enzo, so the audience felt free to applaud and the critics to praise. By the time I left for Italy I had even, I discovered, acquired a little faction of my own. Its members staged a demonstration in my favour while standing

Playing bowls in Recanati, while on a summer holiday from the New York Met.

On board ship—going to Buenos Aires—with the rest of the company, July, 1933

Gualtiero in Bellini's 'Il Pirata'

Radames in Verdi's 'Aida'

in the gallery queue; blows were exchanged, and the *Guardia Civil* had to intervene. So my Spanish tour turned out to be a success after all.

The rest of 1917, after my return from Spain, centred for me—in one way or another—around Pietro Mascagni. I added two more of his operas to my repertory—'Iris' and 'Lodoletta'; and after spending part of the summer singing 'Lodoletta' in his native Leghorn I went with it on a long tour through Italy.

'Iris', in which I sang for a short season at the Chiarella in Turin towards the end of April, is a curiously cramped, contrived piece of work. It was produced for the first time at the Costanzi in Rome, in the autumn of 1899. Although set in Japan, it is of course thoroughly Italian in feeling and style. The pseudo-philosophic theme, with its elaborate symbolism, was not suited to Mascagni's volcanic temperament. It is supposed to be 'thoughtful', but Mascagni was not a man to write opera thoughtfully. He wrote it as freely and spontaneously as one writes a letter, never making a correction. There is the magnificent '*Hymn to the Sun*', with which 'Iris' opens and closes, and there are colourful passages here and there throughout; but as a whole, I imagine that an audience must find this opera somewhat incongruous and disconcerting. However, it provides good opportunities for the principal singers; so personally I was not dissatisfied. But I must admit that the rôle of Osaka—a lecherous Japanese nobleman, the personification of Vice—never did become one of my favourites!

'Lodoletta' was a new work. Mascagni had composed it the previous year, intending it, he said, as a message of love and peace to war-stricken humanity. In tone it is fresh, gentle and idyllic, and it is studded with beautiful melodies; I do not think it quite deserves the oblivion into which nowadays it seems to have lapsed. It had its first public performance on May 2nd, 1917, at the Costanzi, with Rosina Storchio in the title-rôle, and Mascagni himself conducting. Despite the acclaim which greeted it, Mascagni was not altogether pleased with this production. The children's choir—a charming but difficult feature of the opera—had been insufficiently rehearsed, and there were other shortcomings also. So he was delighted when the opportunity arose of giving it a fresh start in his own Leghorn. This time the soprano was Bianca Bellincioni-Stagno, the baritone Giuseppe Noto, the basso Leone Paci; while the rôle of Flammen, the painter, was entrusted to me. It was really a splendid production, and the Leghorn audiences—admittedly predisposed in its favour through their pride in Mascagni—seemed genuinely enchanted with it. We gave nine performances of 'Lodoletta' there in August 1917, as well as several of 'Manon'. During the autumn we took it on tour to Florence and other cities of Northern and Central Italy, ending up in Rome on December 26th, the opening night of the season at the Costanzi.

I have pleasant memories of that August in Leghorn, although this will perhaps be considered a shameful confession. Had I really any business to be enjoying myself at a time when things at the front were going so badly, and the tragic influenza epidemic was sweeping Italy and Europe? The fact remains that I suddenly found myself in a carefree holiday mood. Perhaps it was due to the enthusiastic reception we got, not only from the audiences but from the entire population of Leghorn. Perhaps it was due to the fact that I had been working very hard, without a break, for a very long time; perhaps it was simply an outbreak of youthful high spirits. Whatever the cause, I suddenly became impatient of being just a singer—even a successful singer. I became impatient of having to save up all my strength and energy, all day long, day after day, for the three or four hours of the performance. I became impatient of gargling and siestas and dietary precautions. I wanted to have fun. And so together with Noto, the baritone, and a few other members of the company, I made friends with a group of fishermen. They took us with them when they went out in their boats to fish for *polipi*—octopus —or *ombrina*, a variety of white-fleshed fish, rather like the sea-bass but much larger, which I think is peculiar to the Mediterranean.

We fished for octopus by day and *ombrina* by night, the technique in each case being entirely different. For octopus we would sail out to a point where the sea was about twenty-five or thirty feet deep. Then, through a kind of glass-bottomed bucket, we would peer down through the water. The fishermen could instantly recognize the kind of stone or rock under which the octopus was likely to be hiding. Having tied a small crab as bait on the end of a long stick, they would reach down and dangle this crab in front of the octopus. Greedily, he would emerge from his lair and grasp the crab with his tentacles; whereupon we would promptly pull up the stick, with the octopus self-clamped to the end of it.

To catch *ombrina*, we would set out about midnight. At a fair distance from the shore, each boat in our little fleet would launch five or six tiny white sails, like toy yachts, on the dark water. Each sail had a number of strings attached to it; on one end of the string there was a bait, while we held the other end lightly but firmly in our hands. Every time we felt a tug at one of the strings, we knew that a fish had been caught. We would sit quietly in the boats until most of the strings had been tugged at; then we would draw them in. With sea and sky pitch-dark all around one, it was dazzling to watch the phosphorescent fish rise by the hundred, leaping and quivering, to the surface of the water.

Back on shore, we would have Gargantuan feasts of octopus fried in batter and *ombrina* boiled with lemon, bay leaves, peppercorns and fennel. These dishes would naturally be accompanied by plenty of dry white wine from the island of Elba. The fishermen would teach us their songs, and ask us for ours in exchange. Often we would linger on at table, merrily chorusing, until it was time to go to the Politeama for the evening's performance. Of course this kind of existence was against all the rules of prudence and hygiene, but I enjoyed it so much that for once I didn't care. The success we were having with 'Lodoletta' seemed to indicate that our singing was not impaired. I do, however, remember that after one particularly succulent fish-banquet, I had to keep dosing myself with brandy in order to get through a performance of 'Manon', an experience, I hasten to add, which I have never repeated!

I cannot pretend that I have ever been oblivious of money. Possibly because I was born so poor, it has always mattered greatly to me. As I look back over my life, however, I can think of nothing bought by money that has ever given me the sheer delight of those days and nights with the Leghorn fishermen, out on the sea under the sun or the stars. It would be absurd for me to draw any moral from this. But I feel that, as a simple fact, it may be worth recording.

I now had nine operas in my repertory, but I was greedy for more. So although I welcomed the opportunity afforded me by the invitation of Signora Emma Carelli (the dynamic lady who at that time was director of the Teatro Costanzi) to sing in Rome for the first four months of 1918, I was disappointed to find nothing but old favourites in my schedule: 'Lodoletta', 'Tosca', 'Gioconda' and 'Mefistofele'. Four whole months with no new opera to learn! It almost seemed a waste of time.

CHAPTER VII

ROME AND NAPLES

As things turned out, the 1918 season at the Costanzi proved livelier than I had expected. Thanks to last-minute changes in the schedule, I was able after all to add two more operas to my repertory—Giacomo Puccini's 'La Rondine', and Francesco Cilea's 'Adriana Lecouvreur'.

'La Rondine', an agreeable example of second-best Puccini, may perhaps be described as a cross between 'Manon Lescaut', 'Bohème', 'Traviata' and a Viennese operetta. It has a somewhat curious history. While on a visit to Vienna, in 1914, Puccini was persuaded by a Viennese music publisher to attempt, in collaboration with the librettist of Franz Lehar, a *genre* that was new for him—musical comedy. The finished libretto failed to meet with Puccini's approval, however, and the whole project was still under discussion when war broke out between Italy and Austria in May 1915. All dealings with the Viennese publisher, now officially an enemy, were automatically severed; an Italian firm took over the project and commissioned a new libretto by Giuseppe Adami. But even though the scene was no longer laid in Vienna, the Viennese waltz rhythms in three-four time were still running through Puccini's head, and they found their way into the score.

Set against the background of Paris—the Paris of the Bal Bullier—and the French Riviera under the Second Empire, 'La Rondine' is the story of a noble-hearted courtesan, a pathetic-romantic story of sin, love and renunciation. There is plenty of movement and drama. The music is tender, playful and light; or perhaps I should say deceptively light-sounding, because actually it is quite difficult to sing.

The first performance of 'La Rondine', with Tito Schipa and Gilda Dalla Rizza, took place at Monte Carlo, on March 27th, 1917. Later that year, when it was being produced in Bologna, there was some talk of giving me the rôle of Ruggero, and in fact I went over the score five or six times with Maestro Rosati; but Puccini himself, for a reason that was not precisely flattering to my vanity, decided otherwise. My appearance, he said, was all wrong; I was too rotund to give a convincing portrayal of a romantic lover; this was the first time that his new opera was being sung in Italy, and he wanted it to make a good impression. So Aureliano Pertile got the part instead.

I heard no more of 'La Rondine' until one day in February, 1918 at the Costanzi. I was sitting in the theatre listening to an American tenor named Hackett sing in 'La Bohème'. Hackett was just back from a South American tour during which he had sung 'La Rondine' several times. Puccini happened to be in the audience too. He liked Hackett's voice, and asked Signora Carelli, director of the Costanzi, if it would be possible to insert a few performances of 'La Rondine', with Hackett of course, into the programme of the current season. Signora Carelli gave some non-committal reply, and then came straight to me.

'If we're to do "La Rondine", she said, 'I want you and not Hackett. I'm certain you can do it better. But how are we going to convince Puccini? Anyhow, I don't see how you could manage it. The only time I can fit in the *première* is next week; Dalla Rizza and the other soloists have sung in it before, and I can't expect you to learn a new opera at a week's notice.'

'Well,' I said, 'let me try.'

I knew I had a good memory, but until that evening I had not realized quite how good it was. As I stood at the piano with Maestro Rosati, going over the score, I found that I knew the part already; the five or six times I had read it through the previous year seemed to have riveted it in my head. Next morning, at the rehearsal, I took Puccini by surprise: he was, of course, expecting to see Hackett. But his surprise turned to increasing bewilderment as he discovered that I already knew the part.

'Bravo, bravo!' he exclaimed, when I had finished. 'You'll make a splendid Ruggero.'

'But what about my figure, Maestro?' I reminded him with mock humility.

'I think, after all, that people won't notice the figure when they hear the voice,' he said.

Then we went into the theatre for a full rehearsal with the

orchestra. Hackett arrived while I was on the stage. Amazed and deeply offended that I should have been given 'his' rôle of Ruggero, he turned on his heel and walked out of the theatre without saying a word. He left the following day for Milan, and could not be persuaded to return to Rome for a long time afterwards. I felt very sorry about this episode, but when one is building up a career one cannot afford to refuse an opportunity.

In spite of Puccini's hopes, 'La Rondine' was not the great popular success in Rome that it was to become in New York, where I sang it with Lucrezia Bori several years later. The Roman public much preferred Cilea's 'Adriana Lecouvreur', which I sang for the first time, with Carmen Toschi, Vida Ferluga and Giuseppe Danise, in April 1918.

I had felt a deep affection for Cilea ever since our first meeting in Palermo, where he was director of the Conservatorio. He was a man of stern moral and artistic integrity, a little old-fashioned and perhaps not greatly inspired. The thing about him that appealed to me most was his innocence. There is not very much to be said about his music. It is gently idyllic, lacking in vitality, derivative. Here it recalls Verdi, there Ponchielli, in another place Boito, and throughout, inescapably, Alfredo Catalani. But it has a lyric beauty and melodic elegance of its own with which I felt a certain affinity. A singer is apt to judge music by somewhat personal criteria. The music he prefers is not necessarily the greatest; quite simply, he prefers that which offers most scope for his particular kind of voice.

'Adriana Lecouvreur'—Cilea's masterpiece—was written in 1902. Although belonging to the same period as 'Cavalleria Rusticana', 'Pagliacci', 'Bohème' and 'Andrea Chénier', the predominating influence it betrays is that of Massenet. The libretto is based on a comedy by Eugène Sue. I had been hoping for a chance to sing it ever since hearing Cilea say in Palermo, after a concert in which I had sung the famous '*Lamento di Federico*' from another opera of his, 'L'Arlesiana', that he thought my voice ideally suited for the part of Count Maurice of Saxony.

I think it did prove to be so. I found the nobility and sincerity of the melodic flow of the music so inspiring that I was able to give one of my best performances. Time and again, the orchestra had to stop and let the applause subside, after my first aria, '*La dolcissima effigia*', and in the second act, after '*L'anima stanca*' and the duet with Adriana. The moment of deepest communion with my listeners, however, was too tense and, I venture to say, too sacred for applause. It came in the last act, after the death of Adriana, when I sang, with all the emotion I could summon, the single despairing cry, '*Morta!*' This always seemed to send a shiver through the entire audience, at the same time hypnotizing them into a kind of deathly silence.

With 'Adriana Lecouvreur' I ended my second season at the Costanzi on an exhilarating note of triumph. Almost at once I was off again, on tour with 'Lodoletta', to Naples, Genoa, Turin, Bergamo, and finally Milan. It was now the end of May, 1918. I had never been in Milan before. To some extent, Turin and Genoa had prepared me for my first encounter with this great industrial city. But Turin and Genoa were still recognizably Italian, however different they might be from the Italy of my childhood, whereas Milan appeared to me strange, foreign, overwhelming—more or less the sort of place that I had imagined America to be, except for the vaguely surprising fact that Italian was the language spoken by the inhabitants.

But these were irrelevant impressions. Fundamentally, to me as to any other singer, Milan meant just one thing—the Scala. I had been singing all over Italy for nearly four years, I had made a certain reputation, I had won acclaim, but I had not reached the Scala yet. 'Lodoletta' was being staged at the Teatro Lirico. I would often pause on my way across Piazza della Scala and take a long look at the unpretentious exterior of the as yet impregnable fortress. Clanging and screeching, the trams jerked to a halt in front of it, then lurched forward again in a terrifying headlong plunge. I tried to shut my ears to them, and to listen instead to the imaginary sound of my own voice soaring, above the orchestra, from the stage within. All my petty triumphs seemed to dwindle, to wither away. What did they amount to, if the Scala did not want me? I felt that as long as the Scala remained unconquered, I had achieved nothing.

I left Milan in June 1918 without having set foot in the Scala. Nevertheless, my stay there had not been entirely unprofitable. To begin with, I had received an honorary title: Knight of the Crown of Italy. It did not amount to much, but it was the sort of thing that pleased Costanza. In the second place, I had begun to earn more. For three years, ever since Palermo, my market value had remained stationary at three hundred lire a performance; now, in Milan, it had suddenly jumped to seven hundred. Furthermore, I had signed two contracts for the following year: one with Raoul Gunsbourg for a season at the Casino in Monte Carlo, the other with the Bonetti Company for a season at the Teatro Colón in Buenos Aires. Last but not least, I had begun to make gramophone records.

F. W. Gaisberg of His Master's Voice and the Victor Gramophone Company had come to Milan the previous year to make contacts with artists, and also to erect a local pressing and matrix-mixing plant. With wartime restrictions on fuel and new machinery, this was not an easy matter. However, Gaisberg managed to assemble the plant somehow or other, out of parts scavenged, as he himself has related, from the junk-heaps of Porta Magenta.

The head of this new Italian branch of H.M.V. was Maestro Carlo Sabaino. Mascagni introduced me to him one evening, after a performance of 'Lodoletta' at the Lirico, and he asked me to visit him at his office the following day. There, for the first time in my life, I heard a gramophone record. It was the aria '*Com'è gentil*' from 'Don Pasquale'; the singer was Enrico Caruso, whom I had never heard. I listened to it—I can still remember clearly—with humility and awe.

'Now I want you to come with me to the recording studio,' said Maestro Sabaino. 'I want to try recording your voice. What would you like to sing? Don't worry, this is just an experiment.'

Feeling very excited, I chose Flammen's aria '*Ah, ritrovarla nella sua capanna*', from 'Lodoletta'. The following day, Maestro Sabaino played it over for me. It was a strange experience to sit silently in a chair and listen to my own voice; but what was even stranger was the affinity of tone that I could plainly detect between this record of mine and the Caruso record I had heard the day before. It left me wondering. What had Maestro Sabaino wanted to imply by this juxtaposition?

I met Gaisberg, and we arranged that I should make ten records straight away, mostly famous arias from operas in which I had already sung. These included '*Cielo e Mar*' from my very first opera, 'La Gioconda', with the B flat that had once given me so much trouble; '*Dai campi, dai prati*' and '*Giunto sul passo estremo*', from 'Mefistofele'; '*Recondita armonia*' and '*E lucevan le stelle*', from 'Tosca'; '*Addio alla madre*' from 'Cavalleria Rusticana', and the already mentioned aria from 'Lodoletta'. It required no great insight on my part to guess at the future possibilities of this wonderful instrument, but I was certainly far from guessing that the London headquarters of His Master's Voice would one day have to employ six people to look after my records alone.

As in previous years, I spent most of the summer of 1918 giving concerts to raise money for the Red Cross, and singing informally for the troops at the front. The tide of war had turned for Italy, and victory was in sight. But for me personally, the summer was clouded by the death, on June 10th, of Arrigo Boito. I had never met him, but his opera 'Mefistofele' had become such a part of me that I almost felt as though I had lost a father. When I heard that Toscanini was going to commemorate his dead friend by opening the Scala season with a special performance of 'Mefistofele', I felt terrified at the thought that he might not choose me to sing Faust. I simply could not bear that anyone else should be chosen. My motives were mixed, of course. I wanted to sing with Toscanini; I wanted—wanted desperately—to sing at the Scala. But what I really did want most of all was simply be allowed to share in the commemoration of Boito. I lived in an agony of suspense for several weeks. I lost all enthusiasm for other work, refused several engagements, and went back to Recanati, where I spent my time aimlessly, loitering in the Piazza. At last it came—a telegram signed 'Toscanini'. I had barely time to pack a bag and say good-bye to my family before catching the afternoon train.

Toscanini, of course, was already a legend, and I was awed as well as thrilled by the prospect of meeting and working with this reputedly unapproachable, austere and stormy genius. I intend no paradox when I say that, just because he was so difficult and demanding, I found him easy to work with. It gave me greater satisfaction to sing with him than with any other conductor I have ever known. He always surrendered himself completely to the task in hand, and expected everybody else to do the same. At rehearsals he was indefatigable. His mind ranged over every conceivable aspect of the music; no problem was too vast to be faced, no detail too small to be attended to. He could put magic into the dullest score, and illumine the most difficult. He dealt sternly, even ruthlessly, with laziness and incompetence, but he was quick to show sympathy and understanding if one was plainly doing one's best. He encouraged talent wherever he saw it, and was scrupulously fair. At public performances he was always careful to ensure that the singers got their due share of the applause and credit.

Later on, our paths diverged. His political sympathies were alien to me, and I could never understand the way in which he allowed them to regulate his life. To me, Italy was Italy, no matter what the régime. But I have never ceased to respect and admire him as a musician. I like to think that he had in his possession a small memento that I once gave him. We were both staying at the Savoy Hotel in London at the time. One morning, Toscanini knocked at my door and asked if he might borrow my shaving-brush, as he had mislaid his own. I gladly obliged; then, feeling the impulse to give him a present, I went out, took a taxi to Bond Street, and bought him the most splendid shaving-brush I could find.

Half a century had passed since the first, disastrous performance of 'Mefistofele' at the Scala; now, on that same stage, under Toscanini's direction, we tried to make posthumous amends to Boito. The memorial performance which opened the Scala season on December 26th, 1918 was in every way unforgettable. The title-rôle was sung by Nazzareno De Angelis, and that of Margherita by Linda Cannetti. The contralto, Elena Rokowska, was the wife of Tullio Serafin. All of us, I think, gave of our best; as for Toscanini himself, standing on the podium, he seemed to have been baptized with divine fire.

It was a deeply moving occasion. All who took part in it—singers, musicians and audience—were mourning Boito the patriot, the soldier who had fought under Garibaldi, as well as Boito the poet and Boito the composer. It was only six weeks since the armistice, the victory which he had longed for but had not lived to see. The theatre was a galaxy of diamonds mingled with tears.

For me personally, this production of 'Mefistofele' was to have an unforeseen and important sequel. The name of Toscanini had given it international prominence, and it brought me, in his wake, to the attention of Giulio Gatti-Casazza, manager of the Metropolitan Opera House in New York. But it was only eighteen months later that I came to know of this.

My father was still the bellringer of Recanati Cathedral. All these years, he and my mother had been following my career with trepidation, wonder and pride. My successes had finally convinced my father that singing could be more profitable than a 'good, honest trade' such as shoemaking, and they had helped my mother to overcome her scruples about the sinfulness of singing for money. Of course it is true that success is an easy thing to adapt oneself to; but in the case of my parents, as they gradually grew accustomed to the idea of this new kind of security, it really did help to enlarge their horizon, to dispel their fears, and to reconcile them with the great world beyond the Apennines.

It was high time, I decided, that they should see me for themselves in the framework of this great world; so in February, 1919, I invited them to Naples for my début in 'Fedora' at the San Carlo. I felt very proud, when I met them at the railway station, to see how self-possessed and dignified they looked, in spite of their countrified clothes. With his Sunday suit of rough navy serge, my father wore a pair of hobnailed boots that he had made himself thirty years previously; his home-made shirt of thick flannel was buttoned at the neck, but of course he had no tie. My mother and my unmarried sister both wore their traditional tight bodices and long, full skirts stiffened by numerous petticoats; their heads were covered by white kerchiefs knotted under the chin.

The evening they arrived in Naples, I had to sing in a concert at the Politeama, one of a series organized by the writer Matilde Serao. She gave them a prominent box in the grand tier. When I rejoined them in the interval, I could see that, surrounded as they were on all sides by the silks and satins of Neapolitan society, their unconventional appearance was causing something of a stir. People were obviously wondering why they were there and who they could be. Then something happened which touched me deeply, and which I have never forgotten. I sat down beside them. The audience understood. With one accord they rose to their feet and, turning towards us, gave my parents a prolonged, enthusiastic ovation.

Umberto Giordano's opera 'Fedora' was first performed at the Teatro Lirico, Milan, in 1898, a few months after the same composer's 'Andrea Chénier' had been presented at the Scala. The part of Loris Ipanov was sung on that occasion by an obscure young Neapolitan. Next morning his name was on everyone's lips—Enrico Caruso.

'Fedora' is a drama of love and political intrigue in Tsarist Russia. Melodious and deeply emotional like all Giordano's music, it suited me exactly. The interesting and complex part of Loris gives scope for acting as well as singing, and I was able to identify myself with it completely. One critic observed that, after the duet in the second act, and the great dramatic scene in the third, I wept as though all the misfortunes of Loris were really happening to me.

The tenor's supreme moment in 'Fedora' is the aria '*Amor ti vieta*'. On the first night, I involuntarily broke a rule at the San Carlo. Encores were strictly forbidden; but the audience refused to let the performance go on until I agreed to sing this aria a second time. The applause was so delirious that I felt worried about my parents, realizing that for them it was bewildering and probably terrifying. When I give an encore, I like to vary the interpretation of the aria I am repeating; so, having sung '*Amor ti vieta*' very softly and gently, in *mezza voce*, the first time, I made my second rendering of it ardent and passionate, letting my voice expand and soar. It always gave me a peculiar joy to do this at the San Carlo because of the rare perfection of its acoustics. The encore brought me twenty or more curtain calls.

'The last time you heard me sing in opera,' I reminded my father afterwards, 'you didn't recognize me. I wore a long silk dress and a hat, and I carried a parasol. Remember the Macerata students? Remember Angelica?'

'Yes,' said my father, 'I remember. I was afraid you would come to no good, with all that play-acting.'

There was a twinkle in his eye as he added, 'Well, I suppose you want me to say I was mistaken.'

From Naples I went back to Rome to study the two operas I was to sing at the end of March in Monte Carlo, 'La Bohème' and 'La Traviata'. Both of these operas were later to become favourites in my repertory, so I prefer not to dwell on my painful memories of that particular Monte Carlo season. As a 'tribute' to the Prince of Monaco, who had graciously announced his intention of being present at the *première* of 'La Traviata', Monsieur Gunsbourg insisted that I should interpolate the aria '*Cielo e mar*' from 'La Gioconda' into the middle of the famous drinking scene. This grotesque and meaningless profanation of Verdi was bad enough; but at least it only happened once. What ruined the entire season for me was the fact that every evening the audience would begin to dwindle during the third act, and we invariably sang the last act to an almost empty theatre. Everyone had gone to play roulette.

My partner in 'La Bohème' was the great soprano Lucrezia Bori, who was appearing in public for the first time after five years of retirement from the stage; and the baritone rôle in 'La Traviata' was sung by Mattia Battistini. In conditions so frustrating and humiliating for all of us, we felt quite unable to give anything more than routine performances. There is one fundamental respect in which an opera is like a play—both require that performers and audience collaborate in creating an illusion. If the audience, or most of it, refuses to collaborate, the illusion is destroyed. The performers are no longer heroes, heroines or villains, but merely a set of people paid to go through certain actions on the stage. Without the illusion, they cannot do their job properly, no matter how hard they try. To be paid, as I have said before, is not enough.

In May 1919 I set out for my first transatlantic venture—a five months' season at the Teatro Colôn in Buenos Aires. There was a steadily increasing demand for opera in the great cities of both North and South America, but for the time being there were not nearly enough American singers to meet it; so the way lay open for European impresarios to cross the ocean with their opera companies. These would often include the entire chorus, and might consist of as many as five hundred members. As the Italian companies, at any rate, received no official subsidies of any kind, the financial risk involved was, of course, considerable, as were the possible rewards. The competition was cut-throat, and the methods used by rival impresarios to discredit or outdo each other conformed at times to no law but that of the jungle.

I found these things out for myself, the hard way. Maestro Serafin was connected with the Bonetti Company in an advisory capacity, and it was at his suggestion that I had signed my contract for the Colón. But he gave me no warning. Nor did I feel I needed any; having already been on tour in Spain, I was beginning to consider myself an old hand. The long sea journey was very pleasant. There was another Italian company on board, bound like ourselves for a season in Buenos Aires, but at a different theatre, the Coliseo. We all made friends, and the time passed gaily. But as soon as we reached Buenos Aires it began to dawn on me that my Spanish tour had been, relatively speaking, an idyllic family party, and that this was something very different. Admittedly, it was El Dorado; I was earning far more than I had ever earned in Europe. But could that explain why my shipboard friends from the rival company now looked the other way when they passed me in the street?

CHAPTER VIII

SOUTH AMERICAN SUCCESS

Buenos Aires was my first experience of living in the world of big money. I soon got used to it; one does. Nevertheless, I experienced a few rude shocks in the process.

The first shock was a dispute in which Maestro Serafin joined with Bonetti, the impresario, in taking sides against me. They had decided to open the season at the Teatro Colón with a group of three one-act operas by Puccini: 'Tabarro', 'Suor Angelica' and 'Gianni Schicchi'; and they wanted me to sing in 'Gianni Schicchi'. This would have meant making my Buenos Aires début in a minor and decidedly uncongenial rôle. I was only too well aware of the importance of first impressions; moreover, in recent years a series of famous tenors had sung at the Colón—Bonci, Schipa, Crimi, Di Giovanni, Pertile, not to mention Caruso himself. The audience, would inevitably make comparisons. I did not want them to be too unfavourable. So I refused to sing in 'Gianni Schicchi'; or rather, I reminded Bonetti and Serafin of the clause in my contract which stipulated that my first appearance in Buenos Aires should be in either 'Tosca' or 'Gioconda'. They did not seem to consider this clause as binding; but there it was, in black and white, and I felt that in holding them to it I was entirely within my rights.

They retaliated by not allowing me to sing at all for over a fortnight. The news of this boycott naturally got around, greatly to the delight of Walter Mocchi, the impresario of the other Italian opera company at the Teatro Coliseo. It gave him a chance to ridicule his rivals; and for good measure he began to circulate witticisms, none of them in the best of taste, about my physical appearance. Articles in the local Press hinted at the 'real' reason for the boycott—Bonetti's eleventh-hour decision that I was too fat and ugly to be allowed on the stage of the Colón. Other articles preferred to insinuate that my voice was

Examining the master record after a recording session for H.M.V. in June, 1937

This is the kind of audience to which I often sang. On an August night in 1934, 40,000 people packed the Roman amphitheatre in Verona to hear 'La Gioconda'

Alfredo in Verdi's 'La Traviata'

The Duke of Mantua in Verdi's 'Rigoletto'

Vasco da Gama in Meyerbeer's 'L'Africana'

Pery in Gomez's opera 'Guaranay'

mediocre, my reputation founded on bluff, and that I was simply funking the critics.

At last Bonetti lifted the ban, and I was allowed to make my South American début in 'Tosca'. That night, I must confess, I spent an unusually long time before the looking-glass. I studied my appearance from every angle. Was there any truth, I wondered, in Mocchi's allegations? Was I really a figure of fun on the stage? His barbed shafts had not left me unscathed. Claudia Muzio, the young soprano who was to be my partner, was very beautiful. I felt myself growing self-conscious and shy; but there was nothing I could do about it, except remind myself of what Puccini had said, 'People won't notice the figure when they hear the voice.' I had to face the audience, I had to sing. It was my only defence.

Next morning the critics unanimously declared my performance to have been a revelation, a triumph, sublime, worthy of Caruso. No one said anything about my figure. So much for that, I thought; now I could stop worrying for a while.

I decided to go and visit my brother Egidio, who had emigrated some years before and was living in Buenos Aires. He was the only one of us who had remained faithful to my father's old craft of shoemaking.

'Let's celebrate,' I said. 'I've won a fight.'

'Who were you fighting with?' he asked in astonishment.

I laughed. 'I'm not sure, really,' I said. 'But I won anyway.'

'All right,' he said, 'I'll round up some other Recanati boys; did you know that there are quite a few of them here in Buenos Aires? We'll go and drink a glass or two at the Cantina Firenze. It's an Italian wine-shop—imagine, they even stock Verdicchio!'

That was the first of many wonderful evenings that I was to spend, at one time or another, in one foreign city or another, with a group of emigrant compatriots. On such occasions I have often felt deeply ashamed of myself and my worries. What were my difficulties compared to theirs when they arrived, homesick and unknown, in a totally strange environment, with no qualifications or experience but that of poverty? They worked desperately hard, endured humiliations, and kept their good humour in spite of it all. For their children they earned the privileges of education and opportunity; but they themselves, in most cases, led lives of unremitting sacrifice. I was always proud and glad to meet them because I felt that they personified the best aspects of the Italian character: sobriety, patience, industriousness, and kindness of heart.

In my dressing-room at the Colón one June evening, a few minutes before I was due to go on the stage as Enzo in 'Gioconda', I was handed a cable from Italy: Costanza had given birth to a son. It was in the rôle of Enzo that I had made my début in Rovigo, and I felt sentimental about the name; so I cabled back proposing it to Costanza. Rina and Enzo: my little family was now complete.

We were still at daggers drawn with the Walter Mocchi company, but in spite of everything I continued to find favour with the Buenos Aires public and critics. After 'Tosca' and 'Gioconda', 'Bohème' and 'Mefistofele', I sang one new rôle—that of Gennaro in Donizetti's 'Lucrezia Borgia'—towards the end of the Colón season, in September 1919. 'Lucrezia' cannot claim to be anything but a minor Donizetti work. Dating from 1833, it is a typical by-product of the great *bel canto* period; the libretto is slapdash, the orchestration commonplace, and altogether it seems clear that Donizetti was relying on the singers to make it come to life. There is, however, one great tenor aria, '*Di pescatore ignobile*'.

An unpremeditated incident on the first night of 'Lucrezia' at the Colón brought some comic relief to the macabre sequence of poisonings which constitutes the plot. In the fourth act, when Gennaro is dying—of poison, naturally—there is a highly melodramatic moment when Lucrezia recognizes him as her son. Seizing his head between her hands, she breaks out into despairing lamentations: '*Figlio mio! Figlio mio!*' Ester Mazzoleni, the soprano who was singing Lucrezia, seized my head with such impassioned vigour that she managed to wrench my wig off. She lost her balance and reeled back across the stage, still doggedly singing her '*Figlio mio! Figlio mio!*' the wig still clutched in her hands, while the audience exploded in a gale of laughter.

The Colón season ended that year with a gala performance of 'Tosca'. The President of the Argentine Republic was there, surrounded by members of the Government, the diplomatic corps, and the leaders of Buenos Aires society. The audience gave me a tremendous ovation after '*E lucevan le stelle*', and insistently demanded an encore. The Colón had a ruling against encores, and I tried to respect it; but when the clamour showed no signs of abating, rather than let the performance continue to be held up, I gave in. I naturally expected the impresario to congratulate me afterwards, or at least to give some indication of being pleased with my success; instead, to my utter dismay and bewilderment, I found him in a raging temper. Like Rosina Storchio years before, Bonetti accused me point-blank of having hired a *claque*. This was so outrageous that I lost my temper too, and my brother Egidio had some difficulty in restraining me from hurling a chair at him.

After this episode I felt there could be no question of further dealings between Bonetti and myself; but having already signed a contract with him for a return visit to the Colón the following year, I was in something of a quandary. I was sitting in my hotel bedroom next day, wondering what to do, when there was a knock at the door. It was no other than the rival impresario, Walter Mocchi. He had come hotfoot, after hearing of the incident, with an offer to buy back my contract from Bonetti if I would agree to join his own company the following year instead. In view of Mocchi's earlier behaviour towards me—his jokes about my figure still rankled—I found the whole situation extremely peculiar; but I realized that bygones would have to be bygones, since business was business. I let Mocchi and Bonetti thrash the matter out between them; then I signed a contract with Mocchi for the 1920 season at the Coliseo.

Egidio saw me off at the boat.

'Well,' he said, 'now that you're going back to Italy, how do you feel about the New World?'

'I like it,' I said. 'I like it. But you have to be tough.'

By this time it was fairly clear to me that I was a success, although I can truly say that I never ceased to be astonished at the fact. It was, of course, gratifying. But I was also beginning to discover that success has its own drawbacks—less uncomfortable, to be sure, than those of poverty, but drawbacks nevertheless. The more important one becomes in terms of the box-office, the more oppressively is one hedged in by various kinds of people whom one has no particular wish to see—impresarios, publicity agents, hangers-on. There is no escape. One needs them. But the result is a peculiar kind of loneliness, an abnormal rhythm of life for which I, at least, was certainly not fitted by nature. As any reader of these chapters will by now have concluded, apart from my voice I am a very ordinary kind of person. I was not a leader or a thinker or in any way by temperament a being apart. I was and am a normally gregarious, domesticated Italian. I wanted normal things. I was beginning to feel very tired of always rushing about, of never being with my family for more than a few days at a time, of not having a home of my own.

On my return from South America in October 1919 I spent a fortnight in Recanati. My baby son was a newly-discovered delight. The countryside was at its most beautiful; it was the golden moment of the grape harvest. Superficially, I felt soothed and at peace, but at heart I was restless, impatient of having to crowd my own family into the small, primitive house where my parents still lived, impatient of being a vagabond. I decided to put up with things as they were for another year or so—until after my next South American tour—and then to find a roof of my own, somewhere or other. Rome seemed the most obvious choice. I also wanted to buy a better house for my parents.

But all these plans required money. So at the beginning of November I was off again, to sing in Trieste. I managed to get back to Recanati for Christmas, but it was my last respite for a long time. In January 1920 I sang in Munich; in February, with some misgivings, I returned to Monte Carlo. The manners of the opera-going audience had not improved; people still left the theatre half-way through the performance to go and play roulette.

After that, until the end of May, my time was divided between Milan, Turin, Naples and Florence. In Milan I made a friend, the composer Umberto Giordano, in whose opera 'Fedora' I was then singing at the Teatro Dal Verme. His father-in-law was the proprietor of the Hotel Spatz, at which I happened to be staying, so we saw a good deal of each other. We had long sessions together, going over the score of 'Fedora'. It was a valuable experience for me to have a composer explain his meaning and his intentions in such detail, and I tried my best to interpret them faithfully. Quite apart from this, I greatly enjoyed his company; he was very jolly, and childishly fond of practical jokes, at which he would laugh uproariously.

In later years our friendship grew even closer. Another opera of his, 'Andrea Chénier', was to become my special favourite; of the sixty which eventually formed my repertory, it was the one I most enjoyed singing. When I built my villa in Recanati, Giordano often spent part of the summer holidays there, and we used to go sailing or play bowls together.

I have amusing and affectionate memories of his voracious appetite. One day at luncheon, he noticed that I was on a slimming diet.

'I think I'll follow your example, Beniamino,' he said. 'I need to lose a little weight myself.' (This was an understatement.) 'That stuff you're eating looks quite good. May I have some too?'

The 'stuff' was a particular kind of starch-reduced spaghetti. He ate a large plate of it, and then proceeded to focus his attention on what the rest of the family were eating, which happened to be a *risotto* cooked with mushrooms and white truffles. He let his gaze rest on it for a few moments and then sniffed longingly.

'Listen, Beniamino,' he said at last, 'your spaghetti was good, but this looks even better. I think I'll have a mouthful, just to sample it.'

The 'mouthful' consisted of two heaped plates, after which he calmly worked his way through the remaining courses. For the rest of the holidays he followed the same procedure at every meal: first a plate of 'slimming' spaghetti with me, and then the whole of the normal menu.

On June 15th, 1920, I began my second South American tour—this time under the auspices of Walter Mocchi—with a performance of 'La Gioconda' at the Teatro Municipal, in Rio de Janeiro. The soprano was a Brazilian, Zola Amaro. I spent nearly a month in Rio, singing in 'Tosca', 'Bohème', 'Iris' (with Gilda Dalla Rizza), as well as in two operas which were new for me: Wagner's 'Lohengrin' on June 28th and Alfredo Catalani's 'Loreley' on July 6th.

'Lohengrin' was the only Wagner opera that I ever attempted. I did so at Mocchi's insistence but without having much confidence in my own power to do justice to the music. I felt that it required a different type of voice from mine. But I did my best with it, and I even thought out my own version of the rôle. I made a clear vocal distinction between Lohengrin the mystical

Knight of the Holy Grail, son of Parsifal, and Lohengrin the man, lover of Elsa. At the beginning and at the end of the opera, I tried to give my voice celestial tones, to make it sound like the voice of a god; while in the middle part, when Lohengrin is on earth, I sang dramatically and emotionally, in order to convey his involvement in human struggles.

'Loreley' has this much in common with 'Lohengrin', that its theme is a Germanic legend, and that in composing it Catalani was aspiring, as Wagner did, to a dramatic form of greater substance and vitality than that which prevailed in his day; no special Wagnerian influence, however, is discernible in the actual music. The score was a re-working of an earlier opera of Catalani's, 'L'Elda', written in 1880; the libretto, like Heine's famous poem, was inspired by the legend of the unearthly maiden who sits on a rocky cliff above the calmly-flowing Rhine, combing her golden hair, singing a song, and luring boatmen to their doom.

'Loreley' was first produced at the Teatro Regio, in Turin, on February 16th, 1890; three years later, Catalani died, of tuberculosis, at the age of thirty-nine, in the arms of Toscanini. He had been Ponchielli's successor as Professor of Composition at the Milan Conservatorio. Toscanini held him in high esteem; his son and daughter, Walter and Wally, are named after two of the chief protagonists in Catalani's operas. I fully share Toscanini's admiration for this composer; he was a true musician, and he thought and felt beyond the ideals of his time. Had he lived, he might have become a revolutionary innovator; as it is, he made his influence profoundly felt, even on Verdi and Puccini. His life was sad as well as brief; his operas were rarely performed, and he had many disappointments. Our production of 'Loreley', with Ofelia Nieto in the title-rôle and myself as Walter, got a wonderful reception in Rio de Janeiro; I felt prouder of the posthumous tribute to Catalani than of my own success.

Before leaving Brazil we had a season at the Teatro Municipal in São Paulo, where on August 18th I sang for the first time in Riccardo Zandonai's opera 'Francesca da Rimini'. Based on Dante's immortal rendering of the tragic love story of Paolo and Francesca in the fifth canto of the *Inferno*, the opera nevertheless lacks vitality and is on the whole rather dull. In the São Paulo production the title-rôle was sung by Gilda Dalla Rizza, and that of Gianciotto Malatesta, the betrayed husband, by Segura-Tallien.

Back in Buenos Aires at last, I found myself again caught up in the comic Mocchi-Bonetti warfare; but this time I seemed to be on the winning side from the start. The two companies were installed in the same two theatres they had had the previous year but of course I was no longer at the Colón but at the Coliseo, with Mocchi. This change-over had thrown the opera-going public of Buenos Aires into some confusion. A number of people, presuming me to be still with Bonetti, had taken out subscriptions for the Colôn season; when they discovered that I was to sing at the Coliseo, there was a rush to give back the Colón tickets and buy seats at the Coliseo instead, but in the meantime the Coliseo season had been entirely sold out. This created a pandemonium of protests, last-minute arrangements for extra performances and so forth. It ended with a debacle for Bonetti, and when I returned with Mocchi to Buenos Aires the following year we were able to take over the Colón.

While still at the Coliseo, on September 26, 1920, I sang for the first time in Puccini's 'Madama Butterfly'. The rôle of Lieutenant Pinkerton is, comparatively speaking, so insignificant that it is generally difficult to find a tenor of the first rank who will agree to sing in it—a fact commented on by the Buenos Aires critics in praising my performance. There is an old tenor joke about 'Butterfly': the second act, we say, is the one we like best, because Lieutenant Pinkerton, having abandoned his wife, never appears on the stage at all.

The Coliseo season was coming to an end. I had added four new operas to my repertory in as many months, and now I was looking forward to the restful sea journey back to Naples, to a few peaceful days in Recanati, and then to house-hunting in Rome. But while still in Buenos Aires, I got a letter from New York which induced me to postpone my plans. It was from Giulio Gatti-Casazza, general manager of the Metropolitan, the realm of Caruso and the world's greatest opera house. He offered me a two-and-a-half-months' contract; if I agreed, would I come to New York immediately, to talk things over?

I sailed directly from Buenos Aires. As the ship entered the Hudson, I stood on deck contemplating the sensational Manhattan skyline. This was really the New World at last, I felt: the

New World that people dreamed about in Piazza Leopardi. Well, it would be wonderful to sing at the Metropolitan, and a few months' stay in New York would certainly be an interesting experience. Only I was not really in the mood for new experiences; I was still obsessed by my longing for a home.

As things turned out, New York was to be my home for twelve years.

CHAPTER IX

THE METROPOLITAN, NEW YORK

BEFORE going to New York I knew almost nothing about the Metropolitan Opera House beyond its legendary prestige and its association with two Italians: Giulio Gatti-Casazza and Enrico Caruso. The great Neapolitan singer had been the leading tenor of the Metropolitan since 1903, the dynamic engineer from Ferrara its general manager since 1908. Between them they had made the 'Met' a sanctuary of opera that for a long time had no rival in the world.

The Met. owed its existence to the enlightened patronage of a group of wealthy New York families. Under earlier régimes it had always been run at a loss, but without raising the price of the tickets Gatti-Casazza wiped out the deficit and turned it into a going concern. A supremely efficient and scrupulously honest administrator, he was also a dedicated connoisseur of opera. He raised the artistic level of the Met company and educated the taste of the opera-going public. He gave the public what it wanted—but only up to a point. He forced it to make efforts. He could turn a neglected minor nineteenth-century opera, or a difficult modern one, into a box-office success. He was stern, aloof, peremptory, and altogether somewhat inclined to behave as though he were the Almighty; but his refusal to tolerate the second-rate made him universally respected.

At our first interview this formidable personage treated me kindly but coolly. He doled out some measured compliments to my reputation. In particular, he said, he had been favourably impressed by reports of my singing in the memorial performance of 'Mefistofele' at the Scala. It was fitting that the Metropolitan, in its turn, should commemorate Boito; and he proposed that I should make my New York début in the rôle of Faust. I would have preferred to begin with something less difficult and more exclusively suited to a tenor; but I could see that Gatti-Casazza's 'proposals' were in reality commands, which as a newcomer I was scarcely in a position to dispute; so I said nothing, except 'Thank you', and marched meekly off to a rehearsal.

Santa Cecilia, Parma, Rovigo, the San Carlo, the Costanzi, the Scala, the Colôn—each of these had been a test, a challenge. Each time I had said to myself, 'If I succeed in this, I shall have proved myself.' Yet now, as I prepared to face the audience of the Metropolitan, I felt as though I were still unproved, untried; and so indeed, for this audience which idolized Caruso, I was. Moreover, I thought, since 'Mefistofele' was, after all, primarily a basso's opera, they might not even be curious about me. The opera itself would be unfamiliar to many of them; thirteen years had elapsed since its last performance at the Met, when Chaliapin had made his American début in the title-rôle, only to leave New York a few weeks later vowing that never again would he dirty the soles of his shoes with the slush of Broadway. The critics, I reflected, would probably devote most of their space to raking up the gossip connected with that famous episode, and to comparing the new Mefisto with the great, eccentric Russian; the new Faust was likely to pass unnoticed.

On the night of November 26th, 1920, I faced the ordeal. José Mardones, the Spanish basso, had been assigned the rôle of Mefisto, but he fell ill at the last moment and was replaced by the Russian Adamo Didur. Frances Alda, who in private life was Mrs. Gatti-Casazza, sang Margherita. The conductor was Roberto Moranzoni.

I stood in the wings drinking black coffee and thinking of my mother while Didur sang the '*Prologue in Heaven*'. Then the scene changed to the market-place, and after the drinking-chorus and the Easter Sunday procession, I walked on to the stage with Angelo Bada—my pupil Wagner. At this point I may, perhaps, be forgiven for quoting what one of the New York critics wrote some time afterwards:

'Steady and unperturbed, Gigli sang his opening phrases about the snows of winter disappearing in the soft spring sunlight. It is not a difficult passage; it lies in the middle of the voice and goes neither very high nor very low. There are sixteen measures, then Faust is interrupted by the returning crowd coming to dance on the village square. This was enough. New York knew that a new star had arisen.'

I had thirty-four curtain calls to myself. Next morning, Gatti-Casazza added a further three months to my contract. Caruso sent me a generous message of congratulation. Then someone brought me an imposing pile of incredibly voluminous newspapers. A headline in the Pittsburg *Dispatch* declared: 'Tenor with Queer Name Ranks Next to Caruso.' The New York journals, while more dignified in tone, were still far more enthusiastic than I had dared to hope for. I was especially pleased by what the *Herald Tribune* said about me: 'A loyal Italian, possessed of full faith in the Boito tradition, he disclosed himself as a servant of art and not a mere seeker after personal glory.' The New York *Times* reproached me with 'a persistent disposition to sing to the audience instead of to Margherita', but conceded that I had 'a voice of really fine quality, which he does not often force, still fresh and possessed of colour'. The *World* was cautiously non-committal: 'Gigli may never set the river on fire, but he will certainly prove himself of value at the opera house.' The *Evening Mail* noted 'occasional hints of tremolo, and a certain breathless effort'. But the *Sun* thought that 'Gigli comes very near to the younger Caruso'; and Max Smith in the *New York American* wrote a description of my singing that I still treasure because, modesty apart, I think it was accurate: 'His voice is a lyric tenor of peculiar warmth and mellowness in the middle register, notable for the beauty of its timbre, remarkably elastic, exquisite in *mezza voce,* luscious in full-blooded emission. While Gigli's voice in itself is one of the finest voices of its kind that New Yorkers have heard since the advent of Caruso, the dramatic intensity, the emotional vitality, the expressiveness which inform his singing are even more remarkable.'

The ordeal was over; New York had accepted me. For the time being at least, I belonged to the Metropolitan. It was going to be hard work. There were about a hundred artists in the company; between them, they gave an average of two hundred and twenty performances a season.

On December 3rd I sang in 'La Bohème' with Frances Alda, Didur and the great but ageing baritone Antonio Scotti. He was still a wonderful actor, but his singing voice had deteriorated, and even his admirers, of whom there were many, felt embarrassed by his persistence in refusing to retire. On December 10th I sang in 'Tosca', with Emmy Destinn in the title-rôle and Scotti as

Scarpia; and, on December 17th, in 'Lucia di Lammermoor', with Giuseppe De Luca, José Mardones, and an American soprano, Mabel Garrison. I won praise for all these performances, but it was by no means unqualified. After 'Lucia', for example, the *Herald Tribune* critic wrote: 'Beniamino Gigli was a good Edgardo. That is probably as much as could be said of any contemporary impersonator of the son of Ravenswood. There was once a truly great Edgardo, Italo Campanini, but who cares for ancient history?'

On December 23rd, 1920, I had to sing at short notice in a performance of 'La Bohème'. The opera originally billed for that night had been 'Elisir d'Amore' with Caruso, but it had to be cancelled at the last moment as he was too ill to sing. He had been in constant bad health and pain since September, when a heavy piece of scenery had fallen on him during a rehearsal. On November 11th, half-way through a performance of 'Elisir' at the Academy of Music in Brooklyn, he was almost suffocated by a violent lung haemorrhage, and had had to be rushed away by ambulance. He struggled heroically to recover, or at least to recover sufficiently to sing again, but a few days later he had a relapse. At first his illness had seemed nothing serious; then, almost overnight, it was making world headlines, silent crowds were assembling in the street outside his hotel, old stage hands at the Met would be found weeping in corners.

I had been singing at the Met for exactly a month—it was the day after Christmas—when Gatti-Casazza sent for me.

'Caruso was to have sung in 'Le Prophête' on New Year's Day,' he said. 'Now the performance has had to be cancelled. I want you to sing in "L'Amore dei Tre Re" instead. You have been preparing it, haven't you? Well, you still have four days: that's plenty.'

'Plenty,' I agreed obediently.

'The audience will be disappointed, of course,' he went on. 'You must be prepared for that. The New Year's Day performance is always a special event, and they have been looking forward to Caruso. You won't find it easy to console them.'

Caruso: the name was beginning to haunt me. With all the devotion I felt for his supreme greatness, I could not help wishing that the critics would desist from their glib, if flattering, comparisons. I did not want to live in his shadow. I did not aspire to be his rival or his epigone. I wanted only to be myself—to be accepted as myself.

When, on New Year's Day 1921 I faced the Metropolitan audience, knowing them to be disappointed because I was not their favourite, I felt no ambition to displace him in their hearts. It was only proper that they should be faithful to him, that they should grieve for his sickness. Let them hear me as I am, I thought; let them know me as Gigli, not as someone who is trying to step into Caruso's shoes. For this reason, I think I sang more quietly than usual, as much as possible in *mezza voce,* never seeking to provoke applause; somehow, I felt, it would not be decent. As it happened, 'L'Amore dei Tre Re' lent itself to this mood, for it contains no arias or duets sung to the audience, and affords no scope for mere display of voice.

The opera was new to me, but to New Yorkers it was already familiar, having been presented at the Met on several occasions since its first production there in 1914. The composer, Italo Montemezzi, was a man of superior intellectual powers and of deep feeling for beauty and dramatic expression in music. The poetic tragedy of Sem Benelli which he took as his libretto, while eminently suitable for musical treatment, has considerable literary merits of its own. Set in the period of the barbarian invasions of Italy, it is a tragic story of love and death. Fiora, the heroine (sung on this occasion by Florence Easton) is a personification of Italy as the unwilling bride of her Gothic conquerors. The aged and blind barbarian king, Archibaldo (sung by José Mardones) steals Fiora from her people and plans to marry her to his son Manfredo; but, suspecting her of infidelity with Avito (myself), the old king strangles her, and then places poison on her lips, in order that Avito too may die when he kisses her farewell.

While appreciating the merits of 'L'Amore dei Tre Re', I must confess that I felt more at my ease when, on January 11th, 1921, I sang with Mabel Garrison, Giuseppe Danise and Léon Rothier in another opera that was new for me, 'Rigoletto'. This performance took place at the Brooklyn Academy of Music, where one half of the Metropolitan company used to sing every Tuesday during the season, while the other half played in Philadelphia. Like most Italians, I knew Verdi's famous opera almost by heart long before I ever had to study it. When one thinks of the phenomenal success that it has always had, it is amusing to recall that after its *première* at the Teatro La Fenice in Venice on March 11th, 1851, a Paris journal, the *Gazette Musicale,* condemned it with the words: '*Il n'y a pas de mêlodie*'!

Since coming to New York, I had been too busy to feel homesick; but on January 27th, returning to my dressing-room after the first act of 'Mefistofele', I felt a sudden surge of loneliness, nostalgia and remorse. Lying among the pots of greasepaint on the table in front of me was a telegram from my brother Abramo in Recanati. 'Father died today,' it said.

Tears choked me. 'Not yet! not yet!' I wanted to cry out. 'You mustn't die yet, *babbo*!' He had had such a hard life, and I had been looking forward so eagerly to making his old age comfortable and serene. I had not been an undutiful son; but I had waited too long, and now it was too late. I longed to take the first boat back to Italy and rush into my mother's arms. I longed to be back in Recanati Cathedral, where at that very moment the candles were burning in the nave around my father's coffin. I would have given all I possessed to be able to stand in the organ-loft beside Maestro Lazzarini and sing the '*Ingemisco*' from Verdi's 'Requiem Mass'. What was I doing in this foreign place?

But of course it was impossible to rush back; I had chosen my way of life, and I had to abide by my contracts. Indeed, I had to return to the stage there and then, and sing through three more acts. With a pang I remembered another performance of 'Mefistofele', almost exactly five years before, in Naples, the night my daughter Rina was born. Of all operas, I thought, it was peculiarly fitting that this one, with its attempt to portray man's destiny, should be thus woven by birth and death into the fabric of my own existence.

If there is a bereavement in his family a shopkeeper or a civil servant is excused from work for a day or two, by the laws of common decency, but for actors, musicians, singers, another law takes precedence: The show must go on. To face the audience again, only a few minutes after having learned of my father's death, required an effort of self-discipline of which I would not previously have believed myself capable. Strangely enough, it brought me solace. In the fourth act, Faust is an old man, bent and feeble, with flowing white hair and beard. I had thrown myself back into the part; there was no other way to do it.

But as I began to sing the aria '*Giunto sul passo estremo della più estrema età* . . .', I suddenly felt rapt by an extraordinary peace and sweetness. I felt as though my father's spirit were entering into me and finding expression in my voice.

Caruso was still fighting with death. There was a heart-rending scene on February 26th when, feeling that he had not much longer to live, he asked to see all his Metropolitan colleagues once again to say good-bye. We stood round his bed, trying desperately to be cheerful, but most of his old friends—Lucrezia Bori, Rosa Ponselle, Scotti, De Luca, Didur, Rothier, Pasquale Amato—were unable to restrain their tears. I had, of course, known him very little; but after each of our few meetings, even this last one when he lay struggling with pain, I came away feeling enriched by the generous warmth of his overflowing personality. Everything was exceptional in him, not only his voice.

Gatti-Casazza had planned that Caruso should sing in Umberto Giordano's opera 'Andrea Chénier' towards the end of the season, together with Giuseppe De Luca and Rosa Ponselle; since this was now plainly impossible, and since the Metropolitan programme, once announced, was never changed, he asked me to study the rôle instead. I had been hoping for this opportunity ever since the early days of my friendship with Giordano, at the Hotel Spatz in Milan, although of course I had no idea then that the rôle of the French poet-revolutionary was eventually to become my favourite.

I had never had the time or, to be truthful, the inclination to study history, and the French Revolution was little more than a name to me. I now plunged into reading about it, in order to get the feeling of the part, with what no doubt was a somewhat naïve enthusiasm. The opera is based on the historical fact that the poet André Chénier, despite his support of the Revolution, was guillotined three days before the Reign of Terror ended. Into this bare outline the librettist, Luigi Illica, wove a fanciful story about the young aristocrat Madeleine, who is secretly loved by Gerald, her mother's footman and later a revolutionary tyrant, while she herself loves the poet Chénier. Chénier is arrested; Madeleine, after vainly attempting his rescue, voluntarily takes the place of a condemned woman prisoner in order that she may at least die with him, and they go to the guillotine hand in hand as the final curtain falls.

Although the plot is, therefore, substantially fictitious, Giordano did his best to give an authentic rendering of the period, even going so far as to introduce '*Ça ira*', '*La Carmagnole*' and '*La Marseillaise*' into the score. The music has great enthusiasm, dramatic verve and emotional appeal, and the theme, after all, has nobility. From the very first, from the great *Improvviso* of the first act, '*Un dì all'azzurro spazio*', I felt literally inspired; and Claudia Muzio, who was my partner at the *première* on March 7th, 1921, had tears streaming down her face when she took the curtain calls at the end of the third act.

Our performance was greeted with as much rapturous excitement as if 'Andrea Chenier' had been a new discovery; yet almost twenty-five years had passed since it was first produced, at the Scala in Milan, on March 28th, 1896. Even in New York it had already made three separate appearances. The Mapleson company had staged it in November, 1896; Oscar Hammerstein had revived it at the Manhattan Opera House; and the Boston-National company had given it at the Lexington Theatre in the autumn of 1916. It had not, apparently, aroused much interest on any of these occasions. People said that as far as New York was concerned, I had created the rôle.

I did, in fact, identify myself completely with the rôle of André Chénier. It ceased entirely to be make-believe: I *felt* it passionately. In the third-act trial scene, each time I cried out the words '*Colla mia voce ho cantato la Patria*', I thought of Italy. Like Chénier, I too expressed in song the love I felt for my country.

The almighty Gatti-Casazza had put me to the test and had not found me wanting; or so I concluded when, at the end of my first season at the Metropolitan, he proposed renewing my contract for an entire year. Financial advantage and professional prestige were the two obvious and decisive reasons for accepting, but they were not the only ones, New York itself was a bewildering place, but once inside the doors of the Met., I could almost imagine myself in Italy. Even though fourteen nationalities were represented there, it was so full of compatriots that Italian seemed to be the official language. Artistically, the Met. stood on the highest pinnacle of opera production. It gave its singers great opportunities, and expected them to give great performances in return; I liked both the opportunities and the

My villa at Recanati, from the rear (*right*) and the front (*below*)

My bedroom

The gardens of my villa, a photograph taken from the central tower

challenge. Finally, I liked the idea of spending a large part of the year with the same company, under the same artistic guidance, and in the same place. No European opera house was in a position to offer so much security. With fewer extraneous irritants, I could sing better; with fewer trains to catch, fewer suit-cases to pack, I could at last enjoy some domestic peace.

This I was determined to do. I had not so much as seen my family for over a year. I scarcely knew my children. The notion of making a home in New York took some getting used to, but whatever the difficulties, it was obviously a better solution than no home at all. I had, of course, as yet no guarantee that I would be staying on at the Met when my year's contract expired, but I felt it was probable that I should. In any event, whatever the future might hold, I wanted to be reunited with my family. So I wrote to Costanza asking her to find servants, to pack trunks, and to come.

But not immediately, not until the autumn; for the previous year, never thinking that I would stay so long at the Metropolitan, I had committed myself, for the summer of 1921, to yet another South American tour with Walter Mocchi. After so many months of uninterrupted hard work and unrelieved tension, I felt desperately in need of my mother, of the pale-gold Recanati vineyards, of the orange sails of fishing boats on the calm blue Adriatic. But it was too late to back out, and early in June I embarked for Rio de Janeiro. The months of strain took their toll; I felt in low spirits during the voyage, and on arrival at Rio had to be whisked off to hospital with a violent attack of uræmia. This circumstance provoked a campaign of rumours, circulated as usual by one of the rival companies, to the effect that my voice was permanently impaired, that I had become tone-deaf, that my career was finished, and so forth.

I recovered in time to put a stop to the rumours by singing in Rio, São Paulo and Buenos Aires—twenty-five performances altogether: 'Gioconda', 'Lohengrin', 'Mefistofele', 'Tosca', and a new Mascagni opera, 'Il Piccolo Marat', which had been presented only once before, at the Costanzi in Rome. We gave it its South American baptism at a new Buenos Aires theatre, the Cervantes, on September 20th, 1921. Like 'Andrea Chénier', this opera is based on an episode of the French Revolution; the hero is a *sans-culotte*. The music, being dramatic rather than lyrical, was less suited to my voice than that of 'Andrea Chénier'; nevertheless, our production of it—with Gilda Dalla Rizza as Mariella, myself in the title-rôle, and Gino Marinuzzi conducting—was a great success in Buenos Aires. Mascagni sent me an enthusiastic congratulatory telegram, expressing the hope that I would bring his 'little *sans-culotte*' all round the world with me; but as a matter of fact I never sang in 'Il Piccolo Marat' again.

I returned to New York on October 31st, 1921, in a state of trepidation. This was not caused by the tender prospect of reunion with my family after so prolonged an absence, nor even by the comical one of introducing Costanza—who had never been outside Italy, and had never had a servant before—to housekeeping on a rather grand scale in the apartment I had rented at 140 West 57th Street, near Carnegie Hall. The mechanical organization of life no longer worried me; it had been taken entirely and efficiently off my hands by a newly-acquired secretary, Renato Rossi, an old friend from my student days in Rome.

What perturbed and frightened me was something entirely different. It was the headline appearing in New York newspapers: *Who Will Be Caruso's Successor?* Caruso had died in Sorrento on August 2nd. The debate which immediately sprang up seemed to me irreverent, macabre and unnecessary. It was true, as I have said, that Caruso had reigned over the Metropolitan, but he had done so by virtue of his own greatness, not of any official designation. It seemed absurd to talk as though he had founded a dynasty, as though Caruso the Second would now have to be chosen, crowned, and anointed with holy oils. I felt complete agreement with Gatti-Casazza, who declared, when provoked by the rumpus into doing something he detested, namely giving an interview to the Press: 'There are but two elements, public opinion and time, which can decide who will be the successor or successors to the great artist. The modern theatre has ceased to be a theatre of stars and has become a theatre of the *tout ensemble*. What we aim at is a perfectly-rounded production.'

These wise words proved powerless to mitigate the violence and acrimony of the slanging match which continued to rage between the partisans of the rival candidates for the succession. *Aficionados* and friends of the various eligible tenors aligned themselves in rival teams behind their favourites. The tenors themselves, to do them justice, had no part in this. It was acutely embarrassing to meet a colleague—Martinelli or Chamblée or Crimi or Pertile—in the corridors of the Met, when our respective merits and demerits had been thrashed out in the morning newspapers as pitilessly as though we were about to engage in a boxing match at Madison Square Garden. My own name was being bandied about so often in this connexion—oftener perhaps than any of the others—that I felt obliged to dissociate myself publicly from all responsibility in the matter. I therefore wrote a letter to the *New York Times*—a new departure for me!—in which I said:

'I believe that to speak of this at present, or in any way to mention Caruso's successor, is a sacrilege and a profanity to his memory; it means violating a tomb which is sacred to Italy and the entire world. The efforts of every artist today aim to gather and conserve the artistic heritage received from the great singer, and everyone must strive to do this, not with vain self-advertisement, but with tenacious study for the triumph of the pure and the beautiful. He struggled for this, and we for the glory of our art must follow his example with dignity.'

And to the reporters who badgered me I invariably repeated: 'I don't want to be another Caruso; I just want to be Gigli.'

The tipsters in this strange campaign were prompt to draw conclusions from the fact that Gatti-Casazza asked me to sing on the opening night of the new Metropolitan season. This had always been a privilege reserved for Caruso; after joining the Met in 1903, he had sung on every opening night but one. I think, however, that the tipsters were mistaken, because the opera chosen was 'Traviata'; and since 'Traviata' is a soprano's opera, not a tenor's, I had no reason to feel that a crown was being placed on my head. I simply saw that Gatti-Casazza was wisely and adroitly evading the issue. In point of fact I did ultimately inherit, but not until several years later, the privileged first-night-of-the-season tradition.

The interior of the Metropolitan Opera House is uncomfortable and, to put it mildly, architecturally undistinguished, but on the opening night of the season, in those pre-Depression days, it nevertheless offered a uniquely brilliant spectacle. Behind the dazzling display of jewels and dresses in the thirty-five red-and-gold lacquer caves that form the famous 'Diamond Horseshoe'—the grand tier of boxes rented for the season by the great millionaire families, the Vanderbilts, the Morgans, the Whitneys, the Rockefellers—lay what must have been at that time the world's greatest single agglomeration of wealth.

When, on the night of November 14th, 1921, the curtain rose on 'Traviata', I suddenly realized that in deflecting the interest of this first-night audience from the tenor to the soprano, Gatti-Casazza had been more than adroit; he had been supremely tactful. For, after all, this was the first Met performance since the death of Caruso; and along with its diamonds, the audience visibly wore an air of mourning. The name of the soprano was particularly calculated to arouse curiosity and expectation: it was Amelita Galli-Curci. Until then she had been singing in Chicago; this was her first appearance at the Met.

I found myself devoutly hoping that she would outshine me, for now I felt even more intensely what I had already felt when I replaced the ailing Caruso at the New Year's Day performance—a kind of reticence, a decent reluctance to obtrude myself. Unfortunately, Galli-Curci sang badly. Whatever the cause—whether the rôle of Violetta did not suit her, whether she had failed to study it properly, whether she was not feeling well, or whether she was simply nervous—she succumbed throughout the evening to a distressing tendency to sing flat. The audience made no more than a feebly polite effort to conceal their disappointment with her; and so, despite Gatti-Casazza's strategy and my own desire, the evening was mine—almost by default.

CHAPTER X

AMERICA AND ITALY

On the pretext—a feeble one, since we were now well provided with Italian servants—of lending a hand with the household marketing, I would sometimes slip away downtown by myself and wander among the gloomy tenements of New York's Lower East Side. In Mulberry Street, the main thoroughfare of 'Little Italy', far from the gleaming hygienic self-service supermarkets, I would enter poky little shops where the people spoke Italian and everything smelt of Italy. I would buy Chianti and smoked raw Parma ham and parmesan cheese, herbs such as basil and rosemary and marjoram, *pasta* and olive oil and freshly-roasted coffee, and the long brittle sticks of bread that we call *grissini*. I am a nationalist about food.

But this, as I have said, was only the pretext. What I really wanted to do was talk to the people—those tough, courageous New York Italians who had been forced by poverty to leave the blue Italian sky behind them and fight for survival in these dark, forbidding streets. What heartbreak it must have been, I thought, for an illiterate Calabrian peasant to find himself in this grim place without money, without friends, not speaking a word of the language; finding that even his religion, when he sought its solace in the austere Irish Catholic churches, had become foreign, baffling, difficult of access. How did they do it, I wondered? From what depths of despair did they draw their fortitude?

I rarely had time to attend Italo-American social gatherings; and in any case, since the kind of people I would have met on such occasions would no longer be poor and humble, they interested me less. But I thought continually of the penniless immigrants facing the New World for the first time amid the bleak ugliness of the Lower East Side. Each year, so long as I lived in New York, I always gave a number of benefit concerts in aid of the

Italian Hospital and other charities. I did what I could; but I am well aware that it was little enough.

Four days after partnering Galli-Curci in 'Traviata', I sang with her again, in 'Lucia di Lammermoor'. This time she redeemed herself by a brilliant performance; her voice was peculiarly suited to the music of Donizetti, and Lucia was in any case, I think, her supreme rôle. On November 26th I sang in 'Mefistofele' with José Mardones; and the following day I took part, together with a chosen group of other Metropolitan artists, in a memorial concert for Caruso. It was preceded by a ceremony in which Fiorello La Guardia, on behalf of Mrs. Caruso and her daughter, presented a bust of the great artist to the Metropolitan. The proceeds of the concert, nearly twelve thousand dollars, were sent in Caruso's name to what had been his favourite charity, the Verdi Home for Aged Musicians in Milan. I was reminded of the Boito commemoration at the Scala. Almost everyone, both on the stage and in the audience, had tears in their eyes; and as was only fitting on such an occasion, there was no applause.

The soloists included Frances Alda, Amelita Galli-Curci, Geraldine Farrar, Giovanni Martinelli, Giuseppe De Luca, José Mardones and myself. The programme began with the '*Prelude*' from 'Parsifal', and continued with the '*Requiem*' and '*Kyrie*' from Verdi's 'Requiem Mass'. Of the other items, I remember that De Luca sang Handel's '*Lascia ch'io pianga*', Frances Alda sang César Franck's '*Panis Angelicus*', Galli-Curci sang the Bach-Gounod '*Ave Maria*', and I sang what had been one of Caruso's favourite pieces, Bizet's '*Agnus Dei*'. The orchestra played Chopin's 'Marche Funèbre'; the choir sang the '*Inflammatus*' from Rossini's 'Stabat Mater', and the concert ended with the '*Dies Irae*' from Verdi's 'Requiem'. It was all unforgettably moving, a supreme example of the power of music to penetrate and give expression to those regions of human feeling that lie too deep for words.

In December, 1921, I sang in 'La Bohème' with Frances Alda, and in 'Cavalleria Rusticana' with Rosa Ponselle, who was born in Connecticut of Italian parents, and whose real name was Ponzillo. On December 21st, in 'Tosca', I had my first experience of partnering Maria Jeritza, the great but alarmingly temperamental Viennese soprano who was one of Gatti-Casazza's new acquisitions that season (Titta Ruffo, incidentally, was another). I shall have something more to say about her later on.

On January 5th, 1922, I sang my first new rôle of the season, that of Mylio in 'Le Roi d'Ys', by the French-Spanish composer Edouard Lalo. Gatti-Casazza had laid down an inflexible rule that all operas presented at the Metropolitan must be sung in their original language; so for this opera I had to learn French. The critics, needless to say, did not let slip the opportunity of making uncomplimentary remarks about my accent.

'Le Roi d'Ys' is based on the melancholy Breton legend of a submerged city. The music is sufficiently charming to have made the opera a popular favourite in Paris for many years after its first production there in 1888, but it never really rises above the level of respectable mediocrity. New Yorkers were now seeing it for the first time, but its American *première* had taken place long before, on January 23rd, 1890, in the historic New Orleans opera house which was subsequently destroyed by fire. Lalo, notwithstanding his championship of Wagner in France, was a composer of essentially lyric tendencies, and the Wagnerian form of more or less continuous music that he chose for 'Le Roi d'Ys' seems to have been on the whole outside his scope. To be effective, it would have required a sense of characterization, thematic resourcefulness, theatrical dexterity, in all of which Lalo was patently lacking. He would have done better to have followed the conventional pattern of Italian *opera seria*, which requires the composer only to string together a series of attractive melodies. His real musical gifts can be seen in the overture, and in the '*Aubade*' from the third act, both of them well-known concert pieces. In the overture Lalo had the chance to take a few themes and develop them symphonically at his leisure; in the rest of the opera, one feels that the action is simply getting in his way.

The cast of our New York production was as brilliant a one as the Met could muster: Rozenn was sung by Frances Alda, Margared by Rosa Ponselle, Prince Karnac by Giuseppe Danise, the King by Léon Rothier, and Saint Corentin by Paolo Ananiam. It was no fault of the singers that the opera itself, for all its success in Paris, simply did not appeal to the New York audience. Only at two moments did their apathy kindle into enthusiasm: after the overture, which Albert Wolff conducted superbly, and after my own rendering of the aria '*Vainement, ma bien-aimée*'. It was my luck that the one great aria in the whole opera should have been written for the tenor; and if I was pleased, I was also somewhat embarrassed by the contrast between the tempestuous applause which fell to my lot and the lukewarm clapping doled out to my colleagues.

'Andrea Chénier' had proved such a success the previous year that Gatti-Casazza decided to repeat it, with the same team—Claudia Muzio and myself; and, indeed, for several years after that it remained a fixture in the Met programme. I sang again in 'La Bohème', this time with Lucrezia Bori; and, partnered by her, I made my first Metropolitan appearances in 'Madama Butterfly' and in Massenet's 'Manon'.

The latter was an important occasion for me; the rôle of Des Grieux had been one of my favourites ever since I first sang it in Genoa with the unfriendly Rosina Storchio. Now, of course, I had to sing it in French; to my surprise, the initial effort was rewarded by the discovery that it was really much easier to sing in the original—the words fitted the music better.

A more scrupulous respect for the spirit of the original than I had ever seen in Italy was also evidenced by another feature of this Met version: it retained the spoken dialogue, after the true fashion of *opéra comique* in the more dignified sense of the term. Most European opera houses outside France replace this spoken dialogue in 'Manon' by recitative, thereby arbitrarily converting it into 'grand' opera, according to the French method of classification.

'Manon' had a rather glorious tradition at the Met. When it was first produced there, on January 1st, 1895, the great French tenor Jean de Reszke sang Des Grieux; the following year he sang the rôle again, partnered by Melba, and after a series of mediocre productions there was a spectacular revival in 1909 with Geraldine Farrar and Caruso. Comparisons, it seemed, were inevitable, although this was the sort of criticism that I never could quite get used to. 'Gigli does not look the part of Des Grieux. The unapproachably perfect Des Grieux at the Met remains Jean de Reszke. . . .' Whether or not these critics were old enough to have heard de Reszke themselves, they wrote as if they had. But they did concede that I sang the 'Dream Song' 'beautifully'; that was something. And although I was piqued at being condemned without right of appeal, so to speak, by that epithet 'unapproachably perfect' awarded to Jean de Reszke, I found consolation in this rather touching evidence that a voice long silenced by death can survive in legend.

In February, 1922, I sang in Catalani's 'Loreley', which was being staged for the first time at the Metropolitan. The rôle of Walter was of course already familiar to me—I had sung it on my first South American visit; but this production, which was part of Gatti-Casazza's policy to restore to favour a number of minor works of the nineteenth-century repertory, was superior to the Buenos Aires one. Loreley was sung by Claudia Muzio, Rudolph by José Mardones, Anna by Marie Sundelius, and Baron Hermann by Giuseppe Denise. It proved as great a success as 'Le Roi d'Ys' had been a failure; and again I felt glad that Catalani's memory was being vindicated.

Early in March, 1922, I sang in 'Tosca' with the American soprano Geraldine Farrar; it was her farewell to the stage, her very last performance, and at the end she was smothered in bouquets, which at least helped her to conceal her tears. This final farewell to the public is a heart-rending, long-dreaded moment for every singer, a foretaste of death. We all have to go through with it, and it had better come too soon than too late. It is better that the public should protest, feeling that it is being deprived of something still precious—that it should plead, 'He still sings so wonderfully!'—than that it should shrug its shoulders and say, 'Well, it was high time the old fellow retired anyway!'

On March 18th, 1922, I sang a new rôle that was nevertheless not altogether new for me: it was Des Grieux again, this time in Puccini's 'Manon Lescaut'. Massenet's elegiac 'Manon' retains, I think, much more of the flavour of the Abbé Prévost's story; but Puccini's version, although it is not one of his best works, has distinguishing merits of its own. It is a supreme musical expression of youthful passion and ardour; I think one can sing it well only while one is young.

Junior by nine years to Massenet's 'Manon', having first seen the light in Turin in 1893, 'Manon Lescaut' was an important turning-point for Puccini himself. 'Bohème', 'Tosca', 'Butterfly' were as yet unwritten; his previous opera, 'Edgar', had been a total failure, and he decided that should 'Manon Lescaut' also prove unsuccessful he would give up writing opera altogether. It was not an unqualified success, but at least it provided him with enough encouragement to persevere. There are powerful passages throughout; and the third act, with its great *finale* outside the prison in Le Havre, contains some of the most dramatic passages in modern Italian opera.

It had been in the Met repertory ever since its first production there, with Caruso and the beautiful Lina Cavalieri, in January, 1907. Puccini himself was present on that occasion, *incognito*; but someone recognized him during the interval, and he was greeted with such rapturous storms of applause that he finally had to retire from view in order that the performance might be resumed. This time the critics were kinder to me in their comparisons; those who remembered Caruso in the rôle, they said, would find consolation for his loss in my rendering of it.

The Metropolitan season ended with the company's annual spring tour to Baltimore, Atlanta and Cleveland. On returning to New York I was confined to bed for several weeks with an attack of inflammatory rheumatism. I had given forty-four performances during the season, in thirteen different operas, as well as a number of concerts; and I could scarcely remember when I had last had a holiday. Gatti-Casazza had offered me a new three-year contract. I felt thankful that I had kept the summer free of all engagements. It was with a tremendous sigh of relief that I at last embarked on the *Conte Rosso,* with my family, and turned my face towards the Bay of Naples. I had not seen Italy for two years.

The summer of 1922 was as uneventful as I had wanted it to be. It began with three restful weeks of convalescence at Agnano, a spa near Naples. Here I came to know Maestro Ernesto De Curtis, the composer of many famous Neapolitan songs, such as '*Torna a Surriento*', which were already in my concert repertory. Our acquaintance quickly ripened into deep friendship.

Revived and refreshed by the waters of Agnano, I arrived at last in Recanati. There was sadness as well as sweetness in my first meeting with my mother, and our first hour together was spent in a visit to the graveyard. I gave one open-air benefit concert in Piazza Leopardi during the summer; for the rest, nothing was very different from what it had ever been. I could see that some people began by feeling shy of me, thinking I might have put on grand airs, now that I was rich and lived in New

York; but I found it easy to reassure them. I was delighted to be back among them, on equal terms, playing *boccia* outside the tavern or billiards in the café. A very important part of my holiday consisted in being able to forget, for the time being, about the great world that lay beyond the Apennines.

All summer I had been somewhat persecuted by an extremely heavy piece of luggage—a marble bust of Dante, which the Italian colony of New York had asked me to present to Gabriele d'Annunzio on their behalf. Before leaving Italy in September, I travelled north to Lake Garda to fulfil this mission. D'Annunzio's fantastic villa at Gardone, the 'Vittoriale', is too well known to need description; in any case, I did not see much of it, for I only stayed ten minutes. D'Annunzio, having thrown himself out of a window a short time previously, was still in bed suffering from shock, concussion and other injuries, and felt unable to receive me; but he did send me down a signed photograph of himself, inscribed with greetings and thanks to the 'melodious messenger'. Some time afterwards I was fascinated to read, in an Italian newspaper, a glowing and detailed description of how I met the poet, and of how, in the September sunshine, we walked together in his garden, talking of music, poetry, Italy, Fiume, and our plans for the future!

My new three-year contract at the Metropolitan gave me a sense both of security and of perspective such as I had never known before. I now felt justified in doing something that I had been wanting to do for a long time; I persuaded my old teacher and friend, Maestro Enrico Rosati, to come back to New York with me, on a permanent basis, as my accompanist and coach. I also acquired the services of another secretary, Amedeo Grossi, who for the rest of his life was to prove the prop and mainstay of my existence—a function which his widow, Signora Barbara, now performs with the same unswerving devotion.

Having buttressed myself with these invaluable helpmates, I found it necessary to create yet another post in my rapidly growing establishment—that of physical trainer. The bouts of sickness to which I had fallen victim in Buenos Aires and New York had convinced me that I could no longer stand up to the tremendous strain of work and public life unless I devoted some time each day to intensive physical exercise. I therefore delivered myself into the hands of Mr. H. J. Reilly, a masseur and athletic coach.

Every day, so long as I remained in America, and even when I was on tour, he subjected me to his ingenious tortures.

These tortures, as well as keeping me physically fit, had a further, dual purpose, to strengthen my chest and shoulder muscles so as to accommodate the demands made on them by the vocal cords, and to curb the expansion of my girth. It is an established biological fact that tenors, for glandular reasons, tend to be short and excessively round; while for bassos, who are generally tall and thin, the same law applies in reverse. Only baritones, it seems, are in the happy position of being, from the glandular point of view, normal. Since the tenor's rôle in opera is almost always that of a tragic or romantic hero, this arrangement is rather unfortunate, and most tenors have to wage a constant battle with their tendency to put on weight. I was no exception.

The hard-boiled New York critics showed scant sympathy with my predicament. The *Brooklyn Eagle*, for example, after a performance of 'Andrea Chénier', had observed cuttingly that I looked a 'well-fed poet'. At an early date in the new Met season, I was to sing Romeo; if I was to escape another avalanche of scathing comments, there was no time to be lost. I decided to take Mr. Reilly with me on my October concert tour to Chicago and other cities of the Mid-West.

The exigencies of life in hotels cramped his style by confining him to a sedate routine of massage. Only when I returned to New York and began paying daily visits to his gymnasium, did I realize the full range of his ideas and capacities. The medicine ball, shadow and real boxing, the rowing machine, riding a mechanical horse, sawing and chopping wood, running, general calisthenics—all these formed part of my daily dozen; but they were as nothing compared to the fearsome ordeal that was the climax of every session. This consisted of my being laid flat on my stomach on an iron cradle, with a kind of lifebelt fastened round my waist; Reilly would press an electric button, and the cradle would then proceed, energetically, to rock.

To give Mr. Reilly his due, these drastic methods did produce results. When the Metropolitan season opened in November, 1922, I was twenty pounds lighter. My first appearance was in 'Traviata' with Lucrezia Bori, on the first night of the Brooklyn Academy season. On November 18th I took part in a gala performance of 'Mefistofele' at which Clémenceau, then on an official visit to the United States, was present.

The sensation of the evening was not Clémenceau, however; it was Chaliapin. Breaking the vow he had made never to set foot in New York again, the great Russian had returned to sing the rôle of the Devil, in which he had made his début at the Metropolitan on November 20th, 1907, almost exactly fifteen years earlier. Those who had heard him both on that occasion and on this, declared that he had greatly deepened and broadened his conception of the rôle; I, who was hearing him for the first time, could certainly imagine no finer rendering of it.

To begin with, he looked the part. With his towering, lithe figure, his half-bared breast, and the cruel, terrifying expressions in which he cast his mobile features, the appearance he presented was quite unnervingly diabolical. Diverging at many points from what I knew by now to be the traditional Met interpretation of the rôle, his own rendering of it seemed to me invariably truer and artistically more coherent. In the 'Prologue in the Heavens', for example, instead of emerging among the clouds, he entered from below, huge and menacing, shambling about like a great spider, his long black hair gathered into a sort of scalp-lock that gave his face the look of a Japanese devil-mask. And at the end, instead of descending hurriedly into the pit, he pawed feebly at the celestial rose-leaves that were searing his flesh, crumpled slowly to the ground, and lay sprawling and motionless. Faust had won.

His singing was as great as his acting. His voice was beautiful in texture, perfectly produced, thrilling in range and power; his vocalism was an astounding exhibition of breath control, tonal production and phrasing. The ovation that greeted him when the last curtain fell proved overwhelmingly that New Yorkers had forgiven him his past tantrums.

My own performance was rather submerged on this occasion. Although he amiably yielded me the place of honour in several curtain calls, Chaliapin could scarcely help stealing the show. But I felt such genuine admiration for him that I did not mind.

Chaliapin was a great Mefisto and a great Boris Godounov not only because he could sing—although that, of course, was the primary requirement—but also because he could act. Caruso was a great Canio, a great Rodolfo, a great Eleazar, a great John of Leyden for the same reason. Yet when all is said and done, opera is generally too implausible to be a realistic vehicle for acting. This is the anomalous situation in which every singer finds himself; this is the problem which every singer has got to work out for himself. How can Romeo die convincingly when, having taken poison, he must linger on and on, in a semi-recumbent position, singing as exquisitely as possible?

One can only compromise. The music is the all-important thing; for its sake one must try to act in spite of the absurdities. A good libretto helps. The rest is illusion. The audience must be hypnotized into accepting the make-believe.

For me the problem was more difficult than it can have been for either Chaliapin or Caruso because, although fully aware of its implications, I lacked the talent which helped them to solve it. I was no actor.

I had begun my career by trying, gropingly, to act, and it was a failure. I was criticized for being wooden, and wooden no doubt I was. My acting had probably not progressed very far beyond the level of the burnt-cork-moustache Sunday afternoon entertainments which my brother Abramo used to devise in the parish hall in Recanati. Still, the problem was there, facing me; and gradually I evolved my own approach to it.

Whenever a rôle was assigned to me, I accepted it as a reality —or tried to—blindly and totally, no matter how improbable or inconsistent it might be. I tried to identify myself with it, to become, for the time being, the character I was supposed to impersonate; or if that was impossible, then at least his twin brother, or his dearest friend. I tried to imagine his reactions, to feel with his feelings. I would find myself talking to him, arguing with him. Feeling! That was the keynote of my method, if it can be called a method. I tried to pour feeling into the rôle, to make it come alive through feeling. Not every opera responded to this treatment. 'Gianni Schicchi' never did, for instance, nor 'Iris'. Some rôles defeated me. Others, such as Andrea Chénier, or Puccini's Des Grieux, required practically no effort whatsoever; these were generally (but not always) the rôles I sang best.

Rehearsals, apart from helping me to learn positions on the stage so as not to fall over other people, were never of much use to me. I needed the footlights and the inspiration of the audience, and then I could trust to impulse and throw myself completely into the part. Of course I could and did think out certain fundamental aspects of a rôle beforehand—I have described in an earlier chapter how I did so in 'Tosca'; but I could never foresee exactly how it would work out afterwards, and it never worked out the same way twice. Even when, in giving an encore, I had to sing the same aria over again after a few minutes, I always gave an entirely different version of it the second time—not deliberately, but simply because the first moment had passed and my feelings had now flowed into a different mould. This can scarcely be called acting; but whatever it was, it served my purpose. It enabled me to shed real tears on the stage, to feel real passion and real despair.

When Gatti-Casazza asked me to take the part of Romeo in Gounod's opera 'Roméo et Juliette', I did more in the way of preparation than study the music and go on a slimming cure. First of all, I went to the theatre to see Shakespeare's play, on which of course the opera is based; but although I enjoyed it, the requirements of opera are so different that the fact of having seen it did not really help me very much. I read books about the history of the period, studied costumes of the period in the art galleries, and pondered over photographs of Verona. Above all, I tried to feel with Romeo's heart. Only then did I consider myself ready to ask Maestro Rosati to come to the piano and start going over the score.

All these preparations came to naught, so far as the critics were concerned, through a stupid accident on the night of the *première,* November 24th, 1922. In the fourth act, I lost my footing on the steps of Juliet's bier and tumbled down them unromantically on to the stage. 'Gigli', they chorused next day, 'failed to convince as a tragic lover.' I sighed with wry amusement. When it came to my singing, they were a little more gracious. 'Gigli has found in Romeo a rôle that indulges all the virtues of his voice,' declared the New York *Sun*; but the shade of Jean de Reszke still hovered in the background, providing 'older opera-goers' with 'unforgettable and unbeatable memories'.

The music of 'Roméo et Juliette' is perhaps nothing very wonderful; one suspects that Gounod made it a receptacle for left-overs from his 'Faust'. But it is pleasing and melodic; there are four love-duets; and after all, even the left-overs from 'Faust' are not to be despised. The performance, in which Juliette was sung by Lucrezia Bori, Mercutio by De Luca, Capulet by Didur, and Frère Laurent by Léon Rothier, was conducted by Louis Hasselmans and was a gala occasion. The scenery and costumes were new and magnificent: the Romanesque interiors glittered with golden mosaics, and in the garden scene, great willow branches drooped and shadowed the moonlit wall. The critics found fault; but the audience was enthusiastic, and that was what mattered to me.

On Thanksgiving Day, 1922, I had a strange experience. With Maestro Rosati as my accompanist, I gave a concert in the prison chapel at Sing-Sing to eleven hundred of the inmates. The programme was the identical one that I had sung a few days previously in a millionaire drawing-room on Park Avenue; it included '*M'appari*' from Flotow's 'Marta', '*Lucevan le stelle*' from 'Tosca', '*Recitar*' from 'Pagliacci', and '*La donna è mobile*' from 'Rigoletto'. The convicts sat with rapt attention, and were most appreciative; but their warmest applause was reserved for the Neapolitan songs—'*Ammore che fa fa*', '*Torna a Surriento*', '*Tu ca no chiagne*', '*Tu sola*'—of which they begged me to send them records. Afterwards I was shown round. I saw prisoners at work, sculpturing wood, or threading tiny beads to make ladies' handbags; and I gazed with fascinated horror at the new electric chair in the death house.

I had made a good friend in New York—Commissioner Enright of the New York Police. We got on so well together, in spite of the language difficulty, that I almost felt as though he were my American family. He was always on the pier to see me off when I sailed for Italy, and to welcome me back on my return. I was always glad to help him out by singing in aid of police charities, or to entertain distinguished guests of the city. It may have been in recognition of these services that on November 30th, 1922, he made me Honorary Captain of the New York Police, a title which carried the right to affix a badge with the initials PD (for Police Department) to my car, and to have a police motor-cycle escort on certain occasions. The right of the Commissioner to appoint Honorary Deputies and other non-paid members of the Police Department had been provided for in a 'war measure' passed in 1917 and never subsequently repealed. Of all the honours and titles conferred on me at one time or another in the course of my career, none ever gave me as

Riccardo in Verdi's 'Un Ballo in Maschera'

Des Grieux in Massenet's 'Manon'

Don Alvaro in Verdi's 'La Forza del Destino'

Romeo in Gounod's 'Roméo et Juliette'

These two stills from films show me (*above*) as Enzo Curti in London Film Productions' 'Forget Me Not' and (*below*) in Itala-Film's 'Silenzio: Si gira'

much pleasure as this. Apart from being useful, it was fun. I greatly enjoyed, for instance, being greeted with a friendly 'Hello, Mr. Giggly!' by every traffic cop in New York, and then being waved on past a stream of waiting traffic!

Chaliapin had been away on a tour of the Western States most of the winter; when he returned to New York, we sang together again in 'Mefistofele', on March 13th, 1923. The demand for tickets was so great that a line of would-be purchasers extended all the way down Broadway and across to Seventh Avenue; but most of them were disappointed.

Meanwhile I had been studying another new rôle, that of the Portuguese explorer Vasco da Gama in Meyerbeer's opera, 'L'Africaine' (or rather 'L'Africana', since for some unexplained reason we were for once being allowed to break the Met rule about singing opera in the original language, and were giving it in Italian). I was amused to find a newspaper reporting that I had made a special trip to Portugal to gather background atmosphere; even had I had the time to do so, the opera itself would hardly have warranted such painstaking research. Despite the fact that it was originally intended to commemorate Vasco da Gama's fourth centenary, and that Meyerbeer, from the day in 1838 when Eugène Scribe handed him the libretto, took twenty-five years to finish it, it is a tangle of grotesque absurdities bearing little or no relation to historical fact. The Malabar coast where Vasco da Gama actually landed is transplanted, in the opera, to Madagascar; the inhabitants are referred to as 'Brahmins'. The African slave, Selika, who turns out to be the Queen of Madagascar, acts as though she had been brought up in a Faubourg St. Germain drawing-room; as for the explorer himself, he is a strangely vacillating fellow, unable to make up his mind between a white woman and a dark one, tossed as capriciously on the fluctuating waves of love as his ship is tossed on the high seas. I found it difficult to have much sympathy with him, although I did my best; and I also thought it curious that the rôle of Selika should at one time or another have attracted most of the great tragic actresses of the lyric stage, beginning with Marie Sasse in the original Paris production at the Opéra, April 28th, 1865. The music, with which I had long been familiar—the junior band in Recanati used to play selections from it—is bombastic, pretentious, trivial, completely lacking in any coherent style; there are plenty of musical ideas, more perhaps than in any opera of Verdi's, but they are put in for effect, to impress the public, without any real interior necessity or significance.

Having said all this, I am obliged to add that the rôle of Vasco da Gama became one of the most popular and successful in my whole repertory!

This was perhaps mainly due to the beauty of the one great tenor aria, '*O Paradiso*', which lies embedded in the rest of the opera like a jewel in a rag-bag. Vasco da Gama sings it when, on reaching land at last after his long and perilous voyage, he is suddenly confronted with the dazzling and exotic spectacle of the temples and temple dancers of Madagascar. His feelings at that particular moment were easy enough to imagine, and at the *première* of the Metropolitan revival of 'L'Africana', on March 21st, 1923, I was able to give a rendering of the aria which aroused even the critics to enthusiasm. The names of Jean de Reszke and Caruso, my predecessors in the rôle at the Metropolitan, were of course mentioned; but not to my disadvantage. The title-rôle was sung by Rosa Ponselle. The critics were dissatisfied with her acting; privately I sympathized with her, for as I have said, I thought the rôle of Selika as full of inconsistencies as my own. But the funny thing was that they praised *my* acting. 'For once Mr. Gigli,' etc. And the New York *Globe* declared: 'The real triumph of the affair is the Vasco da Gama of Mr. Gigli. . . . Any success the revival attains is due to him.' I had taken such pains with my Romeo, and they had damned it with faint praise; now, in a rôle that I had practically written off as impossible, it appeared that I had triumphed!

The New York season ended for me that spring on a note of comedy. My last performance at the Met was a matinée of 'L'Africana' on April 21st. At five-past five that same afternoon, together with other members of the company, I was due to leave by train for our annual season in Atlanta. In order to make this possible, the performance had started early, but it had been held up by the storms of applause after '*O Paradiso*'. Encores were strictly forbidden at the Met, but in the end I gave one; it seemed to be the only way of calming down the audience. My voice soared enraptured by the tropical delights of Madagascar, while my mind was fixed in terror on the 5.05 from Pennsylvania Station. If I missed it, I would arrive in Atlanta too late to sing in the opening performance there, which was to be 'Roméo et Juliette'. At 4.52 p.m. I rushed out of the artists' entrance with exactly thirteen minutes in which to catch my train. This was the sort of emergency for which the Police Department badge came in useful; the traffic cops, instead of giving me a summons for speeding, waved me onwards with a smile. I reached the platform at Penn Station, still disguised in the wig and beard, the doublet and hose of a Portuguese explorer, but with half a minute to spare.

CHAPTER XI

THE ARTISTIC TEMPERAMENT

My existence was gradually assuming, if not a routine, at least a pattern. From the beginning of November until the end of April there was New York and the Metropolitan season, sometimes briefly interrupted by a concert tour in other American cities, and always followed by a short operatic season with the Met company in Atlanta, Cleveland, and perhaps Baltimore or Washington. While in New York I often gave concerts at Carnegie Hall, or at the Waldorf Astoria on one of Mr. Bagby's Musical Mornings, or in private houses; and I made records for the Victor Talking Machine Company in Camden, New Jersey. In short, I was kept busy.

For my summers I could choose between work, play, or a combination of both. Work meant a lucrative but strenuous tour in South America, where of course the winter season would be just beginning; play meant lazing on the beach at Porto Recanati; and the combination of both meant a month or six weeks of opera and concerts in various European cities, and a month's holiday in Recanati afterwards. This last solution, while not always feasible, was, on the whole, the one I preferred.

September saw me back in the United States, travelling from coast to coast, or very nearly so, on another concert tour before getting back into harness at the Met. There were variations; but for ten years or so this was to remain the general pattern.

The summer of 1923, divided between Agnano (where I made the acquaintance of Tetrazzini) and Recanati, was a holiday for the most part; but, for the first time since my début at the Metropolitan, I did make a few public appearances here and there in Italy, all of them for charity—'Tosca' at the Teatro Persiani in Recanati; 'Andrea Chénier', with the Irish soprano Margaret Sheridan as Maddalena, in Rimini; and a concert, with Giuseppe

De Luca, at the Augusteo in Rome. While in Rome, I paid a visit to Mussolini; he gave me a signed photograph of himself, with a flattering inscription.

Together with a number of other Metropolitan artists, I had been invited to take part, during September and October, 1923, in the first home-grown operatic venture ever to be staged in San Francisco. This enterprise was the brain-child of an energetic San Francisco Italian, Maestro Gaetano Merola. Filled with a missionary zeal to foster love of opera among his fellow-citizens, but faced with the fact that only second-rate opera companies ever seemed to get as far west as the Pacific coast, he worked out a solution of the problem. He invited the best artists available, individually, to sing the solo parts, and himself trained the chorus, composed entirely of unpaid amateurs. It took them seven months of hard practice to learn eight operas, but they learned them well. There was, naturally, no opera house; the works were staged in the Civic Auditorium. The enterprise was completely self-supporting; there were no subsidies, no funds of any kind available save box-office receipts. Nothing was spent on scenery or costumes; we brought our costumes with us, but the members of the chorus appeared on the stage in their ordinary clothes. This courageous and, indeed, unique achievement proved the great success that it deserved to be, and Maestro Merola was able to repeat it in the years that followed.

On my arrival in San Francisco I was impressed to discover that my title of Honorary Captain of the New York Police carried weight even on the shores of the Pacific. I was met at the Ferry Building by two leading San Francisco police officers, and a squad of motor-cycle police escorted me to my hotel with an ear-splitting screech of sirens!

My fellow guest-artists included Giovanni Martinelli, Giuseppe De Luca, Adamo Didur, and the soprano Queena Mario. We opened the season with 'Andrea Chénier' and closed it with 'Rigoletto'; in between, I sang in 'Mefistofele' and 'Roméo et Juliette'. The rapturous enthusiasm with which we were all acclaimed was profoundly moving.

I have related in an earlier chapter how on this occasion I met once more my old friend, the ex-cook Giovanni Zerri, now proprietor of a little Italian restaurant in San Francisco. This was the moment that he had promised me when, sitting in the garden of a tavern in Recanati, he had urged me to come to Rome, to have faith in my future.

A pleasant incident at the moment of my departure from San Francisco served as yet another reminder of those far-off days of my own beginnings. While some of my colleagues and myself were crossing on the ferry to board the train for Chicago, a girl of sixteen sang Italian songs for us. She had been born in San Francisco, of Italian parents: Tetrazzini had happened to hear her sing when she was fourteen, and had encouraged her to study. I gave her my good wishes for the future, and asked her to tell me her name. Fourteen years later I had occasion to remember it, when Lina Pagliughi became my partner at the Scala.

From San Francisco I travelled across the continent to Montreal, to give a concert; then back to New York, to study my next new rôle—that of Lionel, in Friedrich von Flotow's opera 'Marta'. I was to make my début in it, with Frances Alda and Giuseppe De Luca, on December 14th, 1923, at the Metropolitan.

This naïve, antiquated, humorous and tuneful opera seems to have a way of going underground from time to time, and then re-emerging to astonish everyone with its charm. It had already passed into oblivion when Adelina Patti resurrected it by singing the title-rôle, around 1880 or so, more than thirty years after its first performance, in Vienna in 1847. Caruso and Gatti-Casazza together rescued it from another period of eclipse, and Caruso made the rôle of Lionel peculiarly his own, singing it for twelve successive seasons at the Metropolitan, right up to 1920, the year before his death. In taking it over I was therefore entering directly into Caruso's heritage.

Composed by a German, on the basis of a French libretto about England in the reign of Queen Anne—the sub-title is 'The Fair at Richmond'—and traditionally sung in Italian, 'Marta' is full of silliness, and yet it pleases. Marta, in reality Lady Harriet, is a lady of Queen Anne's Court who for fun disguises herself as a chambermaid and enters the service of Lionel, a Surrey farmer whom she meets at Richmond Fair. Lionel falls in love with her, but the obstacles are obviously numerous, and tragedy seems imminent until he is opportunely discovered to be the heir of the Earl of Derby, when the path is clear for a happy ending.

A curious feature of the opera is the appearance in it, thinly disguised as '*Qui sola, vergin rosa*', of Moore's melody '*The Last*

Rose of Summer', to which Flotow took such a fancy that he simply interpolated it into the score. The rôle of Lionel is an extremely satisfying one for a lyric tenor, as Caruso had obviously discovered; for me, too, it became a permanent rôle, one which I sang fairly constantly throughout the rest of my career. The great tenor aria '*M'appari*' was already part of my concert repertory; when I sang it on the night of my début as Lionel at the Met the conductor, Gennaro Papi, was forced to break the rules and yield to the storm of applause that demanded an encore. The critics were benevolent. 'No one except Caruso,' said one of them, 'ever surpassed his effort.'

Among the revivals of the season, I sang 'Andrea Chénier' with Rosa Ponselle and Titta Ruffo, and a newcomer to the Met—the American baritone Lawrence Tibbett—in the rôle of Fleville. On January 9th, 1924, there was a gala performance of 'L'Amore dei Tre Re' in the presence of the composer, Italo Montemezzi. I took part in it, together with Lucrezia Bori and Didur; there was a ceremony afterwards in which Montemezzi was presented with a silver laurel wreath.

Later in January, 1924, I sang, with Elisabeth Rethberg, Didur and Angelo Bada, in the first New York production of a new Italian opera, 'I Compagnacci' by Primo Riccitelli. It had won a prize offered in 1922 by the Italian Education Ministry, and the world *première*, at the Costanzi in Rome on April 10th, 1923, had been a notable success. Although new, 'I Compagnacci' was not what one might call 'modern'. Riccitelli was a pupil of Mascagni, and his tuneful, melodious opera has many echoes of both Mascagni and Puccini. From my point of view this was just as well, for I have always found really modern opera almost impossible to sing.

'I Compagnacci' was presented at the Met as the second part of a double programme, and the audience no doubt welcomed it as comic relief after the Grand Guignol terrors of 'La Habañera', another modern work which preceded it. The background—Florence in the days of Savonarola—may sound austere and gloomy, but the plot is light burlesque, a comedy about the 'ordeal by fire', with a love theme and a happy ending.

The part of Baldo did not offer very much scope for my voice, except in one lyric solo and in one duet with Elisabeth Rethberg; but the critics—perhaps because this time they were unable to drag in reminiscences of Jean de Reszke!—were unreservedly enthusiastic about my performance. Above all, they said, I showed an unexpected talent as a comic actor!

At the beginning of March, 1924, I gave a short concert tour in the East and Middle West of the United States—Buffalo, Ithaca, Cleveland, Detroit, Fort Wayne, Memphis, New Haven and Paterson. On my return to New York, later in the month, I finally sang the part of Gianni Schicchi in Puccini's one-act opera of the same name—the part I had caused such a fuss by refusing to sing on my first visit to Buenos Aires. I did not like it this time any better than formerly; but I decided that it would be less trouble to sing it and get it over than to oppose the wishes of Gatti-Casazza.

In Europe, outside of Spain and Italy, I was still only a name, a disembodied voice imprisoned in a gramophone record. Max von Schillings, general manager of the Berlin Opera, after hearing me sing at the Metropolitan early in 1924, had urged me to visit Berlin in the summer. I knew the Berlin opera-going public by repute to be musically very discerning and very sceptical, and I accepted the invitation gladly as yet another challenge.

All seats for all performances of the sixteen-day season at the Staatsoper in Unter den Linden were sold out in advance, and the police had to be summoned to prevent the box-office from being mobbed. The season opened with a performance of 'La Bohème', in which the rôle of Mimi was sung by the Russian soprano Sinada Jurjewskaya (who was to die tragically two years later by throwing herself from the Devil's Bridge at Andermatt in Switzerland). Having been warned beforehand of the rigid German custom never to interrupt the music and to reserve all applause for the end of each act, I was totally unprepared for the outburst of applause that followed the last notes of my first aria, '*Che gelida manina*'. I was told afterwards that it was something quite unprecedented in Berlin.

'Tosca', in which I was partnered by Mafalda Salvatini, went somewhat differently. During the first two-thirds of the evening, the audience was reserved. There was no applause during the opening scene. But when it came to the third act, and '*Lucevan le stelle*', there was a wild outcry demanding an encore; and after the final curtain there was a tempest of applause lasting nearly twenty minutes, 'which in vehemence and duration', according to the

Vossischezeitung, 'surpassed anything ever accorded to Battistini'. In 'Rigoletto' I had to give, not one but two encores of '*La donna è mobile*'; I sang it differently each time, three different versions altogether. The critics declared that this was an achievement hitherto unparalleled in the annals of Berlin operatic history.

At my concert at the Berlin Philharmonic there was a kind of stampede. Tickets, it appeared, had been forged, and an unauthorized crowd filled the gangways, while the seated public gave loud vent to their indignation; the police were called in, and I waited on the platform for a quarter of an hour until the tumult subsided. It was all very different from the orderly and rather cold reception that, to tell the truth, I had feared in Berlin.

Telegrams of invitation poured in from other European cities —Leipzig, Prague, Budapest, Munich—but I refused them all except one, for a concert in Copenhagen. I was anxious to get back to Recanati. Busy, if delightful, weeks lay ahead of me; at last I was going to build a home of my own. The apartment on West 57th Street was all very well, but I knew now that nowhere but Recanati could ever really mean home for me. So I had chosen a site, half-way between the town and the Adriatic, on which to build my refuge and retreat. It was a small hill, known locally as Castelletto, affording a wonderful view of the Adriatic and the surrounding countryside. I spent the summer poring over plans with my brother Catervo, who had now settled in Recanati and whom I was leaving in charge of the building operations in my absence.

On September 2nd I was back in San Francisco for Maestro Merola's second opera season at the Civic Auditorium. I sang with Claudia Muzio in 'Andrea Chénier', 'Tosca' and 'Roméo et Juliette', and with Queena Mario in 'Bohème' and 'Rigoletto'. From San Francisco the entire company, braving the huge cyclone then sweeping California, travelled south to give a number of performances in Los Angeles.

Meanwhile I had received a telegram from Puccini in Viareggio, asking me to create the rôle of Prince Calaf in the world *première* of his new opera, 'Turandot', at the Scala the following April. Flattered by such a proof of confidence from the great composer, I naturally accepted; but Puccini died two months later, and the project fell through. In the end it was Miguel Fleta who sang Prince Calaf at the world *première*, and to tell the truth I felt very grateful to him for relieving me of the responsibility, for the rôle was completely unsuited to my voice.

Back in New York for the winter, after concerts in Denver and Detroit, I sang at the opening night of the Brooklyn Academy season in 'Marta', and on the first Saturday matinée at the Met in 'La Gioconda'. Far-off memories crowded on me as I faced a New York audience for the first time in the rôle of Enzo: my début in Rovigo, my dear old midwife landladies, and the terrible B flat at the end of '*Cielo e Mar*'. This time it was not B flat that I had to contend with; once again, it was Caruso's memory. His rendering of '*Cielo e Mar*' had been celebrated; and in 1915, when 'La Gioconda' had last been heard at the Metropolitan, he had sung the rôle of Enzo. Our performance was, I think, a very creditable one, although Rosa Ponselle was taken ill at the last moment and the title-rôle was sung by Florence Easton. José Mardones and Giuseppe Danise were in the cast, and Tullio Serafin conducted; he had joined the Met that season. The critics praised me; but Caruso's supremacy in the rôle, they said, remained unquestioned.

On December 7th, 1924, a great memorial concert for Puccini was held at the Metropolitan. There was an audience of four thousand, including standees; five thousand more had to be turned away. Tullio Serafin, Gennaro Papi and Giuseppe Bamboschek shared in conducting orchestra and ensemble numbers from almost all Puccini's operas, and all the principal singers of the company took part. I sang the first act duet from 'Tosca' with Maria Jeritza, and an aria from 'Manon Lescaut'. Out of the proceeds, Gatti-Casazza sent one hundred and thirty-seven thousand lire to Italy, of which one hundred thousand were destined for the Verdi Home for Aged Musicians in Milan, twenty-five thousand for the municipality of Puccini's native Lucca, and twelve thousand for the erection of a monument to the dead composer.

On January 2nd, 1925, I sang for the first time in Verdi's 'Falstaff'. About my own performance there is not much to say; it is a baritone's opera, and the tenor rôle of Fenton is a small one. Falstaff had always been one of Antonio Scotti's great rôles; in fact, both Verdi and Boito considered him unsurpassed by anyone except Maurel, who had created the rôle in the world *première* at the Scala. Scotti, as I mentioned in an earlier chapter, was already ageing, and was under strong criticism because of his reluctance to retire. On this occasion, however, his friends were overjoyed and his critics routed; he proved conclusively to even the most carping of the latter that he was still able to sing Falstaff a great deal better than any of his juniors.

Scotti's evening of triumph was, unfortunately, to some extent marred by a curious episode. The American baritone Lawrence Tibbett was singing the minor rôle of Ford—a part well suited to him, I thought. At the end of a scene in which Scotti and Tibbett had appeared alone on the stage together, Scotti reaped a well-deserved ovation. He generously insisted on sharing many of his curtain calls with Tibbett; but to our astonishment, there were insistent voices from the audience that Tibbett should take a bow alone. Scotti himself was perfectly agreeable, but Gatti-Casazza insisted that Scotti continue to appear as long as the applause lasted. It was not altogether clear whether Tibbett's partisans formed an organized *claque*, or whether they were genuinely members of the audience who simply felt a patriotic impulse to make a little fuss about an American singer; either way, I think Gatti-Casazza was mistaken in opposing them. In a few minutes, the fact that Tibbett was plainly not being allowed to take a bow alone had flared up into a sensation, and the episode, instead of blowing over lightly, developed into an undignified contest of obstinacy between the audience and the general manager of the Metropolitan. If the performance, already hopelessly delayed, was ever to be resumed, the battle obviously had to be brought to an end somehow; and Gatti-Casazza, with a very bad grace, finally had to allow Tibbett to take his bow after all.

This episode was, of course, manna to the reporters, and the accounts of Scotti's triumph in the papers next day were overshadowed by the rapturous announcements of the 'discovery' of a great new young American baritone. Publicity is a potent weapon; and Gatti-Casazza was obliged to promote Tibbett overnight from the rank of supporting baritone on a fixed weekly salary, to that of a 'star' with astronomical emoluments.

On November 24th, 1924, I was in my dressing-room at the Metropolitan, in the interval between the second and third acts of 'Mefistofele', which I was again singing with Chaliapin, when someone handed me a letter. It was typewritten, and in Italian. The heading read: 'New York, November 1924. Imperial Palace—Invisible Empire—Knights of the Klu Klux Klan.'

The letter demanded that I should send five hundred dollars, within twenty-four hours, to a certain address in Los Angeles. The money, it said, was needed to liberate members of the Klan from prison. It warned me not to contact the police, and ended by guaranteeing that I would not be disturbed in future if I paid the sum demanded.

My first reaction was frankly one of terror; I had visions of my children being kidnapped and held for ransom. When I returned to the stage a few minutes later, I found Chaliapin's realistic impersonation of the Devil even more unsettling than usual. After the performance I telephoned immediately to my friend Commissioner Enright; and from then onwards, for two months, my family and I had a police guard night and day. The police were sceptical about the Klu Klux Klan, and thought the letter more likely to have been the work of the Black Hand—an Italian gangster organization in the United States, which twelve years previously had threatened Caruso. However, investigation revealed the Los Angeles address to be non-existent, and as the days passed and nothing happened, I decided that it must have been a hoax. Were there people who disliked me enough to play such a trick on me? I was forced to conclude that there probably were.

On January 14th, 1925, for the first time at the Metropolitan, I sang the rôle of Count Loris Ipanov in Giordano's 'Fedora'. It had been intended for Giovanni Martinelli, but he fell sick, and I was called on, at short notice, to take his place. My partner was the Viennese soprano Marie Jeritza; Fedora was well known to be one of her great rôles.

Between this lady and myself there had existed, ever since we began to sing together at the Met, what I can only presume to have been a latent conflict of temperaments. In her presence, I always felt tension. I never had any psychological difficulties with my other colleagues, but Madame Jeritza's legendary 'temperament' had a disastrous effect on me. At the least sign of it, something would boil up inside me, and I would suddenly feel capable of becoming every bit as temperamental as she was.

On the night of the 'Fedora' *première*, she hurled herself on me with such abandon in the betrothal scene at the end of Act 2, that I was able to withstand the impact only by bracing myself firmly against a wing support. At the next performance, she wriggled so violently in my supposedly loving arms that I did actually stagger, making the audience roar with laughter at what should have been an intensely tragic moment. Yet another time, again in Act 2, when I was meant to be paying her a formal visit, my top hat dropped on the floor; with a well-placed kick, Madame Jeritza sent it spinning neatly across the stage.

Then came the evening of January 26th. The opera was drawing to an end; it was the scene of my final interview with Fedora; having discovered her to be a spy, I was supposed to spurn her. What happened then exactly I really cannot say. Did my suppressed resentment at the way in which, on all these previous occasions, she had managed to ridicule me on the stage, suddenly find an outlet? Did I miscalculate the force with which I pushed her away from me? Or did she simply slip? All I knew was that she was reeling towards the edge of the stage, and barely saved herself from tumbling over into the orchestra pit. I saw that she was hurt, and tried to help her to her feet, but she rejected my offer violently. She sang on to the end of the scene, and then rushed from the stage in a paroxysm of sobs.

She had wrenched her right wrist in falling on the glass and metal of the footlights, and had abrasions on both legs. 'He did it!' she shrieked, pointing at me. I was really sorry; I apologized profusely and assured her that it was an accident; but in vain. 'He did it! He wanted to kill me! Murderer! Murderer!'

This was too much; I protested.

'Listen to him! First he tries to murder me, then he insults me!' She turned to her husband, Baron Leopold von Popper, a tall, martial-looking Austrian, who always waited for her backstage. 'Defend my honour!' she commanded him. 'Challenge that man to a duel!'

To my relief, I received no challenge from the level-headed Baron; but next day there was an uproar of speculation, both in the newspapers and in the corridors of the Metropolitan, as to whether or not I had 'done it on purpose'. Things went so far that Gatti-Casazza, who normally refused to listen to gossip about any of the Met squabbles, much less intervene in them, felt obliged to issue a statement explaining that I had *not* done it on purpose; but for once, nobody paid any attention to him—it was more fun to let the battle rage. The cartoonists had a field-day; the European press joined in; and Madame Jeritza's wrenched wrist was lost sight of in the furious controversy that exploded between our respective followers as to which of the two of us was the leading artist of the Metropolitan.

I was horrified, but I was powerless to stop it; it was like an avalanche.

More was to come.

Madame Jeritza had declared, the day after the 'Fedora' incident, that she would never sing with 'that man' again, but Gatti-Casazza calmly said 'Rubbish'—his favourite word—and reminded her that she was due to sing with me a fortnight later in 'Tosca'. Whatever powers of persuasion he used, he finally got her to agree.

I need hardly say that on the night of the performance, I took —or thought I took—every possible precaution to avoid offending my susceptible partner. All went well, or at least without mishap, until the very end.

The curtain had fallen; I was on the stage, waiting for it to rise again for the first call. Madame Jeritza was in the wings; I beckoned to her to join me so that we might take our bow together, but she shook her head. The curtain rose, and I took my bow alone. Then I walked off the stage to my dressing-room, leaving all subsequent curtain calls, as I thought, to her. I had attached no importance to the fact of taking the first bow alone. She had done so, as was her right, after the first and second acts; and since in the third act of 'Tosca', with '*Lucevan le stelle*', the tenor rises to pre-eminence, I had thought that when she refused to join me, she was simply indicating that it was my turn.

Alas, I was mistaken. She had, I learned afterwards, refused to join me out of pique, because she thought I had no right to show myself until she had taken all her bows. When I went away, there were calls of 'Jeritza!'; but, declaring tearfully that she had been outraged, she still refused to budge from the wings. The curtain rose and fell twice on an empty stage. Most of the audience went home; but in all parts of the house a fair number of people still lingered—her *claque*, as it transpired—shouting rhythmically, insistently, 'Jeritza! We want Jeritza!'

Fifteen minutes passed, and neither she nor they showed any signs of giving in. Finally Giuseppe Bamboschek, who had conducted the orchestra that evening, took her protectively but firmly by the arm and led her out in front of the curtain. By this time her followers had hypnotized themselves into a kind of delirium. She calmed them down herself by indicating that she wished to say something. She said exactly five words: 'Gigli not nice to me!' Then she collapsed sobbing into the arms of Maestro Bamboschek.

Backstage, her sobbing developed into hysterics. Bamboschek, feeling that the situation had got beyond him, telephoned to Gatti-Casazza, who was already at home and fast asleep. He came at once in a taxi, still muttering 'Rubbish!' and spent a couple of hours humouring and consoling the outraged heroine, with Baron Leopold von Popper a helpless onlooker.

'All right,' said Gatti-Casazza resignedly, when he saw the newspaper headlines the following morning, 'I'll never ask them to sing together again.' And I suppose it was just as well that he never did.

CHAPTER XII

THE WORLD IS MY AUDIENCE

THE episode recounted in the previous chapter may perhaps serve to illustrate one aspect of a singer's daily existence at which the audience, generally speaking, can only guess, the terrific nervous tension and all that results from it, the jealousies, the battles for dressing-rooms, for distinctive rôles, for the centre of the stage, which go on all the time behind the façade of liquid notes and love duets. Most of us manage to keep them under control, but when they do explode, they are all the more violent for having been suppressed. Old-timers at the Metropolitan had a fund of picturesque anecdotes about episodes of this sort, as when for instance, during a performance of 'Carmen'—and in full view of the audience—Caruso gave Geraldine Farrar a shove; whereupon she promptly slapped his face, sat down on the stage, and burst into tears. When such things happen, we can only plead that our life is one of tremendous strain, and hope that our audience will be indulgent.

I mentioned Madame Jeritza's *claque* in the last chapter, because I think that on the occasion described it went too far and did her a disservice; but I must confess that I myself had found it necessary to have a *claque* at the Metropolitan, for the simple reason that everyone else had one. For established singers who had nothing to fear, it amounted to no more than a precaution that one's own legitimate, spontaneous applause would not be submerged by other people's *claques*. Normally speaking, the various *claques* cancelled each other out; they were composed of discerning music-lovers, and their applause was not indiscriminate. But an efficient *claque* could also help to consolidate the reputation of a young singer, or force into retirement a rival whose voice was beginning to decline.

On January 15th, 1925, I sang at the White House, at a reception given by President and Mrs. Coolidge to celebrate the

President's re-election. I was greatly impressed by the dignified simplicity of the building; after seeing it, I felt that I understood Americans better.

On February 23rd I sang for the first time in Verdi's 'Requiem'. I had been brought up on Church music, and had always loved it; so when I stood on the stage of the Metropolitan and sang the '*Ingemisco*' I felt transported in time and space back to the organ-loft of Recanati Cathedral. The 'Requiem' belongs to the peak period of Verdi's achievement, the period of 'Aida'. He wrote it to commemorate the great writer Alessandro Manzoni, whom he called his 'saint'. Ecclesiastical authorities have criticized the 'Requiem' for not conforming to the requirements of liturgical orthodoxy, and it was hardly to be expected that Verdi, who was not by nature a composer of religious music, should fit his genius into the Procrustean frame of ritual. I can only say that I have always felt the 'Requiem' to be a deeply religious work, reverent, inspired, and in certain passages sublime.

I sailed for Europe in April, to fulfil two months of engagements in Germany and Scandinavia—opera in Berlin, Hamburg and Hanover, concerts in Breslau, Copenhagen and Stockholm. Once again I was amazed by the enthusiasm of these people, whom I had always heard described as 'cold Northerners'. By now I was growing accustomed to triumphs and ovations; but to be forced to plead for mercy after half an hour of curtain calls, as in Hamburg, or to be carried to my hotel on people's shoulders after the performance, as in Berlin—these were new experiences for me.

I had only time to snatch a brief three weeks in Italy. On July 1st I had an audience of the Pope in the morning, and was received by Mussolini in the afternoon. Mussolini—it was our second meeting—plied me with questions about the Metropolitan, about the popularity of Italian opera in America, and about the Italian Hospital in New York. I found it quite easy to talk to him about these subjects, but had he mentioned politics I should have been tongue-tied.

On July 13th I sailed for Buenos Aires, where a number of Metropolitan artists besides myself—Claudia Muzio, Frances Alda, De Luca, Didur and Serafin—were taking part in the annual operatic season at the Colón. On August 20th I sang with Claudia Muzio at a special gala performance of 'Loreley', in honour of the Prince of Wales. It was a brilliant and spectacular occasion. The Prince, in scarlet uniform, was accompanied by the President of the Argentine Republic, Dr. Marcello de Alvear. He expressed the wish to congratulate some of the artists in person; and I was accordingly presented to him in the first interval, together with Claudia Muzio and Serafin. He chatted to us very graciously for several minutes, and on parting gave me a gold cigarette-case and said I should come to London.

I sang one new rôle at the Colón that season: Giannetto in 'La Cena delle Beffe', a swift-moving tragedy of the Renaissance period, composed by Umberto Giordano on the basis of a play by Sem Benelli. It had been produced only twice before, once in Rome and once at Rosario in the Argentine. The Colón *première* was on August 31st. It always gave me great pleasure to sing in the operas of my friend Giordano, but 'La Cena delle Beffe', although it is perhaps his most effective work, did nothing to oust 'Andrea Chénier' from its place as my personal favourite. The rôle of Giannetto was too dramatic for my voice.

I had my own good reasons for preferring to sing lyric rôles whenever possible. It was not merely that I sang them better, although that was also a consideration, but they made fewer demands on my vocal resources—or rather, they made the kind of demands that I was best equipped by nature to meet. It was due, I think, to the care with which I always chose my repertory (for example, I invariably refused 'Otello') that I was able to sing in public for forty-one years—a career of unprecedented length for a tenor. Once, when I was already in my mid-fifties, I was asked by another tenor, a good deal younger than myself, to explain why my voice was still fresh, while his was already beginning to harden. 'I think,' I told him, 'that I have always been careful to husband my vocal resources—maybe because I come of frugal peasant stock—while you have been a spendthrift, singing away your capital.'

After a short Brazilian season in Rio de Janeiro and São Paulo, I returned to the United States at the beginning of October and plunged straightaway into a concert tour of the Middle West. Some of the places on my itinerary were new for me—Toledo, for instance, and Milwaukee. I particularly enjoyed the experience of singing in a place called Rome in New York State.

On November 2nd I opened the 1925–26 season at the Metropolitan by singing, with Rosa Ponselle, in 'La Gioconda'. It was the first time that I had really been accorded the full honour of opening the season. 'Traviata', in which I had sung on another opening night four years previously, is a soprano's opera; but 'La Gioconda' belongs to the tenor. It was a favourite choice for Metropolitan opening nights, rivalled in this respect only by 'Aida'.

This time I managed to make the critics omit their usual recollections of Caruso in their praise of my rendering of '*Cielo e Mar*'. The performance as a whole was a splendid example of the team-work which gave the Metropolitan its supremacy over other opera houses. Rosa Ponselle was an ideal Gioconda, and Serafin, in conducting, extracted the last iota of beauty and brilliance from the score. Two hours before the curtain was due to rise, there was a crisis; Jeanne Gordon, who was to have sung the second soprano part, developed a sudden cold. The management hastily telephoned to Margaret Matzenauer, praying she would be at home; fortunately she was, and the performance began on time as though nothing had happened. However, had she not been available, there were no fewer than fifty-one members of the company who were prepared by their contracts to go on the stage at a moment's notice in one or other of the twelve solo parts in 'La Gioconda'. The same system applied, of course, to every other opera in the Met repertory.

Gatti-Casazza was fond of anniversaries, and on November 29th I took part in a gala concert of opera excerpts, sung by all the leading Metropolitan artists, to celebrate the centenary of Italian opera in New York. It was exactly one hundred years, to the day, since Manuel Garcia's company had staged a performance of 'Il Barbiere di Siviglia' at the old Park Theatre.

I had been persistently refusing all invitations to broadcast. The whole thing frightened me. To sing without being able to see my audience was bad enough; but neither to see them, nor even be sure in what form my voice was reaching them—this, I felt, involved too many unknown quantities. A gramophone record was different; I could have it played back to me before it was released, and if I was not satisfied I could insist on re-making it; but in broadcasting I would be letting my voice escape into the air, to be the plaything of invisible forces, before ever it reached the ears of my listeners.

In the end, however, my friends succeeded in convincing me that my fears and imaginings were unscientific and groundless; so on December 27th, 1925, I sang over the air for the first time. It was the Christmas week concert of the Atwater Kent series, and consisted of selections from 'Lucia di Lammermoor' and 'Rigoletto'. An audience of millions! It was an impressive thought! Nevertheless, it took me a long time to get adjusted psychologically, and perhaps, as the following episode would seem to indicate, even technically, to the whole idea of broadcasting.

It was some months later and I had sung over the NBC network. Coming down from the studio, I was engaged in conversation by the small boy who operated the lift.

'Are you the guy that just sang?' he inquired.

My secretary interpreted this for me, and I nodded.

'Do you mind if I give you a bit of advice?'

I bowed.

'Well,' said the boy, 'I listened in on you and your voice came over too powerful. Next time, don't stand so close to the mike, see?'

I thanked him with my best smile.

'That's okay, buddy,' he said, 'I straighten out a lot of amateur singers.'

The stage, the platform, the audience—these were now my whole life. I lived in them, by them, through them, for them. Outside of them, I had time for very little else. Indeed, I was aware of very little else. I never really got to know America or the Americans; I simply did not have that much mental energy to spare. I had to concentrate on one thing only, if I was to do it well. In my apartment on West 57th Street I lived in a completely Italian atmosphere, with Italian servants and Italian cooking. When I was not engaged in a performance or a rehearsal or the study of a new rôle, when I was not resting or being pummelled in Mr. Reilly's gymnasium, I found relaxation in a few very ordinary pastimes—going to the cinema, playing poker, taking my children to Coney Island and shooting clay ducks, looking after my stamp collection. It was an old Italian, a member of the chorus at the Metropolitan, who had introduced me to the joys of stamp-collecting; I derived great satisfaction from poring over my albums, although unfortunately they did not meet with the approval of my wife, who considered them a waste of money.

The Italian contingent at the Metropolitan was growing larger every year. Recent recruits included Toti Del Monte and Tita Ruffo, while Ezio Pinza and Giacomo Lauri Volpi were heralded for the following season. I sang with Tita Ruffo in the Met *première* of 'La Cena delle Beffe' on January 2nd, 1926. The opera was much more suited for him than it was for me; he had a splendidly dramatic singing voice, and was a magnificent actor. His Neri was an impressive study in madness, and I think it was in no small measure due to him that 'La Cena delle Beffe' proved such a remarkable success in New York.

On January 11th I sang at St. Patrick's Cathedral in a Pontifical Requiem Mass for the Queen Mother Margherita of Italy, who had died shortly before. January 27th was the twenty-fifth anniversary of the death of Verdi; we commemorated him at the Metropolitan with a special performance of his own 'Requiem'.

On February 1st I left New York for a month's recital tour on the Pacific coast—Seattle, Portland, San Francisco, Los Angeles, Pasadena. I was to have given a concert in Detroit on the way back; but when I arrived there, on February 23rd, I found a heavy plain-clothes guard waiting to escort me to my hotel. The police had received a note which said: 'If Gigli wants to adorn a slab in the morgue, let him try to sing in Detroit. We will cut this canary's throat. [Signed] True Friends of Italy.'

The motive underlying this threat was difficult to guess at. No one paid much attention to the 'True Friends of Italy' part of it. The Detroit police, like their colleagues in New York on a previous occasion, thought it might be the Black Hand. But why? Someone else suggested the hypothesis of a link-up with the notorious mutual jealousy of two rival impresarios; while according to yet another theory—not, I may say, too seriously propounded—it was the work of the followers of a jealous rival!

I did not like yielding to threats; but I could not help feeling a certain amount of shock, and I decided that in circumstances of nervous strain I could not do justice to myself on the concert platform. Reluctantly—for I had grown particularly fond of Detroit audiences—I decided to cancel my recital; and with the police guard still forming a thick hedge around me, I left that same evening for Buffalo.

Perhaps some writer of detective stories might find inspiration in this mysterious episode. I never got to the bottom of it.

At the end of May, 1926, I sang for the first time in Havana. It had been a Caruso stronghold, and I knew that I faced a critical audience; but all went well, and my success received official consecration when President Machado of Cuba invited me to sing at the wedding of his daughter Angela on July 1st.

There was one rather trying evening when, almost suffocated by a severe cold, I had to force myself to sing through a performance of 'Rigoletto'. I felt thankful when I got to the end of it without disgracing myself; but the audience, to my dismay, were so pleased with me that they refused to let me go home until I sang '*O Paradiso*' from 'L'Africana'. I tried to explain to them, in bad Spanish, about my cold; but they pretended not to understand. Finally I gave in, wondering if I would have any voice left by the morning. Then I hurried back to my hotel, took an aspirin and some grog, wrapped a woollen scarf round my throat, and went to bed. Shortly afterwards I heard a commotion in the street underneath my window; a crowd seemed to be gathering; there were shouts of what was, unmistakably, my name. 'Sing "*O Paradiso*" again!' they were calling out. 'Please, Señor Gigli, sing "*O Paradiso*" again!'

I decided that if they wanted to hear me in 'Marta' the following night, enough was enough. I pulled the blankets over my head and shut my eyes.

Provided that I felt well enough, I never liked to refuse a song. I have a happy memory of an August night in Venice later that summer. I had given a concert in the beautiful eighteenth-century Teatro La Fenice; it was in aid of charity, and the price of admission had been high enough to make it into one of the fashionable events of the season. When the concert ended it was nearly midnight, but there was a huge crowd waiting outside the theatre—working-class Venetians, the humbler kind of tourist, young people—all obviously hoping to hear me sing. On an impulse, I said to them, 'I'll sing for you in Piazza San Marco.'

Luckily, we found some kind of band still playing in the Piazza, and the conductor readily agreed to accompany me. Meanwhile the news seemed to have spread; people poured into the Piazza from all corners. Standing in front of the golden cathedral, under the velvety moonlit sky, I sang '*Giunto sul passo estremo*', '*Lucevan le stelle*', '*O Paradiso*' and '*M'appari*'. The acoustics of the Piazza were wonderful. Venice on a summer night is wonderful. My audience was wonderful. I felt wonderful, if a little tired, when I finally said 'Good night'.

The autumn and winter months of the 1926–27 season at the Metropolitan were as busy as ever, but relatively uneventful. The Klu Klux Klan, the Black Hand, and the 'True Friends of Italy', all left me in peace, but Commissioner Enright insisted on providing me with a constant plain-clothes guard as a precaution. To show my gratitude, I gave a Christmas party for the orphans of New York policemen who had been killed while on duty during the previous year. I dressed up as Santa Claus, and I think a good time was had by all, because my small guests arrived at three-thirty in the afternoon and did not leave till midnight!

In October, before the Metropolitan opening, I had gone on my usual autumn concert tour, including a recital at the Maine Festival in Bangor; and in January and February, 1927, I undertook a more far-flung tour that ranged from Philadelhia to New Orleans, and from Havana to Cincinnati. If I sometimes found these tours fatiguing, it was not so much because of the singing or even the travelling; it was the inevitable and generous hospitality that I encountered everywhere, the receptions, the banquets with the Italian colony, the sea of new faces every day, that often used up my last scrap of energy. But there was no escape, and it would have been ungracious to seek one. It was all part of the game. Sometimes, too, there were unexpected rewards—as when, for instance, in Baltimore, I met an Italian carpenter who turned out to have been my classmate in the primary school in Recanati!

The highbrow critics were inclined to find fault with the programmes I offered in my recitals. I did nothing to educate the public taste; there were too many old chestnuts, and so forth. These criticisms never worried me. I was not catering for the critics; I was catering for the general public.

Sometimes I was able to awaken an interest in music among

people who had not felt it previously. A local newspaper in Dallas, Texas, for instance, reporting a concert I had given there, described the ovation I got—the audience on its feet, waving programmes and handkerchiefs, shouting and clapping in a deafening roar of applause. 'Probably Mr. Gigli is used to it,' the paper observed, 'but such enthusiasm was until now unheard of in Dallas. The Dallas public used to be apathetic at recitals. Mr. Gigli's concert marks the overthrow of the indifference, scepticism and bad humour that had been the common denominator of local recital audiences for many years.'

Furthermore, I always felt very strongly that the concert audience must get what it wants. If '*La donna è mobile*' comes into the deplored category of old chestnuts, that simply means that successive generations have recognized it as being one of the most beautiful and haunting melodies ever written. I cannot see that this constitutes a valid reason for not singing it, or for 'educating' audiences to a point where they no longer want to hear it.

The same can be said of all the other 'old chestnuts' that I liked to include in my recitals, such as '*Questa o quella*', '*Celeste Aida*', '*Che Gelida Manina*', '*O Paradiso*', '*M'appari*', '*Giunto sul passo estremo*', '*Vesti la giubba*', the 'Flower Song' from 'Carmen', '*Una furtiva lagrima*', '*E lucevan le stelle*', the '*Improvviso*' from 'Andrea Chénier', '*Donna non vidi mai*', from 'Manon Lescaut', '*Cielo e Mar*', '*Spirto Gentil*', from 'La Favorita', the '*Lamento di Federico*' from 'L'Arlesiana', Gluck's '*O mio dolce ardor*'; and, of course, the Neapolitan songs. What would the critics have liked me to sing instead of these, I wonder? I was happiest of all when my concert developed into a kind of family party, with the audience relaxed, excited, calling out to me to sing their favourites.

It was quite a long time since I had had a really suitable new part, and I was delighted when Gatti-Casazza asked me to sing Wilhelm Meister in 'Mignon', the tuneful, romantic opera for which the French composer Ambroise Thomas had found inspiration in Goethe. Its freshness and fragrance may have faded a little since it first appeared at the Opéra-Comique in Paris in 1866, and nowadays producers may tend to embalm it as a Second Empire period piece rather than take it seriously; but to me these considerations were immaterial. Its tender, wistful melodies and lyric sweetness were ideal for my voice, and that was what mattered to me.

There was a full house for our *première* on March 10th, 1927, at the Metropolitan, where 'Mignon' had not been previously heard since 1908. Curiously enough, my predecessor in the rôle of Wilhelm Meister had been Alessandro Bonci, the former employer of my old friend the cook, Giovanni Zerri!

We succeeded, I think, in giving a spirited performance; it was certainly received with great enthusiasm. I reaped special applause at the end of the third act for a feat of which, I confess, I did feel rather proud. In order to save the gipsy girl Mignon from the flames, I lifted her in my arms and carried her bodily across the stage, singing all the time. The prima donna, Lucrezia Bori, weighed considerably more than a feather; so I took this achievement as evidence that I was not wasting my time in Mr. Reilly's gymnasium.

I had grown so accustomed to hard work that I found it very difficult to remain idle during my holidays. In the summer of 1927, for example, I gave sixteen benefit performances in Italy. In Rome I took part in an ex-pupils' concert to celebrate the fiftieth anniversary of the Accademia di Santa Cecilia, which was attended by Princess Mafalda, the King's daughter, and her husband the Prince of Hesse. I gave an improvised moonlight concert, lasting from midnight to 2 a.m., for fifty thousand people in Piazza Colonna; and I sang Mascagni's '*Stornelli Marini*' at a great concert in the Augusteo, conducted by the maestro himself.

In Recanati, I organized and sang in six performances of 'La Bohème' at the Teatro Persiani, for the X-ray equipment fund of Recanati Hospital; and on August 21st, at Osimo, a little harbour on the Adriatic near Recanati, to raise money for restoring the medieval castle, I sang in a concert pageant re-enacting the safe return from the Battle of Lepanto of a certain Paolo Gigli. This was a sixteenth-century Recanati fisherman who, together with 106 companions, had set sail from Osimo in a galley, to fight the Turks, returning long years afterwards, with the six other survivors of the expedition, to become a legend in Recanati. There are, of course, no records to show whether this adventurous fisherman was an ancestor of mine, but I like to think that he was.

But the big event of that summer for me was the completion and house-warming of my Recanati villa. To tell the truth, I was rather overawed by the final result; I felt that, in my absence, Catervo and the architects had let their enthusiasm carry them a little too far. There were sixty rooms altogether, and twenty-three bathrooms, besides a swimming-pool, a Roman bath and an aqueduct; in the kitchen there was a refrigerator large enough to hold food for twenty people for a year. Was that really necessary, I wondered uneasily? Were we ever likely to be besieged for so long?

I was, however, entirely delighted to find myself owning land—fields, meadows, orchards, vineyards. How I wished that my father could have lived to see them! The estate comprised at that time (it has since been increased) some seven thousand acres, and included seven great farms, linked by about fifty miles of road, all built specially. Since that year, the estate has provided pigs and poultry, fruit and vegetables, wheat, dairy produce, and wine of several kinds—including, needless to say, Verdicchio!

I had bought my mother a pretty little house of her own in Piazza Leopardi, and I think it gave her pleasure; but she was frankly terrified by the scale and dimensions of my establishment. 'How will you ever be able to pay for all this, my son?' she murmured anxiously. 'Where will you find the money?'

We were sitting, I remember, at the top of my house, in a little belvedere from which, on fine days, one can see right across the Adriatic to the Dalmatian coast on the other side.

'Don't worry, Mother,' I told her. 'Every brick in the walls of this villa, every square inch of land, as far as you can see and beyond, has been paid for already by a note of music that I've sung somewhere, at some time or another.'

My return journey to New York that September was enlivened by the presence on board of the great Sicilian comic actor Angelo Musco and his company, bound for an American tour. Half-way across the ocean there was a severe storm, during which one of my pet parrots amused everyone by shrieking, entirely on his own initiative, 'Don't worry! Don't worry!'

I was glad that the itinerary of my autumn concert tour afforded an opportunity of returning to Detroit and making amends for the recital that I had been obliged to cancel a year and a half previously. I also sang at Ann Arbor and Pittsburgh, and crossed the Canadian border to Winnipeg and Montreal.

At Christmas I again gave a party for the orphans of New York policemen and firemen. Remembering how last time my guests had left at midnight instead of 6 p.m., and feeling that I was getting too old for such prolonged jollifications, I decided to hold this year's party on board the Cunard liner *Anaulia*, so that I could be the one to leave. But Mayor Walker dropped in, and got me playing with an electric train; and my plans for retiring early were forgotten.

With the passage of years, the once-burning question of 'Caruso's successor' had died down at the Metropolitan. Caruso had been Caruso, and was now enshrined in memory; the living were themselves. I was Gigli; my name meant something on its own merits and that was the way I had wanted it to be.

But impresarios have a fondness for publicity-catching labels. It was with a feeling of grim amusement that I read two advertisements that appeared on the same day in the same musical section of the same New York newspaper.

One said: 'Gigli, the world's greatest tenor, will sing at a benefit recital for the Italian Hospital on Sunday afternoon, February 19th.'

The other said: 'Martinelli, the world's greatest tenor, will sing at a benefit recital for the Relief Society for the Aged at the Waldorf Astoria Hotel on February 26th.'

On February 24th, 1928, with Lucrezia Bori and Giuseppe De Luca, I sang for the first time in the broadcast version of an entire opera, 'La Traviata'. It is strange to remember now how revolutionary we felt.

On March 10th I took part in the Metropolitan *première* of Puccini's 'La Rondine'. I had not sung it since that first time at the Costanzi. The other soloists were Lucrezia Bori, Editha Fleischer and Armand Tokatyan. Once again I witnessed the phenomenon of an opera which had elicited only a cool response on one side of the Atlantic, being enthusiastically and in fact rapturously received on the other side. I often puzzled over these occasional but striking differences in taste. In Rome, the critics had as good as implied that the less said about 'La Rondine' the better; in New York they now declared that 'La Rondine' was vastly more entertaining than most of the shows on Broadway, and that if only a Broadway theatre would stage it, it could run for years.

Might it be, I wonder now, that the Americans took a fancy to 'La Rondine' because it was the nearest Puccini ever came to writing a 'musical'?

In the summer of 1928 I crossed the Atlantic four times. I had a South American engagement in July and August, so there was nothing for it but to take my Italian holiday before and after those months. In June there would be the first wheat harvest in my own fields at Recanati, in September the first grapes from my vineyards would be trodden in the winepress; I could not bear to miss either of these solemn events. In June, too, I had promised to sing in the presence of the King and Queen of Italy at a gala concert inaugurating the Carducci monument in Bologna. I was surprised to find myself perfectly at ease in the presence of Their Majesties; it must, I concluded afterwards, have been my long acquaintance with the King of Ys and the Queen of Madagascar that had given me such confidence!

The Colón season was a particularly fruitful one for me that year, for it gave me the chance to sing in two new rôles, both of which delighted me: Riccardo in Verdi's 'Un Ballo in Maschera', and Nemorino in Donizetti's 'L'Elisir d'Amore'.

The *première* of 'Un Ballo in Maschera' took place in Buenos Aires on July 20th. D'Annunzio once called this opera 'the most melodramatic of all melodramas', and perhaps he was right; the libretto is almost a parody of grand opera absurdity. But the absurdities are swept away in a torrent of music, and the libretto is ennobled by the genius of Verdi.

It was originally called 'Gustavo III', but during the rehearsals for its first production, in Naples in 1858, an attempt was made on the life of Napoleon III, and Verdi was ordered by the Neapolitan police (this was before the union of Italy) to change both title and libretto. He refused to obey, and there was a tremendous row, in which the whole population of Naples took sides. In the end Verdi agreed to change the name, but left the libretto as it was, except for a few minor concessions which made nonsense of the whole thing.

So the action of 'Un Ballo in Maschera' may take place in either Naples or Boston; Riccardo, Earl of Warwick, is Governor either of Naples or Boston; Adelia may be called Amelia and

Renato Reinhart. To crown the geographical confusion, the plot hinges on something that is supposed to have happened in Sweden! But the music is magnificent, so what does it matter?

From the heroics of 'Un Ballo in Maschera' I turned to the droll simplicity of Donizetti's comic masterpiece, 'L'Elisir d'Amore'. This I sang for the first time, in a performance conducted by Serafin and with the Argentine soprano Isabel Marengo, on August 11th, 1928, at the Colón. Based on a French farce called 'Le Philtre', it is the story of a timid, clumsy village swain who spends his last penny on buying, from an itinerant quack, a love potion for his fickle betrothed. The style is that of Italian *opera buffa* of the first half of the nineteenth century. Sprightly choruses alternate with wistful melodies and clowning by-play. The inspired music is light as air, the whole effect one of artless spontaneity.

As had previously happened when I sang the rôle of another rustic lover—that of Lionel in 'Marta'—I won laurels for my comic acting as Nemorino; but of course the climax of 'L'Elisir d'Amore' for me was the great tenor aria '*Una furtiva lagrima*'. At the Colón *première*, the performance was held up for fifteen minutes while the audience demanded an encore, although they knew perfectly well that the rules of the theatre forbade it to be granted. The Press reports next day were so enthusiastic that thousands of people wanting to buy tickets had to be turned away from the Colón box-office.

The 1928–29 season at the Metropolitan was again a fairly uneventful one for me. I did not sing anything new, but by this time I had an extensive repertory on which to draw; and the public seemed to like hearing me in the same rôles again and again. I made my customary midwinter coast-to-coast concert tour, and accompanied my colleagues on the customary opera tour in the spring; but I shall not weary the reader with a detailed account of all my journeyings. My own head reels when I try to remember them!

Nor shall I attempt to recapitulate in these pages all the moments that have been precious to me—the forty curtain calls after 'Manon Lescant' in Rio, the unprecedented three encores of '*La donna è mobile*' when I sang 'Rigoletto' in Budapest, or of '*E lucevan le stelle*' when I sang 'Tosca' in London.

Now that I am an old man, sitting alone in my garden, I like to think back over these things which were my life. For me, each one of them is a separate, unique memory; but to anyone else, they must appear a repetitious chronicle.

The summer of 1929 began and ended with a tour in Central Europe: in May and June, concert and opera in Zurich, Budapest, Munich, Berlin, Hamburg and Stockholm; in September, opera in Prague and Vienna. In between, there was Italy: Recanati, benefit performances here and there, and one unforgettable new experience—singing 'Marta' to an audience of forty thousand people in the great Roman amphitheatre at Verona. They had come by special excursion trains from all over Italy to hear me, even from Sicily and the furthest end of the peninsula. Every member of the audience had been given a candle on entering the Arena, and when I emerged on the spot which two thousand years earlier had already been a stage, I saw the flames of forty thousand candles quivering in the August night.

The year 1929 witnessed the Wall Street crash, and the first ominous rumblings of the Depression could already be heard at the Metropolitan. I had never been tempted to play around with stocks and shares, for I had inherited the cautious attitude towards money of a peasant from the Marche. I did not go quite as far as to hide it under the mattress; but I had transferred all my earnings to Italy, and after sinking a large part of them in my property at Recanati, I had lodged the rest with a trustworthy banker. But a number of my colleagues at the Met lost all their savings, the most pitiful case being that of Antonio Scotti, who was too near the end of his career to have any hope of being able to make a fresh start.

There was no visible evidence of Wall Street panic, however, in the resplendent crowd that thronged the Metropolitan when I sang in 'Manon Lescaut' on the opening night of the season, October 28th, 1929.

Lucrezia Bori had made her original New York début, with Caruso, as Puccini's Manon, on the Met. opening night of 1912; not until now had she appeared in the rôle again. An opening night always puts singers on their mettle, and this performance was in every way exceptional. What we did not know was that we were singing the dirge of the golden era of the Metropolitan.

On November 29th, 1929, I made my début as Don Ottavio in

Mozart's 'Don Giovanni', which was being revived at the Metropolitan after an absence of twenty-one years. The critics had long been begging Gatti-Casazza for it, but I think it was against his better judgement that he finally decided on the revival. 'Don Giovanni' was not an opera for the yawning maw of the Metropolitan. Ideally, it should be sung only on small, intimate stages such as that of the Teatro La Fenice in Venice. Mozart contrived it expressly to suit the Prague theatre, which had only seven singers and no regular chorus.

We all did our best in our respective rôles—Serafin as conductor, Ezio Pinza as the Don, Elisabeth Rethberg as Donna Elvira, Editha Fleischer as Zerlina, Pavel Ludikar as Leporello, myself; but I think everyone realized that we failed to bring it off. Personally, of course, I had not had much experience of the very special style of singing that is required for Mozart. Moreover, I felt quite unable to sympathize, much less identify myself, with the personality of Don Ottavio. As a betrothed lover, he seemed to me quite unbelievably stupid in his tolerance of the carryings-on of Don Giovanni.

Of the two great tenor arias '*Dalla sua pace*' and '*Il mio tesoro*', which because of their difficulty are sometimes omitted, but which I sang in the Met production, I think I did make a success of the first. That is as much as I can fairly claim for my performance as Don Ottavio.

On December 28th, 1929, I sang in 'Manon Lescaut' with Frances Alda. It was her farewell to opera, after twenty-two years at the Metropolitan. Born in New Zealand, she had met and married Gatti-Casazza in Milan, when he was general manager of the Scala, and had accompanied him to New York. She had made her Metropolitan début in 1908, as Gilda in 'Rigoletto', with Caruso as the Duke of Mantua. Her parting had an extra undertone of sadness and finality because she had been divorced from Gatti-Casazza the previous year; now her break with the Metropolitan was complete. I wondered if she had chosen the rôle of Manon for her leave-taking because Manon's end in the story permits such a torrent of sorrow.

After a prolonged concert *tournée* that took me back and forth for two months between Canada and California, I returned to New York to sing Nemorino in 'L'Elisir d'Amore' on March 21st, 1930. Nemorino had been one of Caruso's great rôles; he alone had sung it at the Metropolitan, and it had remained his until that tragic November night in Brooklyn when a broken blood-vessel in his lung forced him to give up in the middle of the performance, and the audience was dismissed. For almost ten years afterwards Gatti-Casazza had refused to let anyone else sing Nemorino, and 'L'Elisir d'Amore' dropped out of the Metropolitan repertory. That I should now be chosen for its revival was, I knew, the greatest honour that the Metropolitan had to offer me.

Rodolfo in Puccini's 'La Bohème'

Manrico in Verdi's 'Il Trovatore'

Don José in Bizet's 'Carmen'

Count Loris Ipanov in Giordano's 'Fedora'

Over the years I have often been privileged to be able to visit homes and hospitals and sing for the war-wounded

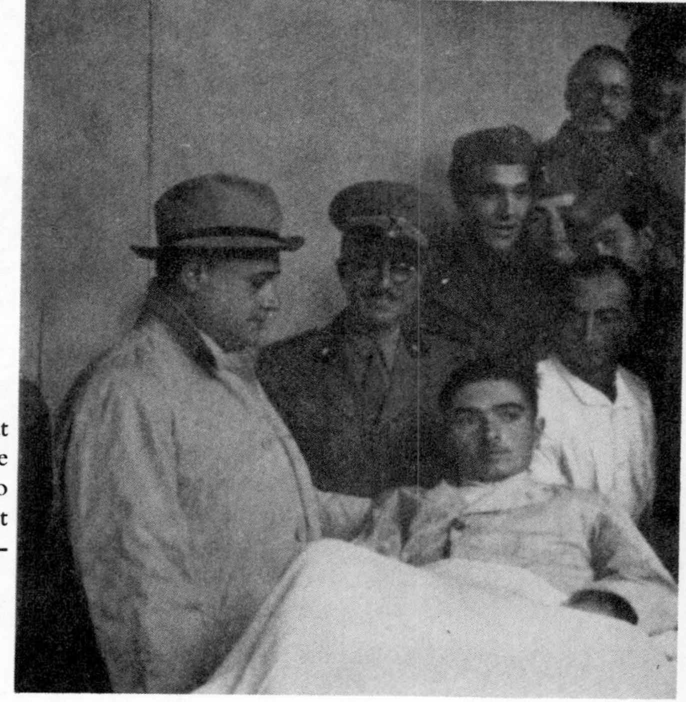

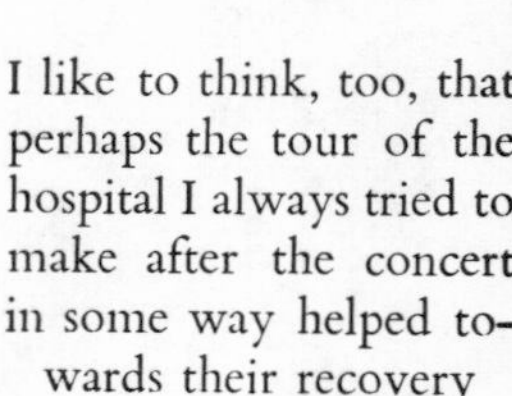

I like to think, too, that perhaps the tour of the hospital I always tried to make after the concert in some way helped towards their recovery

CHAPTER XIII

FAREWELL TO THE METROPOLITAN

I WAS forty years old, and had spent quite a considerable part of my life in travelling. I had been to places that, with my poor knowledge of geography, I had never even heard of until some impresario told me I was to sing there, places such as Winnipeg, Rosario in the Argentine, or Phoenix, Arizona. Yet the two great cities of whose existence everyone was aware even in Recanati, the two foreign cities that symbolize 'travel' to most Italians—of these I still knew nothing. I had never been to either Paris or London.

This omission I was finally able to repair in the early summer of 1930, when I gave two concerts at the Salle Pleyel, in Paris, and sang in four operas at Covent Garden.

My first encounter with the French public and French critics was, perhaps, less happy than the subsequent occasions when we got to know each other better. The contact which I normally found so easy to establish with concert audiences eluded me in the Salle Pleyel. It was plain that this was the most critical audience I had ever faced; and I was not surprised to find myself subjected in the Press reports the following day to a barrage of reproaches for my 'theatrical defects', my 'lack of style', and my bad taste in choosing Toselli's '*Serenade*' and '*O Sole Mio*' as items in my programme. Well, I sighed as I departed for London, no doubt this first visit to Paris had been good for my character. I did not feel depressed, however; only determined that next time I would find a way to make the French like me.

My cool reception in Paris had made me somewhat apprehensive of the fate in store for me among the 'cold English'. To my immense relief I did not find them cold at all, only disconcerting. My first appearance at Covent Garden was in 'Andrea Chénier', with Margaret Sheridan. When I sang '*Un dì all'azzurro spazio*', the applause stopped the performance, and I had to repeat my aria; and after I had left the theatre, the crowd mobbed a car, under the mistaken impression that I was inside it. But then I sang in 'Tosca', with Iva Pacetti, and when the last note of '*E lucevan le stelle*' died away, and I waited for the applause, there was none, not even a hand-clap. The orchestra continued to play, and I felt so chagrined and mortified that I had difficulty in singing to the end of the act. What could have happened? In other opera houses '*E lucevan le stelle*' always meant at least one encore, if encores were allowed; and if not, at least ten minutes' interruption for applause. To be given no applause at all was a disaster that had never happened to me before. What had I done to displease this English audience?

But then the final curtain fell, and the applause broke out in a wild storm; it was like the bursting of a dam. They called me back again and again; clearly, I had not displeased them. But why had they kept silent after '*E lucevan le stelle*'? The mystery was not solved for me until the following morning, when I read the Press reports. The critics praised the audience for having had the 'good manners' to refrain from interrupting the performance by applauding in an open scene.

Now I understood. At the end of '*E lucevan le stelle*' the music flows on continuously, whereas there is a pause in the music, a natural interval for applause, so to speak, after the '*Improvviso* in 'Andrea Chénier'. I felt great admiration for the civilized attitude which drew such fine distinctions as to when applause was permissible; but alas, it made no allowances for the human frailty of singers! Fortunately for me, the Covent Garden audience could sometimes forget what the critics called its manners; some years later, at another performance of 'Tosca', I had to sing '*E lucevan le stelle*' three times.

Incidentally, I always greatly enjoyed reading the English critics; they invariably found something new and surprising to say about me.

'All his notes are genuine coins from the mint,' wrote one critic in appraising my début at Covent Garden. 'He rang them on the counter one after another, like good golden sovereigns.'

Another critic on the same occasion found a comparison which delighted me even more: 'Gigli sings with his whole body, at once active and easeful,' he wrote, 'like a good tennis player serving.'

I began to see myself in a new light!

Besides 'Andrea Chénier' and 'Tosca', I sang 'Marta' and 'La Traviata' during my first Covent Garden season. Rosa Ponselle was memorable in 'La Traviata', but the performances as a whole were makeshift ones, decidedly inferior in quality to those of the Metropolitan. On later visits to London, however, I found the standard much improved.

I have many happy memories, dating even from this first visit, of London hospitality, especially of Sunday evenings at the house of Sir Louis and Lady Sterling in St. John's Wood, where visiting musicians had an opportunity of meeting English people as well as each other. I remember finding a common interest with John Drinkwater in our stamp collections!

Later that summer, in a series of benefit concerts, I continued to explore the wonderful settings for open-air music which the centuries have bequeathed to Italy. Singing in Piazza San Marco in Venice and the Roman amphitheatre at Verona had already given me a startling revelation of such possibilities. I sang again in Piazza San Marco, to an audience of twenty thousand. But the Boboli Gardens in Florence were new to me, and it was a new experience to sing with a chorus of nightingales in the background! I was told that musical entertainments in the Gardens were a tradition going back to the days when Florence was ruled by the Medici. Great concerts had been held there to celebrate the marriage of Anna de' Medici to Ferdinand of Austria in 1652, and that of Cosimo III to Margaret of Orleans; and when the Archduke Francis of Lorraine or King Ferdinand IV of Naples came on state visits to Florence, the leading *castrati* of the day were summoned to entertain them in Boboli. After hearing these tales, I felt that I could almost see spectral figures moving past the cypresses or beneath the boxwood arches in the moonlight.

The last concert that I gave, before sailing for New York at the end of August, was held in the courtyard of the Maschio Angioino in Naples, the great medieval fortress built by the Angevin kings. The concert was in aid of the victims of a recent earthquake. To solemnize the occasion, the vast edifice was entirely draped in velvet and cloth of gold, and heralds in Renaissance costume sounded trumpets to salute the arrival of the King's cousins, the Duke and Duchess of Aosta, who had come to hear me sing.

I had been looking forward to my return visit to San Francisco that September, where Gaetano Merola's pioneering operatic venture had now become established as an annual civic event. I felt rested and well pleased with my summer, and had no presentiment of tragedy.

Perhaps I have been fortunate in that my sorrows have always come to me suddenly. Perhaps it is a blessing to be spared the agonies of waiting and anticipation; but I could find solace neither in these thoughts nor in any others when, on September 24th, 1930, a few moments before going on the stage to sing 'Mignon' at the Civic Auditorium in San Francisco, I was handed the cable which told me of my mother's death.

When I kissed her good-bye in Recanati, only a few weeks earlier, I had been able to say 'See you next year, Mamma', with perfect confidence, for I could find no trace in her of failing health. She had died quickly and peacefully, with children and grandchildren gathered round her bedside; life had often treated her harshly, but death had been gentle with her. She was eighty-three years old. I had no grounds for complaint. Nevertheless, my losing her was the supreme tragedy of my existence. No other relationship could make up to me for her. No subsequent joy has ever been able to dispel the dark cloud that gathered over my life that September evening in San Francisco. When my mother died, I had to learn to face solitude.

I sat for a few minutes in my dressing-room, with my head between my hands, staring at the cable. I could not allow myself to weep just yet, for if I started I knew I could not stop.

Then I walked out on to the stage and sang.

Throughout the 1930–31 season at the Metropolitan there blew the cold wind of the Depression. Season tickets were not renewed, box-office queues dwindled; fewer New Yorkers could afford the luxury of opera. One rumour followed on the heels of another. The Chicago Opera Company was bankrupt; would the Met be able to weather the storm? Most people—such was the confidence inspired by the father-figure of Gatti-Casazza—never doubted that it would.

Meanwhile, work went on as usual. The Met continued to make new acquisitions. It fell to my lot that season to partner two rather sensational young sopranos—Lily Pons and Grace Moore—on the occasion of their New York début. To accompany a young singer through this test, and to witness her triumph, was an experience in which I always found a peculiar satisfaction; I had not forgotten the anxieties and terrors of my own beginnings.

Lily Pons had never been heard before in the United States, and was in fact still practically unknown. Born in Cannes, of Franco-Italian parentage, she had been discovered by the tenor Giovanni Zanatello singing in a small opera house in Montpellier, and brought to the attention of Gatti-Casazza. With her début in 'Lucia di Lammermoor' on January 3rd, 1931, she became deservedly famous overnight. She was romantically pretty, somewhat in the style of Lilian Gish; and her voice possessed a quite extraordinary range. High F had no terrors for her. The climax of her performance in 'Lucia' came with the Mad Scene; the audience went wild, and applause crashed on her from every part of the house. Among those present was the poet Paul Claudel, then French Ambassador in Washington. Next day the critics hailed her with all the rapturous phrases in their vocabulary, but with one reservation; she was, they said, no Patti.

With Grace Moore I sang in 'Manon' on March 11th, 1931. She lacked the vocal range of Lily Pons, but she too had remarkable physical beauty. What was more, she had great charm and sweetness of personality; her tragic death some years later was a great blow to me.

On March 6th I sang the rôle of Osaka in Mascagni's 'Japanese' opera 'Iris', which was being revived after an interval of sixteen years; I myself had sung it on only one previous occasion, fourteen years earlier, in Turin. When first produced at the Metropolitan, on October 16th, 1902, with Mascagni himself conducting, it had made an immense impression, and it retained its popularity when Caruso sang it in 1908, and Toscanini conducted it in 1915. But taste, one was forced to conclude, fluctuates; our revival was a failure. Neither critics nor audience attempted to conceal their boredom. 'Dull and bad,' was one succinct verdict, 'although the singers did what they could.' Another critic asked what was, perhaps, a pertinent question, though I would not have wholly subscribed to its implications: 'Admitting that few new operas are of any permanent value, would not a production of the most ephemeral or discordant modern work be preferable to the exhumation of an opera which cannot possibly be given the breath of life or have a vital interest for a modern audience?'

I had a refreshingly new experience when on my usual mid-winter concert tour. I was about to give a recital at the Mayflower Hotel in Washington, and as I happened to be staying in the hotel, I decided to take a short cut through the kitchen to the auditorium. Almost unconsciously, to test my voice, I burst into a snatch of song; but I was immediately terrified into silence by an angry voice shouting, 'Shut up that noise!' It was the Swiss *chef* of the Mayflower, who thought that one of his cooks was violating the rule against singing while at work!

When I sailed for Europe on May 6th, I had an eminent fellow-passenger on board the *Aquitania*, Governor Franklin D. Roosevelt. Together with Rosa Ponselle, I gave a concert in his honour.

The Covent Garden season of May and June, 1931, was notable for its all-round excellence and for the participation of Chaliapin. I sang in 'Rigoletto' with the English soprano Noel Eadie, and in 'La Bohème' with Odette de Foras and Mariano Stabile.

From London I went to Paris, where I fared somewhat better than the previous year at the Salle Pleyel; and from Paris to Berlin, where I sang in 'La Traviata' at the Staatsoper. Then I went back to Italy and faced what had to be faced—Recanati without my mother.

When I returned to New York in October, 1931, it was to find an atmosphere of tension and anxiety. Otto H. Kahn had just resigned from the presidency of the Metropolitan Opera Company, a position he had occupied since 1918, and Paul D. Cravath had been elected to succeed him. Both Cravath and Gatti-Casazza were forced to issue public denials of the rumours now finding their way into the newspaper headlines about impending disaster at the Metropolitan. I shared the concern of my colleagues for an institution so important to all of us; but I had as yet no idea that a year of major decisions lay ahead of me, or that the coming season, my twelfth at the Metropolitan, was also to be my last.

I went ahead with my commitments, which were much the same as any other year. Together with Lucrezia Bori, I opened the Philadelphia season on November 4th, in 'Manon', and immediately afterwards I appeared at the Metropolitan in 'Elisir d'Amore'. In a performance that was part of Gatti-Casazza's campaign to bring opera to the suburbs, I sang 'Madama Butterfly' in White Plains on November 13th; I sang 'Don Giovanni' at the Met, 'La Gioconda' in Brooklyn, and 'La

Traviata' in Hartford, Connecticut. I sang in 'L'Africana' for the Italian Hospital, and in 'Mignon' for the Grenfell Medical Mission to Labrador. I was nearly mobbed by an audience of ten thousand after a recital in Boston on December 13th. I attended the traditional Christmas Eve party at the Metropolitan, and as was customary for the soloists, I gave a gold present—cuff-links or a bracelet—to each of the one hundred and nineteen members of the chorus, to each of the ninety-three members of the orchestra, and to each of the forty-odd stage-hands, call-boys and wardrobe attendants.

On New Year's Day 1932, at the Metropolitan, I sang in a matinée of 'La Bohème' with Lucrezia Bori. The entire performance was broadcast, which at that time was still something of an experiment. It proved successful beyond all expectations. Millions listened throughout the country and we were deluged with congratulatory letters. This encouraged the management to make Saturday broadcasts a regular feature, and in the first three months of 1932 these earned $150,000 for the Metropolitan. That they were also winning a new audience for opera, the following episode may serve to illustrate.

During the New Year's Day performance of 'La Bohème', a woman rushed up to the window of the Met box-office and asked for a ticket. The seller pointed out that the matinée was already half over. 'Yes, I know,' she said. 'I've been listening to the first two acts on the radio, and it's so wonderful, I want to see the rest of it.'

In January and February 1932, I went on my usual coast-to-coast concert tour. To my surprise, I found no falling-off of audiences; from Toronto to Chicago, from San Francisco to New Orleans, from El Paso, Texas to Kalamazoo, Michigan, the theatres were always sold out.

On March 16th, 1932, I appeared in what was to be my last new rôle at the Metropolitan, that of Elvino in 'La Sonnambula', by Vincenzo Bellini. Although it contains some of the loveliest music in all opera—arias such as '*Ah non credea mirarti*', '*Come per me serena*', or '*Ah non giunge*', or the wonderful blending of voices in the duet of the second act—'La Sonnambula' is seldom produced, for the simple reason that the leading soprano rôle is one of inordinate difficulty, and singers trained to its demands are rarely to be found. It was, however, a perfect medium for displaying the extraordinary talent of Lily Pons. At the same time Gatti-Casazza found a pretext for a kind of centenary celebration in the fact that it had been performed for the first time one hundred and one years earlier. Moreover, with Marcella Sembrich and Italo Campanini, it had figured in the programme of the very first Metropolitan season, in 1883; Caruso had sung it there in 1905, again with Marcella Sembrich; and there had been two other revivals, in 1910 with Elvira de Hidalgo, and in 1916 with Maria Barrientos.

'La Sonnambula' has this in common with 'Don Giovanni', that it can never be quite itself in a vast theatre such as the Metropolitan; its pure, tender beauty requires, ideally, a smaller, more intimate setting. Lily Pons, however, gave such a dazzling performance as Amina—so fragile and sensitive a portrayal of delicate young womanhood, so brilliant and crystalline a vocal rendering—that the production was completely justified in spite of its shortcomings. I myself greatly enjoyed singing the rôle of the sleepwalking heroine's harassed lover, and to let my voice follow Bellini's lovely melodic curves was an experience of intense fulfilment. But I was well aware that the laurels, on this occasion, were not mine.

The season came to an end, as usual, in April; I sang in the concluding performance, which was 'L'Africana', with Elisabeth Rethberg. Serafin conducted with his customary verve; I had an ovation after '*O Paradiso*' and nothing seemed amiss. But although I did not know it for certain at the time, it was my farewell to the Metropolitan.

The crisis had come at last. At the beginning of April, 1932, Paul Cravath, president of the Metropolitan Opera Company since the previous October, had made an official announcement. 'Reduced receipts due to the prevailing financial depression,' he said, had 'practically wiped out the company's capital of $550,000 and most of its reserve, leaving it with insufficient funds to assure another season.' An 'earnest effort,' he continued, would be made to work out a plan of reduced expense 'and other measures', so that in spite of everything there might still be opera in New York the following winter.

At the same time it was learned that all employees of the Metropolitan Opera House, from soloists to ushers, would be asked to take a 'voluntary' salary cut of 25 per cent if the 1932–33 season should be decided on. This was the chief economy measure proposed to avert closing down. An earlier 'voluntary cut' of 10 per cent had already been proposed the previous December. There was, of course, nothing voluntary about these cuts, they were decided by the management and all concerned had no option but to give their consent.

These proposals were the rock on which I split with the Metropolitan. My behaviour in doing so was widely criticized, a fact I resented at the time; but now I have enough detachment to realize that my critics were to some extent justified. I did act unwisely—above all, tactlessly. People cannot be expected to see behind appearances, and appearances were against me. It looked as though, after a happy and fruitful association that had lasted twelve years, I were leaving the Metropolitan in the hour of its distress, over a question of money.

That, however, was not the way I saw it; but it would be both painful and pointless to exhume the dead bones of ancient quarrels. The manner of my parting from the Metropolitan remains one of my few regrets. I acted, quite frankly, in a fit of pique. I am ready now to admit that it was unwarranted.

I would like to stress the fact that I fully shared the general anguish about the survival of the Metropolitan. Had I been asked to help, in my own way and at my own discretion, I would gladly have given, not a quarter but half my salary to an emergency fund. I would equally gladly have given extra performances for nothing. I found it intolerable, however, that my contribution should be demanded as a right, decided for me in advance, stopped out of my salary. I found it intolerable that my hard-earned contract, which had still three years to run, should be—to all intents and purposes—scrapped. I felt angry at this high-handed approach. I suddenly felt that I wanted to revolt against the almighty Gatti-Casazza.

This upsurge of resentment stirred into wakefulness another feeling that for some time had been lying dormant—my nostalgia for Italy. I had never wanted to spend my whole life in a foreign country, and now I suddenly found myself longing intensely for a glimpse of the changing seasons in my trees and fields at Recanati. I had never seen my almond trees in bloom; and so long as I stayed in America, I never would. Until now it had been a dream; suddenly it struck me, with the force of a revelation, that the dream was within my reach.

Even so, it took me weeks to reach a decision. Beneath the surface of my anger with Gatti-Casazza there was an undertow of loyalty to the Met, which had given me so much. Against the potent attraction of Recanati, I had to weigh the big financial risk involved in a return to Europe. Night after night I lay awake, tossing from one argument to another, unable to make up my mind.

Finally, one night, as I lay uneasily between sleep and wakefulness, I saw—or dreamed I saw—my mother. 'Come back to Italy, my son,' she said—or I dreamed that she said. 'You have been among strangers long enough.' Then she was gone—or the dream was gone; but in that instant I knew that my mind was made up.

Next morning I tore up my $300,000 contract with the Metropolitan, gave notice to my landlord, and booked my passage to Italy. It was April 30th, 1932. I never saw Gatti-Casazza again.

CHAPTER XIV

HERE, THERE AND EVERYWHERE

Now that the decision was taken, I felt impatient to put the past behind me and think about the future. But there were still some commitments to fulfil before I could leave the United States. I had promised, for example, to sing in a performance of Francesco Marcacci's opera 'Evangeline', which was being produced in May at Temple University, Philadelphia, to commemorate the fiftieth anniversary of the death of Longfellow. The last act of the opera is set in Philadelphia, and the libretto, by Antonio Lega, is based on Longfellow's poem of the same name. Marcacci himself, who was to be present, had appealed to me to take the rôle of Gabriele; and I felt I could not refuse this homage to the great American poet who had translated Dante into English and had loved Italy so much.

On June 1st, 1932, I finally sailed for Europe. It was not a joyful departure, nor an entirely sad one. I was fully aware of all that I owed America, not least the financial independence that was now enabling me to leave it. But the past was past; like the Manhattan skyline, as we forged into the Atlantic I put it behind me. I turned my thoughts to the summer that lay ahead.

In Italy opera showed no signs of a slump. Invitations to sing had been pouring in from here, there and everywhere; I had to refuse most of them for lack of time. The first offer I accepted was from Mascagni; he was conducting his own operas in a summer musical season at Leghorn, and asked me if I would sing my old rôle of Flammen in 'Lodoletta'. I still treasured fifteen-year-old memories of 'Lodoletta' and Leghorn, and wondered if I would succeed in recapturing the enchantment of midnight expeditions with the fishermen. But, somehow, this was not possible. When I had made friends with the fishermen I was young and unknown; now, inevitably, I stayed at the best hotel, and had secretaries, and everything was different. I could only wander down to look at the boats, and stand there for a while, thinking melancholy, middle-aged thoughts. Now I was successful; then I had been happy.

From Leghorn I went to Torre del Lago, where Puccini is buried, and sang twice in a Puccini festival; from there to Parma, where I took part in a concert entirely devoted to the music of Verdi. In September I sang in the centenary performance of 'L'Elisir d'Amore' at Donizetti's native Bergamo.

It was, however, in Verona, at the annual opera festival in the Arena, that I found the most striking contrast to the crisis I had left behind in New York. The organizers of the festival, in their apparent determination to surpass their own previous standards of lavishness, had managed to get a subsidy of 150,000 lire from the government, and had staged a spectacle which, however dubious in its artistic merits, certainly delighted the crowd. And what a crowd it was! The State Railways put on special popular-priced trains from the five chief points of the Italian compass, and gave a 50 per cent reduction on regular trains. Thirty to forty thousand people swarmed into the Arena every night.

Throughout the festival, which lasted from the end of July to mid-August, two operas alternated—'L'Africana', in which I sang with Margherita Carosio, and 'Un Ballo in Maschera', which had Aureliano Pertile in the tenor rôle. Two thousand performers took part in 'L'Africana' alone, and fifteen assistant scenographers worked behind the scenes to solve the difficult problems of stagecraft which the Verona amphitheatre presents. Indeed, the attention devoted to scenography was such that the singers, I felt, were reduced to mere accessories.

This year, I learned, experimentation had been abandoned; the effect aimed at was one hundred per cent realism. A rajah rode in state on a fake elephant; torrential rain drummed on the luxuriant vegetation of a tropical forest; but above all, there was the ship and the shipwreck. This scene alone cost fifty thousand lire, a third of the entire subsidy. Pericle Ansaldo, technical stage director of the Rome Opera, had attempted an exact reproduction of a fifteenth-century galleon, with its full complement of sails. The stage proper formed the main part of the deck, but the poop was constructed separately, and designed to roll, pitch and swerve. This movable part could hold about forty people. Behind it all was the 'ocean', with mechanical waves. The 'ship' navigated wildly, as if split in two, out of tune with both wind and waves, not to mention the orchestra. The bulk of the crew squatted securely on the main deck, which was *terra firma,* while the principals and some of the chorus ducked and slid down the rocking cabin hatchways.

Were these extraneous contrivances really necessary to draw the crowd? I wondered. I was all for making opera popular; but I could not help feeling that this production of 'L'Africana' came perilously near to being a circus, with '*O Paradiso*' thrown in as an afterthought.

In the autumn of 1932 I went on a long recital tour of Germany, Holland, Denmark and Switzerland. At the German frontier I discovered that I had forgotten my passport; I explained the situation to the German frontier guards, and sang a few bars of '*La donna è mobile*' to convince them that I was telling the truth. They let me pass.

In Nuremberg, when I got to the end of my concert, the audience refused to go home until I sang the entire programme over again—as an 'encore'. In Berlin, I had an audience of twelve thousand at my concert in the Sportpalast. In Copenhagen, the Danish royal family came to hear me sing in 'La Bohème', and the King received me afterwards in private audience.

The most memorable episode of the whole tour, however, was in Frankfurt, where I got a letter from an Italian boy imploring me to visit his father in hospital. This old Italian, who had lived for many years in Frankfurt, importing oranges and lemons, had had both legs amputated two days previously, and was now dying. I went to the hospital and sat at his bedside. He begged me to sing just one note. I sang the whole of '*Spirto Gentil*' from 'La Favorita'. 'Thank you,' he said. 'Now I can die happy.'

In Rome, two days before Christmas, I at last found an opportunity of paying my respects to Don Lorenzo Perosi, the great composer of Church music, whom I had revered ever since my childhood in Recanati. It was difficult to approach him, for he had withdrawn almost completely from contact with the world, and lived the life of a recluse. I stood outside his door and began to sing, very softly, one of his own compositions, the '*Dies Iste*'. '*Nova mater novam prolem, nova stella novum solem . . .*' Suddenly the door opened and Don Lorenzo stood before me, with tears pouring down his cheeks. It was a great moment for me. I told him about Maestro Lazzarini and the boys' choir in Recanati Cathedral, and how we had loved to sing his music; and then how disappointed I had been when I got to Rome and found I was too old to be admitted into the Sistine Chapel choir, of which Don Lorenzo was director. He asked me to sing something else for him; I sang Bizet's '*Agnus Dei*'. Then he played on the piano for me, a new composition of his own—'*La festa al villaggio*'. Hours passed, and when at last I left, it was to find that I had caused a sensation; not for years had Don Lorenzo consented to receive a visitor.

That same evening, I was invited by King Victor Emmanuel and Queen Elena to sing for them at Villa Savoia. Two of their daughters were also present: Princess Mafalda, who was later to die tragically in Buchenwald, and Princess Maria. I sang Gluck's '*O mio dolce ardor*', '*Una furtiva lagrima*', '*M'appari*', and Curti's '*Prima notte a Venezia*'; and then, at the Queen's request, the 'Dream Song' from 'Manon', an aria from 'Le Roi d'Ys', Toselli's '*Rimpianto*', and Pergolesi's '*Tre giorni son che Nina*'. The Queen inquired about my concert tour in Germany; she seemed motherly and simple. The King questioned me closely about America and the Depression, on which he was obviously far better informed than I was. I found myself revising the impression I had formed of him in Bologna. Despite his tiny stature he was, I decided, rather intimidating.

I had worked out an agreement with the Italian Government which more or less neatly filled the gap created by my break with the Metropolitan. I undertook to give about eighty operatic performances a year, all over Italy, without binding myself by contract to any single opera house.

And so, one snowy night at the end of December 1932, I found myself—after fourteen years' absence—back in the Scala. The opera was 'Andrea Chénier', the conductor Victor de Sabata, the soprano Gina Cigna, the baritone my old colleague from the Metropolitan, Giuseppe Danise. The composer, my friend Umberto Giordano, was in the audience; his Andrea Chénier was my favourite rôle, but he had never before had a chance to hear me sing it.

I felt a little nervous. Audiences differ, and the only one I really knew intimately was the audience of the Metropolitan. It was a long time since I had faced a critical Italian public, and then only as a young 'revelation', not as an internationally-known celebrity. (The summer audiences of open-air opera are apt to be indulgent.) To my anguish, I could feel that my nervousness was affecting my singing. The '*Improvviso*' of Act I came and went without stirring even a ripple of applause; and this coldness persisted throughout Acts 2 and 3. I felt desperate; to fail at the Scala now—what a humiliation that would be! I put a supreme effort into my singing in Act 4, and after '*Come un bel dì di maggio*', I won the audience at last. But it had been touch and go.

After that first hurdle, all went well. I sang fifteen times altogether at the Scala during the season—'Rigoletto', 'Manon' and 'Tosca' as well as 'Andrea Chénier'. They brought the biggest box-office returns of a decade. I sang 'La Gioconda' in Rome, with Gina Cigna and Gianna Pederzini, and also in Parma; 'L'Africana' in Genoa, and 'Manon Lescaut', with Rosetta Pampanini, in Turin. The critics in Turin treated me almost as severely as their Parisian colleagues had done; but the public came to hear me notwithstanding.

I celebrated my forty-third birthday, on March 20th, by taking a quick trip to London to give my first concert at the Albert Hall. I felt in a party mood and enjoyed myself thoroughly. By ten o'clock the audience was in an uproar, with those who wanted me to sing '*Questa o quella*' trying to shout down the partisans of '*Celeste Aida*'. I did my best to please everybody.

Resuming my Italian engagements, I sang 'Tosca' in Rome with Claudia Muzio, 'Rigoletto' in Palermo, 'Manon Lescaut' in Venice, and 'Lucrezia Borgia' in a gala centenary performance at the Maggio Fiorentino festival in Florence.

I then managed to fit in three concerts in Copenhagen before sailing for Buenos Aires on May 25th. I had not been to South America for five years; there too, opera had been adversely affected by the Depression. Disaster in one form or another had overtaken most of the old operatic companies, and this time the Colôn season was to be under the direct management of the municipality of Buenos Aires. The Director of the Rome Opera had been asked to form the company. He based it mainly on Claudia Muzio and myself; among the other members were Ebe Stignani, Carlo Galeffi and Gilda Dalla Rizza.

The Argentine President, General Justo (whose father came from Italy and was called 'Giusto') heard me sing in 'Andrea Chénier' at a gala performance celebrating the twenty-fifth anniversary of the Colón; and I sang 'Lohengrin' in Rio de Janeiro, to commemorate the fiftieth anniversary of Wagner's death. The most exciting event of the season for me, however, was my début as Don Alvaro in Verdi's 'La Forza del Destino', at the Colón, on July 5th.

For years I had been hearing legends about this opera. Superstitious colleagues warned me never to sing in it because, they said, it was under a spell; it had the Evil Eye. So I was rather curious to see what would happen. As a matter of fact, several things did happen, but with no untoward results beyond the interpolation of a comic element into this old Spanish tragedy of true love and innocence thwarted by a cruel Destiny.

At the end of the first act, Don Alvaro throws his pistol to the ground, proving to Leonora's father that he is unarmed, but the weapon goes off by accident and Leonora's father is killed. The sound of my exploding weapon was to have been provided by a stage-hand, hidden under a table, firing an airgun. I threw down my pistol, I cried '*Eccomi inerme!*', but nothing happened; the stage-hand under the table had fallen asleep. Leonora's father fell, mortally if inexplicably wounded; the orchestra played on; finally he expired. I had been pouring forth my horrified despair over the corpse for a good thirty seconds, when there was a loud report backstage. This belated attempt by someone to remedy the situation provoked peals of laughter from the delighted audience.

I was amused to discover recently that the same misadventure once befell Caruso, although I must admit that he showed more resourcefulness in dealing with it than I did. The following passage is taken from a letter he wrote, in English, to his American wife, after a performance of 'La Forza del Destino' in Havana, in June 1920:

'At the moment which I throw down the pistol, at the end of the first act, the people inside of the stage dont shot and I make a big noise with my mouth like this, BUUUM!!!! and I kill the father of Leonora. You can imagine the public how laughing! That assure the success of the night, because the public put himself in good humor because saw me laughing.'*

* From *Enrico Caruso*, by Dorothy Caruso.

Mario Cavaradossi in Puccini's 'Tosca'

A scene at a rehearsal of Donizetti's 'L'Elisir d'Amore' at the Rome Opera House

My daughter Rina gives me a helping hand in making up as Rodolfo in 'La Bohème' at Covent Garden in 1946

But to continue with my own story. In the interval, I tripped and fell over an iron bar; that was nothing. In the third act Don Alvaro, gravely wounded in the wars, is borne on a stretcher to the front of the stage. It is supposed to be a moment of pathos. Just then, one of the stretcher-bearers lost his footing and let the stretcher drop. I rolled ignominiously to the ground. There seemed to be nothing for it but pick myself up and climb back on the stretcher again; but the pathos was gone. I sang '*Solenne in quest' ora*', I sang '*O muoio tranquillo*', with all the tones of anguish I could summon, but it was no use; the audience was helpless with laughter.

'Well, surely that's enough of the Evil Eye for one night,' I said to myself; but there was more to come. In the fourth act Don Alvaro, now a monk, is challenged to a duel by Leonora's brother, Don Carlos. Supposedly outraged by his insults, I bent to snatch up a sword. There was an ominous cracking sound; the skin-tight breeches I was wearing had split right up the back. Fortunately the damage was concealed by my monk's habit!

After all these mishaps, I began to think there might be some truth in the superstitious legend. But the music of 'La Forza del Destino' belongs to Verdi's great period; and I decided that if only for the sake of '*O tu che in seno agli angeli*', it was worth putting up with the caprices of a poltergeist.

October, 1933, found me with the Scala company in Berlin, for a fortnight's season at the Charlottenburg Opera House. Hitler, Hess and Goebbels attended the gala performance of 'Tosca', in which I sang with Rosa Raisa, on October 13th.

From Berlin I went on a recital tour of Scandinavia, visiting Oslo for the first time; and from Oslo I went back to London for another concert at the Albert Hall. It was completely sold out. In spite of the fact that I was suffering from nervous exhaustion and fatigue, I found more favour with the English critics on this occasion than I had ever done before. 'Gigli by his soft phrases transformed the Albert Hall into an intimate music-room,' wrote the *Manchester Guardian*, and it added: 'Gigli's voice is for quiet moonlit nights; he should have sung in Illyria to the Duke.' I felt suitably grateful for these unusual compliments!

A certain atmosphere of comedy had surrounded my arrival at Victoria Station. A large crowd of people, mostly Italians, had come to meet me, and the moment I stepped off the train they clamoured for me to sing. I tried to comply, but a majestic station official intervened. 'What's this all about?' he demanded. 'It's Gigli singing,' someone explained. 'Well, I don't care who it is,' said the official, 'he can't sing here. This,' he added importantly, 'is Victoria Station.'

I was sorry to have to disappoint the people who had waited for me; and as my taxi drew away from the kerb, I sang a few high notes, for fun, as a farewell. Just then a couple passed by. They had not seen me, but they heard my voice.

'I told you so, dear,' said the woman to the man. 'It *is* Tetrazzini.'

The wheels of success and of international sleeping-cars bore me on and on, from one town to another, from one theatre to another, from one concert platform to another. Now and then I managed to snatch a few days in Recanati, but there never seemed to be time for the long, deep, idyllic plunges into rural peace and quiet that I had dreamed of when leaving New York. European concert managers were no less inexorable than their American counterparts, no less ingenious in devising merciless itineraries; and I myself could not afford to slacken the pace. The more money I earned, the more expenses I had, the more demands made on me, the more people came to depend on me, the faster the money got spent. So I had to keep going.

After singing at the Albert Hall, I returned to Central Europe—Germany and Hungary—for another three weeks. On November 22nd, 1933, Goebbels attended my concert at the Scalatheater in Berlin; and four days later, when I sang there again, I saw Hitler, Goebbels, Frau Goebbels, and the French Ambassador François-Poncet, all sitting in the front row. Afterwards Hitler shook my hand and told me he liked Italian music very much.

Together with the soprano Giannina Arangi-Lombardi, I opened the Rome opera season in 'Lucrezia Borgia'—its centenary was still being celebrated—on December 26th. Mussolini had attended the dress rehearsal on December 23rd; and the King, the Prince and Princess of Piedmont, and Princess Maria of Savoy were all present in the royal box on the opening night. I sang again for the King and Queen a month later, at an evening reception in the Quirinal Palace. From January until May, 1934, I was busy keeping my bargain with the Italian Government; I sang opera in Rome, Naples, Genoa, San Remo, Turin, Florence,

La Spezia and Milan. At the Scala I sang in 'La Forza del Destino' with Iva Pacetti and 'Romeo e Giulietta' with Mafalda Favero; the latter work had not been heard in Milan for twenty-three years.

In May and June I was off on tour again: opera in Vienna and Budapest, concerts in Copenhagen, Paris and London. In Paris I had an audience of ten thousand at the Vélodrome d'Hiver; Charles Munch conducted the orchestra of the Concerts Lamoureux. At last, it seemed, I had found the way to make the French like me; at the 'Vél' d'Hiv'' there was no trace left of the coldness with which they had received me on previous occasions at the Salle Pleyel. This time I might almost have been a cycling champion!

In other years my return from New York to Italy had marked, theoretically at least, the beginning of the 'holidays'; but now that there was no such landmark in my calendar, there seemed to be no definite point at which to stop, and I went on singing right through the summer. I sang in the Roman amphitheatre at Pola, in the Sala della Ragione at Padua, in the Piazza del Comune at Cremona—here I took part in six open-air performances of 'La Gioconda' commemorating the centenary of Ponchielli. Then came the Arena in Verona—'La Gioconda' again, and 'Andrea Chénier' with Maria Caniglia, three weeks altogether. In September there was the third International Music Festival in Venice, with Serafin conducting Verdi's 'Requiem' in the Piazza San Marco, to an audience of ten thousand; and lastly, at the beginning of October, there was 'La Favorita' at the annual Donizetti festival in Bergamo. In between times, I managed to get to Milan and make a complete recording of 'I Pagliacci', with Fred Gaisberg, for His Master's Voice—the first full-length opera I ever recorded.

In October and November I made an extended concert tour of the British Isles, starting off in London, at the Queen's Hall, and working northwards, through Birmingham, Sheffield, Manchester, Middlesborough, Nottingham, Newcastle-on-Tyne, across the border to Scotland—Edinburgh, Glasgow, Dundee, Aberdeen; then over to Ireland—Belfast and Dublin—and back, through Bristol, to London. Someone nicknamed me 'the non-stop tenor'! On previous visits I had never got further than London; and I was greatly impressed by the warmth and enthusiasm of audiences in other English cities. In Manchester I was so carried away by the response of the public that I found myself still singing when, after the concert, I got out into the street!

In Scotland I had hoped to see the hills of Lammermuir, because of their associations with Donizetti's Lucia; but I was disappointed. I did pass them in the train on my way to Aberdeen, but it was at night, and I saw nothing.

I made a bad mistake on my first day in Scotland. Someone asked me: 'Do you know "*Annie Laurie*"?' I said, 'No, who is she?' When they told me, I lost no time in learning the song, and was able to surprise my audiences with it before leaving Scotland. To Ireland I came better prepared; my Irish-American friends among the New York police had long ago taught me '*Mother Machree*'.

The way back to Italy was a roundabout one, leading through Paris, Hamburg, Copenhagen, Berlin, Prague, and then Paris again, where I sang for the first time at the Opéra, in two rather undistinguished performances of 'Traviata' and 'Rigoletto'.

The year 1935 was the Bellini centenary—a hundred years since the young Sicilian composer's sad, lonely death, on September 24th, 1835, at Puteaux in the Parisian suburb of Saint-Denis. The Rome Opera chose to commemorate him with a production of 'Il Pirata', a minor work but already prophetic of 'Norma', which was to follow it four years later. I sang the rôle of Gualtiero, and Iva Pacetti that of Imogene; our *première* was on New Year's Day 1935.

The action of 'Il Pirata', which is involved and melodramatic, takes place in thirteenth-century Sicily. Gualtiero, Count of Montaldo, is driven from one misfortune to another by his feud with the Angevin kings, until in the end he kills himself and the heroine goes mad. This final scene of Imogene's madness is, musically speaking, one of the most moving in the whole of opera. 'Il Pirata' was very popular with Italian patriots at the time of the Risorgimento; they saw in Gualtiero's rebellion against the Angevin dynasty a symbol of their own revolt against the domination of the Austrian Empire.

When first performed, at the Scala, on October 27th, 1827, the success of 'Il Pirata' was instantaneous, and decisive for Bellini's subsequent career; but it is rarely given nowadays because of its extreme difficulty. Bellini designed the part of Gualtiero for a tenor named Rubini, who had a fantastic vocal range; Reina, his successor in the rôle, was unable to sing it until Bellini agreed to transpose several arias a few tones lower. It is still a risky and arduous undertaking for any tenor; the score dictates such vertiginous leaps from low to high notes and from high to low, that one sometimes feels one's vocal cords are going to break. It was certainly not an ideal rôle for me, but I felt that I had to make the effort as an act of homage to Bellini.

By this time there was scarcely a theatre in Italy with which I was not familiar. January to April 1935 was another intensive Italian season; I sang in opera all over the country, from Trieste to Bari, from Palermo to Genoa. Mussolini brought Pierre Laval to hear me sing in 'Mignon' at the Rome Opera; and when I sang 'Il Pirata' in Palermo, the Mayor came with eighty guests—English Boy Scouts who happened to be camping nearby. I sang 'La Traviata' with Claudia Muzio, 'La Forza del Destino', 'Manon' with the Brazilian soprano Bidú Sayão, 'La Bohème' with Pia Tassinari, the inevitable 'Marta' and 'Andrea Chénier', and 'La Favorita' with Giuseppina Cobelli—this last, in Genoa (where it had not been performed for twenty-four years) and in Rome, was a production of epoch-making quality.

In May, 1935, I went to Berlin to make my first film. It was to be an Italo-German co-production, directed by Augusto Genina. I had a certain amount of stage fright, mainly because I feared—as I had feared before my first broadcast—that the sound-track might distort my voice; but in the end I was reassured.

The amount of work involved was enormous, for I had to make two complete versions, German and Italian; and since I did not know German, this meant learning by heart long strings of what were, to me, meaningless sounds. Of course, the rather novelettish plot was merely the pretext to enable me to do a lot of singing. A famous tenor meets and falls in love with a simple young girl (played by Magda Schneider). They marry. One day, by chance, she encounters the man who was her first love. Unlike the tenor-husband, he is young and handsome. The husband sees that they are still mutually attracted, and is ready to sacrifice his own happiness and withdraw from the scene; but in the end the girl realizes that she loves her husband, and decides to stay with him after all.

The musical part included scenes from various operas—

'Marta', 'Aida', 'Rigoletto', 'Lohengrin', 'La Forza del Destino', 'Elisir d'Amore'—and a new song, '*Non ti scordar di me*', written specially for the film by Ernesto De Curtis, which immediately became a popular 'hit'. The outdoor shots were taken in Hamburg, on the Transatlantic liner *Bremen.* In both German and Italian, the film was called 'Forget-me-not'.

This film had such an extraordinary success that in the next few years I followed it up with fifteen others, all of them, to tell the truth, very much alike. From the chorus of horror with which my films were invariably greeted by the film critics, I was forced to conclude that, judged by the standards of cinematographic art, they were bad. I did not really mind. I had no ambitions to be a film star. Not only did the films earn a lot of money for me; they won me a vast new audience which I would otherwise never have reached. All the world over, they were seen in towns and villages too small or too remote ever to be included in a recital tour; and even in great cities, they brought my singing to people who for one reason or another—lack of money or education or interest in music—had never seen the inside of a concert hall or an opera house.

This was made plain to me by the thousands of letters I received—so wildly enthusiastic that at a certain point they ceased to gratify and began to alarm, as when a woman wrote to me from Berlin, telling me that in *one month* she had seen 'Forget-me-not' sixty-seven times!

I met Hitler again while working on the film in Berlin; he came to a reception at the Kaiserhof following a benefit concert which I gave. On this same occasion I made the acquaintance of Richard Strauss and Franz Lehar.

In June 1935 I returned to Buenos Aires for a three months' season with a rather heterogeneous company, consisting mainly of French singers from the Opéra-Comique in Paris, but with a sprinkling of other nationalities—the German soprano Vina Bovy Fischer, the Brazilian Bidú Sayão, and a few Italians. Ernest Ansermet directed the *ensemble*, if such it can be called. The result was not, on the whole, very satisfactory; we had not had enough rehearsals together, and the general standard was lower than in previous years at the Colón. I sang in a number of familiar operas, and I also appeared in one new rôle—in Gounod's 'Faust'—with Nerina Ferrari, on September 10th.

I could not help wishing that chance might have led me earlier to the discovery of this most melodic of all operas. Beautiful and, for the tenor, profoundly satisfying though it is, I had identified myself too closely and too long with the other Faust, that of Boito's 'Mefistofele', to be able to enter as completely as I would have wished into a rôle which, while apparently identical, was so subtly and so intrinsically different. However, this was a purely private feeling; I tried to sing my best in spite of it, and to let my audiences suspect nothing. The music was so ideally suited to my voice, that I think I succeeded.

I have one uncomfortable memory of the Colón *première* of 'Faust'. Margherita is in prison, and insane with grief. In her delirium, she snatches handfuls of straw from her pallet and scatters them on the floor. Approaching to comfort her, I slipped on the straw—I was wearing new shoes—and fell full length, very painfully, on the stage. Whenever an accident happened in front of the audience, I always tried to camouflage it by making it seem part of the action; so I remained prostrate in Margherita's cell, and dragged myself across the floor to her, as though in great humility, at the same time wondering uneasily if I had fractured my spine.

At the end of October, 1935, I went back to Berlin for the German *première* of my film at the Ufa Palast am Zoo, and stayed on to give a few concerts and opera performances. Dr. and Frau Goebbels attended one of my recitals, while Hitler came to my benefit concert for the *Winterhilfe* on November 29th, and afterwards gave me a signed photograph of himself. That evening I also met the great pianist, Walter Gieseking.

CHAPTER XV

AMERICA ONCE MORE

My little family was growing up. In order to be with my children as much as possible when not on tour, I had bought a house in Rome. In Rome, too, I had my secretary, my accountant, my lawyer, my doctor; I had become a respectable middle-aged citizen of the city in which I had arrived—penniless, hungry, but full of hope—almost thirty years before. I did not over-romanticize my youthful memories; I could still recall clearly that I had not enjoyed being hungry. Nevertheless, something had been lost or stifled with the passage of the years. It was not merely that I no longer had the time or the inclination to press my nose in wonder against the shop windows in the Corso, or to stare hypnotized at the Punch and Judy show in the Pincio, or to watch the sunset from the Trinità dei Monti. What filled me with occasional melancholy was the realization that nothing seemed wonderful to me any more. My own success had been so extraordinary that it had blunted my capacity for astonishment. I had been applauded by too many crowds, fêted at too many banquets, decorated with too many ribbons. I enjoyed it, I thrived on it, I needed it all; but I had also grown used to it. Sometimes it seemed to me that to have too much was like having nothing; or even less than nothing.

The year 1936 was the year of the conquest of Abyssinia, of sanctions, of the Spanish Civil War. I had no concern with politics and could scarcely be held accountable for them, but the fact remained that I was an Italian. Regretfully I decided that it would be more tactful not to visit England for the time being.

Having recently had a surfeit of travelling, I found it a great relief to be able to spend most of the winter in one place—Rome. I opened the opera season on December 26th, 1935, in a revival of Mascagni's 'Iris', conducted by the composer himself. It was a gala performance, planned as a kind of homage to Mascagni. The theatre was decked with masses of red, white and green flowers and foliage—the colours of the Italian flag. The entire company, including the soloists, joined in singing the '*Hymn to the Sun*'. The production was a spectacular success, and a personal triumph for Mascagni. It was not so very long since I had seen 'Iris' fail utterly to stir the audience at the Metropolitan, and once again I felt puzzled by the apparently capricious waxing and waning of this opera's popularity.

Another 'homage' paid that season by the Rome Opera to a living Italian composer was the revival of Francesco Cilea's 'Adriana Lecouvreur', brilliantly conducted by Serafin. Cilea was present at the *première* on January 14th, 1936; when he reluctantly consented to appear before the curtain at the end of the second act, the entire audience rose to their feet and gave him a prolonged ovation. As for myself, I had always liked the part of Count Maurice of Saxony; and I think that perhaps I did it justice, for I had altogether twenty-five curtain calls in the course of the evening.

On February 7th I had the pleasure of witnessing my daughter Rina's début as a singer. It was on a modest scale, at a benefit concert in Rome; and as she was already engaged to be married, I thought that would be the beginning and end of it. I was far from imagining that she would one day emulate me and make a career in opera. I take a great pride in her now, but I must admit that she got very little encouragement from me. Being a somewhat traditional Italian father, I would have liked my son to follow in my footsteps; the disciplined irregularity and exhausting emotions of a career on the operatic stage were not what I would have wished for my daughter. Nature, however, decided differently. My son Enzo successfully resisted all my attempts to interest him in music, while Rina, at the age of three, could not be kept away from the piano.

The month of April was devoted to a recital tour in Germany, during which I visited several places that were new to me, including the valley of the Ruhr. I spent the whole of May in Berlin, making a film called 'Ave Maria', and in June I went to Munich for another film called 'Du Bist Mein Leben'. While in Berlin I sang at a big reception given by the Italian Ambassador Attolico. Among those present were Goering, Ribbentrop,

Marshal von Blomberg, and the Kaiser's son, the Crown Prince, with his wife.

By the time I had finished with film-making, there was not much of the summer left to spend in Recanati; even so, I could not stop singing. On Sunday mornings, at High Mass, I would sometimes climb up into the Cathedral organ-loft and join the choir. I sang several times in the Piazza where in the old days people used to interrupt my games by asking for 'just one little song, Beniaminello'.

On September 25th, in the nearby town of Jesi, I took part in a performance of Pergolesi's delightful *opera buffa* 'La Serva Padrona'.

In October I gave another cycle of concerts in Germany, and in November—I am almost ashamed to confess it—made yet another film. I also met Hitler again in Berlin, after a benefit concert at the Scalatheater. These encounters, I need hardly say, were always brief and formal in the extreme. I knew nothing about his political activities, and never had occasion to exchange more than a few polite words with him. If I record my contacts with him and other Nazi leaders, it is because they belong to a period that has already passed into history. Now that their names have acquired so sinister a context, it is curious to visualize these men listening to 'Tosca'; yet that is how I knew and saw them.

During the 1937 winter season I sang mostly in the three great Italian opera houses—Rome, San Carlo and the Scala. I opened the Rome season on December 26th in 'Lohengrin', with Franca Somigli, Ebe Stignani and Armando Borgioli. Another notable Roman production that winter was 'Rigoletto', in which I sang towards the end of January with Toti Dal Monte and Mario Basiola. When I sang in 'Manon' at the Scala, I found my old Metropolitan colleague, Giuseppe De Luca, in the part of Lescaut. Like Claudia Muzio, Serafin, Giuseppe Danise and myself, he had now returned to Italy.

Goering and Frau Goering came on an official visit to Rome in January, 1937, and I sang at the concert which the City of Rome gave for them in the Capitol on January 15th. The occasion was surrounded with all the pomp that Italian municipalities seem to be able to conjure up whenever there is an excuse to parade it. Out of the moth balls come the velvet and gold brocade tapestries and hangings, and the Renaissance costumes designed, one is invariably told, by Michelangelo. Pages and heralds are tricked out in this finery, supplied with tasselled silver trumpets, and lined up in rows to impress the important visitor. Such devotion to the glorious past has its comical aspects, but on the whole I like it. After all, why not? Present-day existence is drab enough.

Never to force my voice, never to attempt rôles that I considered beyond its scope, had always been one of my cardinal principles. Now, however, I was confident that it had grown sufficiently robust and mature to undertake certain arduous rôles about which I had long felt hesitant. One of these was Radames in Verdi's masterpiece 'Aida'—a difficult, challenging part, but I prepared it very carefully, and at last I felt ready to sing it. The *première* was to be on March 28th, 1937, at the Rome Opera House, with Maria Caniglia, Mario Basiola and, as conductor, Serafin.

Like many Italians, I am inclined to be superstitious about death. I have what I think must be an atavistic dread of hearing it mentioned unnecessarily; at the very least, this brings bad luck. I was therefore not too pleased to find, on the morning of the dress rehearsal of 'Aida', that the post had brought me a black-bordered mortuary card bearing the legend:

Today
BENIAMINO GIGLI
Departed This Life

Knowing only too well the extent to which singers can be carried away by professional jealousy, I concluded that some colleague was playing a practical joke. This thought, even more than the card itself, upset me so much that I began to feel it was indeed an ill omen for the dress rehearsal. I spent the morning in a state of extreme nervous agitation. Several hours passed before I could bring myself to look at the card again. When I finally did so, I noticed something that I had previously overlooked—a line of small lettering at the bottom: 'The little angel was only three months old.' So it was a genuine announcement after all. I felt greatly relieved, and a bit ashamed of having suspected my colleagues unjustly. The identity of my three-months'-old namesake, however, was still a mystery to me.

I recovered from this disturbing episode in time to acquit

myself honourably at the dress rehearsal of 'Aida'; and the *première* was as great a triumph as I could have wished for.

A few weeks later, in the train to Milan, I exchanged a few words with the sleeping-car attendant. Travelling as often as I did, I knew them all by sight; but this one I even knew by name, for he had once told me that he was called Gigli like myself.

'Yes,' he sighed, as though picking up the thread of an earlier conversation, 'it was a sad blow to us, losing our little Beniamino. We had named him after the Signor Commendatore in the hope that it would bring him luck. Did the Signor Commendatore get the card we sent?'

Shortly after my début as the Egyptian prince Radames, I appeared on the stage of the Rome Opera in the guise of yet another exotic hero—Pery, head of a tribe of South American Indians, and protagonist of 'Guarany', an opera by the Brazilian composer Carlos Gomez.

First produced in Milan on March 19th, 1870, 'Guarany' enjoyed a tremendous vogue for twenty years. Snatches of it were played by all the village bands in Italy and whistled on all the street corners. Then its popularity suddenly declined. Now, after half a century of oblivion, it was being revived to commemorate the centenary of the composer's birth.

Gomez, who may perhaps be described as an epigone of Verdi, was a curious example of musical cross-fertilization. Born in Brazil of Portuguese parents, he showed such early and remarkable promise that the Emperor, Don Pedro of Braganza, sent him to Italy to study music at the Milan Conservatorio. After becoming famous overnight with a revue in Milanese dialect, 'Se sa minga', he composed 'Guarany' at the age of twenty-one, and spent the rest of his life trying in vain, with a series of other operas, to live up to this first success.

The libretto of 'Guarany' is based on a novel of the same name by the Brazilian writer José de Aleucar. The scene is laid in Brazil, near Rio, about the year 1560. The action hinges on the love story of Pery, the young Indian chief, and Cecilia, the beautiful daughter of the Portuguese Governor. A gang of savage Indians and Spanish desperadoes plot to kidnap Cecilia and hold her for ransom; but Pery outwits them and rescues her, and the evil-doers are brought to justice.

The music is easy and tuneful, if little more, and the opera as a whole shows that Gomez had a true dramatic instinct. The rôle of Pery is not without difficulty, being based almost entirely on the top vocal register. Our production, which included Attilia Archi, Mario Basiola and Giacomo Vaghi as well as myself, and was brilliantly conducted by Serafin, had its *première* on April 15th, 1937.

In May I went on a brief *tournée* to Budapest, Vienna and London. Back in Milan, where I was joining the Scala company for their June visit to Berlin and Munich, I sang in three concerts: a Goethe memorial concert celebrating the 150th anniversary of the poet's stay in Milan, with an appropriate programme consisting of selections from 'Faust', 'Mefistofele' and 'Mignon'; a factory concert—my first—in the Savoia-Marchetti plant at Sesto Calende; and a Gomez centenary concert at the Scala, in which my partner was Lina Pagliughi, the girl I had heard singing on the San Francisco ferry boat in 1923.

The words 'triumph' and 'unprecedented' tend to get threadbare, yet when I think back to the Scala opera season in Berlin and Munich in June, 1937, I can find no other terms to describe it. I sang in 'Aida' and Verdi's 'Requiem', both of them conducted by Victor de Sabata. In Munich, de Sabata was crowned with a laurel wreath. Hitler and Goebbels attended a performance of 'Aida' on the final evening of the Berlin season at the Deutsches Opernhaus; Gina Cigna and Ebe Stignani sang Aida and Amneris. I had seen plenty of enthusiastic German audiences before, but never quite such frantic delirium. At the end of each act the entire audience was on its feet, shouting and waving handkerchiefs. Hitler applauded tirelessly, and at the final curtain he sent enormous bouquets, tied with the national colours of Germany and Italy, to all the principal artists. This provoked the audience to new outbursts of applause. After the performance Goebbels gave a reception in the foyer of the theatre to the entire Scala company. Innumerable toasts were drunk to the Scala and its artists and the glory of Italian music. The members of the company subscribed thirty thousand marks towards the replacement of the Zeppelin *Hindenburg*, which had recently crashed in flames as it was about to land in New York.

On August 1st, 1937, I shared with Toti Dal Monte the privilege of founding a tradition which has since become world-famous—the summer season of open-air opera in the Baths of

Caracalla in Rome. The inaugural opera was 'Lucia di Lammermoor'.

Music for the masses in historic settings, under the calm sky of Italian summer nights—now that we are used to it, it seems such an obvious idea; yet it had never, apparently, occurred to anyone until a few years previously, when an orchestra conductor, Maestro Bernardino Molinari, began to organize symphonic concerts in the Basilica of Maxentiuso, overlooking the Roman Forum. The idea caught on quickly, and soon in the whole of Italy there was scarcely a Greek or Roman ruin, or even a presentable medieval piazza, that did not have its 'musical summer'.

The Caracalla opera season has proved the most flourishing of all these enterprises. Popular prices and a high artistic standard have combined to ensure its success. Every night throughout July and August, over twenty thousand people crowd into the majestic ruins of the baths which the Emperor Caracalla built in the third century A.D., on a scale of unparalleled magnificence, for the benefit of the citizens of Rome.

What was once the Caldarium, or Hot Room, is now the massive roofless stage, flanked by two monumental towers. The 'curtain' is formed by lights that prevent the public from seeing the changes of scenery in progress behind them; but scenery is in any case almost superfluous, for the ruins themselves can be made, by an imaginative use of lighting and a few basic properties, to produce almost any effect.

The acoustics at Caracalla, perhaps inevitably, fall something short of perfection. When one sings on the left side of the stage, there is a treacherous little breeze that carries one's voice away from the audience. In an opera house, a defect of this kind would torture me with worry; but at Caracalla it does not seem to matter. The Caracalla audience is lenient. It does not care too passionately about the tenor's B flat. It is content to sit among the ruins and the flowering oleander trees, and hear music wafted to it across the air of a balmy August night.

I was working harder than ever, so hard that I was losing weight rapidly—forty pounds in a single year! My film directors were visibly relieved. I was now, they assured me, 'much more photogenic'.

In August 1937 I at last achieved a long-treasured dream.

I organized a 'musical summer' of my own in Porto Recanati. The new stadium—the 'Arena Beniamino Gigli'—lent itself admirably to open-air opera; and helped by Umberto Giordano, I produced and sang in a series of performances of 'Andrea Chénier', with artists, chorus and orchestra from the Scala company. Giordano conducted, and the venture was such a success that I decided to make it an annual event.

I spent October in Rome, making a film—my fifth!—at Cinecittà; and in November and December I gave eighteen recitals in England, Ireland and Scotland. This left me only a fortnight to learn the two new rôles in which I was shortly to appear at the Rome Opera: Fritz Kobus in Mascagni's 'L'Amico Fritz', and Lionetto in Cilea's 'La Gloria'.

'L'Amico Fritz', in which I made my début—with Licia Albanese as Suzel and Vincenzo Bellezza conducting—on December 23rd, 1937, was to become my favourite Mascagni opera. Mascagni wrote it in 1891, as a kind of protest against the critics who had hinted that half the success of his first work, 'Cavalleria Rusticana', was due to the magnificently dramatic story by Verga which had supplied the libretto. For his second opera he was determined to find a modest, undemanding plot that would provide an unobtrusive background for the music, and no more. He explained this one day, in the train between Naples and Cerignola, to the music publisher Sonzogno. 'Here,' said Sonzogno, taking a booklet out of his pocket, 'have a look at this.' It was a sentimental farce called 'L'Amico Fritz'. Mascagni read it at once and declared with enthusiasm that it was exactly what he needed.

With one-dimensional characters and an almost non-existent plot, 'L'Amico Fritz' was undoubtedly a contrast to the powerful drama of 'Cavalleria'. It belongs rather to the *genre* of idyllic comedies such as 'L'Elisir d'Amore' and 'Don Pasquale'. The music is an unbroken flow of melody; I found it perfectly suited to my voice.

On Christmas Day, 1937, in a concert—the first of its kind—broadcast by Radio Vaticana over a network of thirty European and American stations, and entirely devoted to the music of Lorenzo Perosi, I sang Don Perosi's latest work 'Natalitia', a cantata for tenor, choir and orchestra.

There were some notable revivals at the Rome Opera that

season: 'Fedora', in which I sang with Giuseppina Cobelli, and 'Mefistofele', with the great bass Nazzareno De Angelis in the title-rôle. It was the first time he had consented to sing in public since the tragic death of his wife ten years previously.

On January 15th, 1938, I made my début in Francesco Cilea's 'La Gloria', which had not been heard in Rome since its first performance there in 1909, and which Cilea had completely revised in the meantime. It is a somewhat wooden story of fourteenth-century Siena.

Cilea was present at the *première*—shy, more than a little deaf, and terrified of the limelight. The applause was tremendous; there were thirty-one curtain calls altogether, and I was very glad for Cilea's sake that the revival proved such a success, but privately I could not help wondering why. Undoubtedly it was well sung—the cast included Maria Caniglia, Tito Gobbi and Armando Borgioli; and there is melody and passion in the second act. On the whole, however, the score seemed to me greatly inferior to that of Cilea's other operas, 'L'Arlesiana' and 'Adriana Lecouvreur'.

This 1938 season, both in Rome and at the Scala, was, I think, exceptionally brilliant. I can recall several productions for which even the most jaundiced critics had nothing but praise. In Rome there was 'Un Ballo in Maschera', with Gina Cigna and Armando Borgioli as well as myself; 'La Bohéme', in which I sang with Licia Albanese; Verdi's 'Requiem' with Maria Caniglia, Ebe Stignani and Nazzareno De Angelis as the other soloists; and 'La Gioconda', in which Gina Cigna sang incomparably. In Milan there was 'Marta' with Mafalda Favero, 'Lucia di Lammermoor' with Lina Pagliughi, and 'Aida' with Gina Cigna—a production which several critics declared to be the best 'Aida' ever heard at the Scala.

My last memory of Hitler dates from the time of his state visit to Italy in 1938. The Governor of Rome, Prince Colonna, gave a reception for him in the Capitol on the afternoon of May 6th. The pomp and splendour of the costumes and uniforms, fanfares and parades, far outshone anything that had been staged for Goering. The Piazza del Campidoglio was a mass of pink and white azaleas. Hitler drove up with the King in the royal carriage; then, alighting, he gave his arm to the Queen, and they led the *cortège* through the magnificent rooms, ablaze with lights and

A proud moment in my life. I am presented to Queen Elizabeth II at the 1952 Royal Command Variety Performance in London. On my right is Maurice Chevalier

A snapshot taken of me with two of my brothers, Abramo and Catervo

Sing: Certainly, anywhere: even on Dover station upon my arrival in Britain for my 1954 tour

fragrant with thousands of roses and Madonna lilies, to the Salone Giulio Cesare, where Maria Caniglia and I sang for them. I began with '*E lucevan le stelle*' and ended with Di Capua's '*Aria Napoletana*', while her programme included excerpts from 'Aida' and 'La Bohème'.

There is a reference to this occasion in the recently-published memoirs of Hitler's valet. Hitler, it seems, thought the pageantry utter nonsense, and was bored to death by the entire proceedings. He was also extremely annoyed because the Italian royal family sat with him in the front row at the concert, while Ribbentrop and other Nazi leaders were relegated to the row behind. Altogether, the Führer had nothing but contempt for the Italians who thought—however mixed the feelings of some of them may have been—that they were doing him honour.

In June 1938 I returned to London for a four-week season of Italian opera at Covent Garden, directed by Vittorio Gui. It was my first Covent Garden appearance for seven years. I sang in 'Rigoletto' with Lina Pagliughi, who was making her London début; in 'Tosca' with Iva Pacetti; and in 'La Bohème' with Lisa Perli. I also sang at a reception given by the Italian Ambassador, Dino Grandi, for the Duke and Duchess of Gloucester.

It was during a performance of 'La Bohème', on June 13th, that I acquired a reputation as a fireman. Rodolfo and Marcello, shivering in the garret, decide to light the stove. I stuffed it with a bundle of old newspapers, struck a match, and shut the little door. Then I sang on. Mimi arrived; I took her hand, and had got about half-way through '*Che gelida manina*' when I heard a loud crackling noise coming from inside the stove. My eye travelled along the pipe, which extended almost to the footlights; it was spouting flames and smoke in the direction of the audience. Still singing, I took the bottle of water which was standing on the table in readiness for me to sprinkle on Mimi's face when she fainted, and emptied it on the leaping flames inside the stove; its only effect was a momentary splutter.

The situation was plainly serious, but I was determined that the performance should not be interrupted. I had not yet finished my aria; approaching the wings, I sang out '*Please fire, Please fire, Please fire*', in tune and time with the orchestra. Someone handed me a jug of water, but it proved as inadequate as the bottle had done. Meanwhile the audience was behaving with admirable calm; some people were smiling, and once I smiled back, but no one stirred. Mimi began her song '*Si, mi chiamano Mimi*', but I paid no attention to her. I was back at the wings, pleading 'Water! More water!' This time an immense bucket was produced, and I finally managed to quench the flames. The episode was safely over, and there had not been a single break in the continuity of the music. Next morning the *Daily Herald* had a headline: 'Gigli Puts Fire Into "La Bohème"!'

In Milan, during the spring of 1938, I had made a recording for His Master's Voice of the whole of 'La Bohème', with Licia Albanese; and in July, while singing at Caracalla in the evenings, I spent four afternoons making a recording of 'Tosca'. The recording took place, not in a studio, but on the stage of the Rome Opera; the conductor, Oliviero De Fabritiis—a Puccini specialist—felt that this would ensure greater theatrical authenticity.

The recording of an opera takes much longer than a straight performance; every passage is registered four or five times, or more if necessary, in order to reach perfection. We were about a third of the way through when the soprano, Iva Pacetti, suddenly collapsed. The doctor ordered her three days' rest, a delay which would have upset our arrangements hopelessly, because there was a four-day time-limit on our use of the opera house, and this was already the second day. I rushed off with Fred Gaisberg of H.M.V. to get Maria Caniglia. It was a hot afternoon, and we found her taking a siesta. Almost before she had wakened up properly, she was standing at the microphone on the stage of the Teatro dell'Opera. Of course, we had to start the recording all over again; but we managed to finish it on time.

The Manhattan skyline had changed a little in six and a half years; and so, no doubt, had I. 'Gatti's Gone So Gigli's Back, Forty-Two Pounds Lighter' was the headline that greeted me in the *New York Post* when, at the beginning of October, 1938, I stepped off the *Rex* on my first return visit since I left the Metropolitan.

It was good to find a telegram from Mayor La Guardia welcoming me to New York; but I had about thirty-five engagements to fulfil all over the United States before I could avail myself of his welcome.

First of all there was to be Gaetano Merola's opera season in

San Francisco and Los Angeles. I stopped at Detroit on the way, to make a broadcast for the Ford Motor Company, with the Detroit Symphony Orchestra under Eugene Ormandy. This broadcast was important for me. It was my first contact with the American public after a long absence. Would my old friends remember me, I wondered? And the people who had never heard me before—would they be interested? The response was reassuring; I got enthusiastic letters from several thousand listeners. And Samuel Chotzinoff wrote in the New York *Evening Post:* 'Mr. Gigli definitely belongs to opera, and it is to be hoped that the Met will let bygones be bygones and take advantage of the singer's return, in the interests of Verdi, Donizetti and Massenet. There appears to be no tenor better qualified by nature at the moment to cope with the suavities and elegances of the music of these masters.'

It was pleasant, on arriving in San Francisco, to find a new opera house and old friends. The War Memorial Opera House was on the small side, but its acoustics were excellent. I saw it as a monument to the courage and imagination of Gaetano Merola, the founder of San Francisco's now firmly-established operatic tradition and, happily, still its moving spirit. I greatly enjoyed meeting him again; and I also enjoyed my reunion with another, still older friend, no longer cook but *chef* and restaurant proprietor —Giovanni Zerri.

I sang on the opening night, with Elisabeth Rethberg, in 'Andrea Chénier'—the very rôle in which I had opened Maestro Merola's first season in 1923. The critics were kind enough to say that they liked me even better this time. I also sang in 'Marta' with Mafalda Favero, in 'La Bohème' and in 'La Forza del Destino'; in a benefit concert at the Civic Auditorium for the San Francisco Symphony Pension Fund; and in 'Andrea Chénier' at the Shrine Auditorium in Los Angeles.

At a party in Hollywood given by the voice teacher Dr. Marafioti—an old friend of Caruso's and owner of a wonderful collection of Caruso souvenirs—I met a number of former Metropolitan colleagues who had now settled down in the movie capital and were working there. I got several screen offers myself, but saw no possibility of accepting any of them. Where would I find the time?

Then came two and a half months of zigzagging back and forth across the continent, giving recitals, greeting old friends and making new ones. I worked my way northwards up the Pacific coast from Pasadena, through Portland, Oregon, to Spokane, Seattle and Vancouver; then across Canada to Toronto and Montreal, down through New England, New York, New Jersey, Pittsburgh and Washington to New Orleans and over to Havana; then back in another sweep through Texas, Colorado and Michigan. Half-way along, I had spent a week in Chicago, singing with the Chicago City Opera in 'Marta' and 'Aida'.

It was not only the Manhattan skyline that had changed. I felt increasingly, in the course of this long recital tour, that the musical knowledge and taste of the American public were changing and evolving. No doubt this was due to the influence of the radio; whatever the cause, I found it very encouraging.

Meanwhile I had arranged with Edward Johnson, general manager of the Metropolitan since Gatti-Casazza's retirement a few years previously, to give five performances there during January and February 1939.

It was unexpectedly touching to be back in New York, to be constantly recognized in the street by total strangers and greeted with a friendly 'Hello, Mr. Gigli!'. I enjoyed meeting my old trainer, H. J. Reilly, and being complimented by him on my new slim figure—achieved, as I did not fail to point out, entirely without the aid of the diabolical contrivances he considered so necessary to one's physical well-being.

There were sad moments too, as when I went to visit Antonio Scotti or Pasquale Amato, once my seniors at the Metropolitan, great names in their day, but now retired from the stage. They had lost every cent in the Depression. Amato managed to eke out a living by teaching singing in American schools; Scotti depended on the generosity of friends. In both cases it seemed a hard fate after a lifetime of hard work, a pitiful anti-climax to an illustrious career.

I returned to the Metropolitan on January 23rd, 1939. The opera was 'Aida', which I had never sung in New York before; the other soloists were Elisabeth Rethberg, Bruna Castagna and Carlo Tagliabue, the conductor Ettore Panizza. Every seat was occupied, and there was a full complement of 'standees'. To face this Met audience once again, after all that had happened, was admittedly a nervous and emotional ordeal for me. I felt some tension as I embarked on '*Celeste Aida*', but I regained confidence quickly as the aria carried me forward, and the wild ovation that greeted my final B flat brought tears to my eyes. So the New Yorkers were faithful to me. It was a wonderful moment.

When the fourth act ended, and I emerged from the tomb in which I had been buried alive with Aida, to face the light, not of day but of the Met chandeliers, the scene was overwhelming. I had endless curtain calls; I gave up counting them. The entire audience was on its feet, clapping, stamping, shouting, howling. In my whole life, I have had few experiences as joyful or as heartwarming as that welcome back to the Metropolitan.

'More Mature in Voice, the Great Tenor Gets a Carusoesque Reception'—thus the headline of Samuel Chotzinoff's article in the *Evening Post*. The critics, as usual, had their little reservations, but on the whole they were generous. On a few points they all agreed: my voice, they said, had lost some of its 'sweetness' and 'lush freshness', but had gained in range, in variety of expression, in artistry and in dramatic power. Well, I thought, it was not a verdict that I could quarrel with.

The critics liked me better in the other operas I sang—'Tosca', 'Lucia di Lammermoor', and 'Rigoletto'—and no doubt they were right; I was fully aware that no matter how hard I strove for perfection in the rôle of Radames, it could never be completely congenial to my voice.

Each one of those five evenings at the Metropolitan was an emotional upheaval for me. I realized what an integral part of my life it had been—more than any other single opera house, my spiritual home. I felt love in my heart for the wonderful audience. Yet at the same time I felt melancholy because my contemporaries were scattered, and there were so many new faces in the corridors. I was growing older, and the past could not be recaptured nor reconstructed. I had chosen to make my life elsewhere. Regrets were useless. All the same, I told myself, it was just as well that my passage was already booked, that I was giving only five performances at the Met. A few more, and the roots that I had pulled up in 1932 would start entwining themselves afresh around those ugly yellow brick walls at the corner of Broadway and West 40th Street.

CHAPTER XVI

THE FRONTIERS CLOSE—BUT OPEN AGAIN

For me, as for so many millions of people, 1939 was the end of an epoch. As a singer, I was called on to make so few sacrifices, compared to those of others, that it would ill become me to dwell on the repercussions that six years of relative immobility and isolation were to have on my career. I feel that I cannot ask the reader to accompany me step by step, from concert hall to opera houses and back to concert hall, through those tragic years of massacre and destruction. I did what I could in the way of benefit recitals and performances for the troops; and, of course, the opera house carried on as normally as possible. In their own way, they were rendering a service; the need for music is perhaps deeper in time of war than at any other. But the details of my doings, so far removed from the mainstream of world events, would make, I fear, a tedious chronicle.

When I think back to 1939, I remember how happily it began for me, with my return visit to the Metropolitan. The first shadow fell before I left New York, when I learned of the death of Pope Pius XI, to whom I had been profoundly devoted. The American Cardinals Dougherty and Mundelein were fellow-passengers on the boat to Naples; they were coming to Rome to attend the Conclave. During the voyage, at a solemn Requiem Mass for the dead Pope, I sang excerpts from Verdi's 'Requiem'.

The six or seven 'normal' months that followed seem to have got telescoped in my memory, as though they had been impelled in a headlong rush towards the fatal September. March was devoted to a concert tour of the British Isles. I developed influenza, and at the last recital, on April 2nd in the Albert Hall, I sang with a temperature of 102°. I had to change my clothes from head to feet three times during the evening, each time spreading layers of paper under my shirt, in an effort to keep my chest dry; even so, I had to give up before the end. I felt so sorry to disappoint my public that I hurried back to London, after a short opera season in Rome and Milan, to give another Albert Hall concert at the beginning of May.

The Covent Garden season in May and June that year was exceptionally brilliant. I sang in 'Tosca' with Gina Cigna and Mario Basiola, in 'Traviata' with Maria Caniglia and Basiola, and in 'Aida' with Maria Caniglia and Ebe Stignani. This last production was conducted by Sir Thomas Beecham, the other two by Vittorio Gui. Never in my experience of Covent Garden had there been such harmony between conductor, soloists, chorus and orchestra. As I said good-bye, I already found myself looking forward to 'next year'; but seven years were to pass before I could return.

Maria Caniglia and Ebe Stignani were my partners again, later that summer, in 'La Forza del Destino' and 'Aida' at Caracalla. There, too, the season had what in retrospect appears like a before-the-deluge splendour. Mussolini came often, sometimes with important foreign guests, sometimes in one of the cheapest seats, alone and incognito until the first interval. By the following year the black-out had descended on the ruins and the oleanders, and the Egyptian trumpets were silenced. When they sounded again, in 1946, it was to an audience of khaki-clad Allied soldiers and somewhat threadbare Romans.

World events tended to dim the importance of private anniversaries; nevertheless, it was with some emotion that I appeared on the stage of the Teatro Sociale in Rovigo, towards the end of October 1939, to celebrate my silver jubilee as a singer. Exactly a quarter of a century had elapsed since the night when, on that same stage, full of apprehension about the final B flat in '*Cielo e Mar*', I had made my début. This time the opera was 'Lucia di Lammermoor'; it had not been possible to arrange for a performance of 'La Gioconda'. I had often told myself that twenty-five years of public singing would be enough, and that my silver jubilee would be the proper moment to say farewell to the stage; but now that I had attained this date, the notion seemed ridiculous. I felt in full possession of my powers, far more so than on that October night of 1914. Moreover, I had received no hint that my audiences thought otherwise. There seemed, all things considered, to be no good reason for retiring. What would I do with myself all day? My estate in Recanati gave me great pleasure, but I had never had time to learn much about the running of it; that was safely in the hands of experts, and for me it had remained something of a toy. As long as I continued to have voice and strength, life without singing did not seem conceivable. I put the thought away from me.

On December 9th, 1939, at the Rome Opera House, I made my début in Verdi's 'Il Trovatore', with Maria Caniglia, Ebe Stignani, Gino Bechi and Italo Tajo. The conductor was Oliviero De Fabritiis. The rôle of Manrico is *lirico spinto* to an even greater degree than that of Radames in 'Aida'; from beginning to end I had to sing with my diaphragm, a feat which in earlier years I would not have attempted. Some of the top notes required of the tenor verge dangerously close on mere vocal exhibitionism. In other ways, however, the rôle of Manrico is an attractive one, full of romantic fervour and love for humanity. I did my best to interpret it as I think Verdi intended—I tried, in other words, not to shout it, but to sing it.

It was now, of course, more or less impossible to go abroad, and I spent the whole of 1940 singing in opera and concerts all over Italy. There were some notable revivals, such as 'La Rondine' with Mafalda Favero and 'Loreley' with Gina Cigna—both of these in Rome, early in January; and later that same month, 'Adriana Lecouvreur' at the Teatro La Fenice in Venice. There was an excellent production of 'La Forza del Destino' at the Scala in February, with Gina Cigna, Armando Borgioli, and Tancredo Pasero as well as myself; there was 'Lohengrin' in Trieste with Pia Tassinari, and 'La Favorita' at the San Carlo in Naples.

April brought me back to the Scala in two new rôles: Dufresne in Leoncavallo's 'Zaza', with Mafalda Favero, on April 26th, and Giovanni Riada in 'Maristella', a little-known opera by Giuseppe Pietri, on April 27th. Both of these must be described as minor works, and I had no occasion to repeat either of them after that one season at the Scala; but each in its different way had melodic charm and achieved a satisfactory, if modest, success. 'Zaza' had not been heard in Milan since its world *première* forty years previously, when Rosina Storchio had sung the title-rôle and Toscanini conducted. The libretto—a story of youthful romance in Paris—was written by Leoncavallo himself. 'Maristella' dated, like 'Zaza', from the beginning of the century. It had already been performed in Milan two years previously, at the Castello Sforzesco, but this—in the presence of the composer—was its baptism at the Scala. It is a charming story of life in Naples, based on some verses by the great Neapolitan dialect poet, Salvatore Di Giacomo. I found the tenor rôle extremely congenial to my voice, full of beautiful melodic phrases, and with one lovely aria, '*Maristella*', which I promptly added to my concert repertory.

October 26th, 1940, was the fiftieth anniversary of the *première* of 'Cavalleria Rusticana'. Twenty-five years previously, at the San Carlo in Naples, I had sung the rôle of Turiddu on the occasion of its silver jubilee. It was now my pleasure and my privilege to sing the same rôle in the jubilee performance, conducted by Mascagni himself, at the Teatro Comunale in Florence. The other soloists were Bruna Rasa and Carlo Tagliabue. Mascagni's one-act opera 'Zanetto', which is set in Renaissance Florence, was given as a curtain-raiser. It was a great evening for the illustrious and venerable maestro—perhaps the supreme moment of his career; and I was very proud that he should have asked me to share it.

Italy had entered the war in June, 1940; and it was perhaps with the desire to strike a suitable note of austerity that the directors of the Scala chose Donizetti's opera 'Poliuto' for the opening night of their first wartime season, December 26th, 1940.

Based on a text of rare nobility and grandeur—the tragic drama 'Polyeucte' by the great French seventeenth-century poet Pierre Corneille—'Poliuto' reproduces the Cornelian conflicts between love and duty, between one duty and another, in a musical exaltation of Christian martyrdom. The action takes place at Mytilene in Armenia, in A.D. 257.

Written in 1838, 'Poliuto' is of particular interest because it shows us such an unfamiliar aspect of Donizetti; it was not, however, destined to achieve the popularity of his comic masterpieces. Never performed frequently, its last previous appearance in Italy had been at the Costanzi in Rome, under Mascagni's baton, in 1904.

The Scala production did the fullest possible justice to Donizetti's music. I sang the title-rôle, and Maria Caniglia sang Paolina. Tancredo Pasero and Gino Bechi were the other soloists, and the conductor was Gino Marinuzzi. It was a triumphant success. Yet despite this success, I have never heard of any other opera house—with the solitary exception of Rome, where I sang in a few performances in December, 1942—undertaking to produce it since. Do opera-house managers cling to the conviction that the public wants nothing but comedy or romantic melodrama? No one could believe this who had witnessed the acclaim with which the Scala audience greeted 'Poliuto'.

I had been eager to sing the rôle of Federico in Francesco Cilea's opera 'L'Arlesiana' ever since my first meeting with Cilea, in Palermo in 1915; but I had to wait twenty-six years for the opportunity to come my way. It was not until February 3rd, 1941, at the Rome Opera House, with Gianna Pederzini, Rosa Mamai and Tito Gobbi, that I finally made my début in this appealing rustic opera. When 'L'Arlesiana' was first performed, in 1897, at the Teatro Lirico in Milan, an unknown young tenor named Enrico Caruso created the rôle of Federico.

The culminating moment of the tenor rôle, and perhaps of the whole opera, is the beautiful '*Lamento di Federico*' in the second act. I had the privilege of spending many hours going over the score with Maestro Cilea, and in particular studying the way in which this famous aria should be sung. Some critics afterwards reproached me for introducing into the concluding phrase of the aria a B natural which they could not find in the score. I did it with Cilea's full consent. Federico is expressing all the pent-up sorrow of his life; I felt convinced that this called for a dramatic *crescendo* at the end of the aria, not a lyrical fading-away. '*Mi fai tanto male—ahimè!*' No, I could *not* let my voice trail off on that *ahimè*! I had to sing a B natural if I was to sing it at all. Cilea not only came round to my point of view; he told me that he liked it much better than what he had written himself. The audience seemed to like it too, for they invariably demanded an encore.

In April 1941 I spent a week in Berlin, singing in 'Un Ballo in Maschera' and 'L'Elisir d'Amore' at the Charlottenburg Opera House, and giving benefit concerts for the Red Cross and other charities. In May I took part in the annual Florentine music festival, the 'Maggio Fiorentino', with 'La Bohème', 'Un Ballo in Maschera' again, and a new rôle—Franco Alfano's 'Don Juan de Manara'.

This opera had not been heard since it was first performed at the Scala in 1913. It belongs to Alfano's best period, and he understandably refused to resign himself to its initial failure. He worked on it for many years, revising and rewriting it; it was this new version that we gave in Florence. On two points at least I can claim some small share in the revision. I was able to study the score of 'Don Juan de Manara' with Alfano, as I had studied 'L'Arlesiana' with Cilea; and I drew the composer's attention to the difficulties I encountered in singing the rôle as he had written it. The first difficulty was the *recitative*. The half-sung half-spoken dialogue of grand opera is normally confined to the middle notes of the vocal register; but Alfano wrote his *recitative* as though it were an aria, full of A flats and B flats and grace notes. I thought this absurd, and as we were friends, I took the liberty of telling him so. He finally agreed to bring all my *recitatives* in 'Don Juan de Manara' back to the normal middle register.

Another point on which I had some discussion with Alfano was the duet between tenor and soprano in the second act. I felt certain that the music would be much more effective if the soprano were left out of it, and the duet transformed into an aria for the tenor. Here, too, I succeeded in convincing him; and on the night of the *première*, my aria '*Tu Verdi in un bel ciel*' won, I think, more applause than anything else.

There was, however, plenty of applause all round on the evening of May 28th, 1941, at the Teatro Comunale in Florence—applause for Iva Pacetti, Gino Bechi and Italo Tajo; for Serafin, who had taken his usual infinite pains with the orchestration; and for Alfano himself, the composer whose twenty-eight years of faith in his own work were at last justified and rewarded. For the revival of 'Don Juan de Manara' was more than a success, it was a triumph. Yet here, as with a number of other operas, the question remains: Why, if this opera was such a success, have we never heard it since? Why has it not become popular?

In the case of 'Don Juan de Manara', I think that the explanation is not far to seek. While possessing qualities to win the appreciation and enthusiasm of a musically sophisticated, highly discriminating public such as that of the 'Maggio Fiorentino', it lacks the elements necessary to give it a wider and more lasting popular appeal. It is the story, based on historical fact, of a reformed libertine—reformed, indeed, to such a degree that he becomes a saint. The trouble is that we have to take his libertinism on trust; as we see him, he is reformed from the very start. There is no conflict, no situation, no drama worth speaking of; there is very little vitality. From the first raising of the curtain to its final descent, this Don Juan marches steadily forward on the path of virtue. In 'Poliuto', sanctity is won only after a tremendous struggle; here it is too easily come by. One is forced to admit that Alfano's opera, like its hero, is a little dull.

In July 1941 I visited Croatia for the first and last time. I sang 'Aida' in Zagreb and 'La Traviata' in Ljubljana. Afterwards I returned to Rome to make a film; and the rest of the year, until December, was devoted to fairly routine opera throughout Italy.

In Rome, on December 3rd, I took part in a performance of Mozart's 'Requiem'. It was held, not in a theatre, but in the superbly appropriate setting of the Basilica of Santa Maria degli Angeli, the beautiful church which Michelangelo, with a few masterly architectonic gestures, conjured out of the ruined Baths of Diocletian. Victor de Sabata conducted—brilliantly and movingly, I thought. The critics, however, were of a different opinion. They reproached De Sabata with too slow a *tempo*; and as for me, they did not mince words. Let me abandon, they said, once and for all, the mistaken notion that I was capable of singing Mozart.

They liked me better in 'Carmen'; and no doubt they were right. Never in all my career did I throw myself so completely into any rôle as I did into that of Don José—at any rate on the night of the dress rehearsal. No audience has ever heard me sing it as I sang it then; but the critics were there, and some of them—oh miracle !—wept.

That night I was carried away, inspired. I lost myself in the rôle. It was all so true, so close to the core of human passion, that I had no need to act. I was really in love with Carmen, tortured by jealousy of Carmen, consumed with longing for Carmen. By the time we got to the tremendous scene in the fourth act when Don José begs, entreats Carmen to come away with him—'*Sì, Carmen, sì, c'è tempo ancora*'—and she refuses, I had lost all recollection of the tenor Beniamino Gigli. I *was* Don José. Love and despair welled up from my heart and almost choked me. I had tears in my eyes and a lump in my throat. I trembled all over. Finally I broke down. The emotion was too much; singing had become impossible.

Offstage, friends revived me with brandy and told me that everyone who had heard me was weeping. I managed somehow to get to the end of the performance; but I realized that there is a point beyond which a singer must not lose himself in a rôle. For actors it may be different, but one cannot sing when one is choking with tears.

With Gianna Pederzini as Carmen and Serafin conducting, the *première*—on December 23rd, 1941—was of course a success all round; but I could not allow myself, then or at any time since, to recapture the pathos of the dress rehearsal.

The emotional control I had learned in 'Carmen' proved useful when a few months later, on April 7th, 1942, I sang in 'I Pagliacci' at the Rome Opera House; for it is almost as fatally easy to let oneself be carried away by the rôle of Canio as by that of Don José. With a kind of animal instinct of self-preservation, I had always refused this highly dramatic rôle—a favourite of Caruso's—when Gatti-Casazza proposed it to me at the Metropolitan. At that time I felt it would put too great a strain on my voice. But in 1934 I had ventured to make a recording of it; and the fact that I now felt able to sing it in public gave me conclusive proof that my voice was stronger than it had ever been before.

In self-defence, singers must sometimes be on their guard against the imprudent proposals of managers and impresarios. The latter are interested in immediate results, while the singer has to think far ahead. Unsuitable rôles can cause permanent damage to both voice and career. Toti Dal Monte is a case in point. In 1918, when I sang with her in 'Lodoletta', she had a beautiful lyric soprano voice, perfect for the romantic heroines of 'La Traviata' and 'La Bohème'. Her impresarios, however, persuaded her that her imposing physique would be somewhat incongruous in these fragile rôles, and they urged her to turn to other operas—'Il Barbiere di Siviglia', 'Rigoletto', 'Lakme', 'La Sonnambula'—where the heroine is not supposed to be a consumptive.

This meant that she had to force her voice into the mould of a *coloratura* soprano, and as such she achieved world fame; her greatest rôle of all was Lucia di Lammermoor. Then, after enduring the strain for years, her vocal cords finally slackened, and she found herself unable to sing *coloratura* any longer. Her natural, lyric soprano voice was still intact, but her impresarios clamoured only for 'Lucia', and to the consternation of the public, she suddenly vanished into premature retirement.

Another point on which I had always stood firm was my refusal to sing the operas of Rossini. The fact that Rossini came from my own province of Marche—he was a native of Pesaro, which is only a little further up the Adriatic coast from Recanati —did not blind me to the fact that his operas were not suited to my temperament. It seemed to me that in all of them, with the possible exception of 'Guglielmo Tell', he treated the tenor as a kind of spineless *coloratura* soprano.

When the directors of the 'Maggio Fiorentino' festival asked me to sing in Rossini's 'Messa Solenne', I told myself that I did not need to object to his religious music as much as I did to his operas; nevertheless, it was only with reluctance that I finally agreed. Having once accepted, I of course did my best; all the same, I was rather surprised that my singing at the *première*, on May 7th, 1942, at the Teatro Comunale in Florence, should inspire the critics to shower me with their most gracious compliments. I thought I sang Mozart's 'Requiem' rather well, and hey had detested it; but in Rossini's music, which I felt myself temperamentally so unsuited to interpret, they found my voice 'divine'.

The year 1943 brought great upheavals in Italy: the Allied landings, the fall of Mussolini, the armistice, the German occupation, the Partisans, the Resistance movement. I had never been able to make head or tail of politics, and I felt so bewildered by all these happenings that I would have liked nothing better than to stay quietly in Recanati until the war was over.

However, it was plainly not a time for following one's personal inclinations. The country was rent asunder; the South was cut off by a barrier of fire and steel; Milan and Turin had been shattered by bombardments; in every town and village of Italy, death walked the streets.

Opera was certainly far removed from most people's thoughts, and indeed in most places it had become an anachronism. The Scala lay in ruins, a burned-out shell. For this very reason, the Rome Opera House had to carry on. It was entreated to do so by hundreds of people, not only from Rome but from all over Italy, who depended on opera for their livelihood. Orchestra, chorus, scene-shifters, electricians, call-boys—all of them needed opera if they were to feed their families. The soloists were not, for the most part, in financial straits, but obviously there could be no opera without them. The directors of the Rome Opera appealed to those of us who were available—Maria Caniglia, Tito Gobbi, myself, others. I could see no good reason for refusing the appeal.

And so, not only was there an opera season during that strange, tragic winter of 1943–44 in the 'Open City'; it was a season of unprecedented length—over seven months. From November 1943 to June 1944, I sang in 'Aida', 'Lohengrin', 'La Traviata', 'Mefistofele', 'Manon', 'Fedora', 'Tosca', 'Un Ballo in Maschera'. The sound of the Allied artillery grew closer every day, and we still sang on. It would, I suppose, have been difficult to find a more wildly inappropriate opera for the evening of June 2nd, 1944, than 'Un Ballo in Maschera'. We ended at 1 a.m. on the morning of June 3rd. By eight o'clock the German occupation troops were in flight, and twenty-four hours later the Fifth Army entered Rome.

Having 'sung for the Germans', I now discovered, to my astonishment, that I was a traitor. The accusation did not come from the Allies, but from my own countrymen. Threatening crowds besieged my house in Rome; for months I did not dare to leave it.

One day an English officer came to investigate. 'Of course I sang for the Germans,' I told him. 'I sang for everyone. I sang for the English and for the Americans. I sang under the Fascist government, as I would have sung under the Bolsheviks or anyone else that happened to be ruling Italy. I don't see how that makes me a traitor. Do you?' He laughed, and went away.

This unpleasant situation lasted for about nine months. By the spring of 1945, things were calmer. I began to appear in public again. On March 12th I sang at a concert in the Teatro Adriano, in aid of the refugees. Many people asked me afterwards, 'When are you coming back to the Opera?' To myself I thought 'I'll wait till I'm asked'. I did not have to wait long.

On May 5th, 1945, after an absence of eleven months, I returned to the Rome Opera House in 'La Forza del Destino'. On May 10th, emboldened by the memory of my success in the 'Messa Solenne', I sang in another of Rossini's religious works, the 'Stabat Mater', at the Accademia di Santa Cecilia. At the end of

June I sang 'La Bohème' at the San Carlo, and had my first glimpse of a sadly bomb-scarred, war-worn Naples. In July I sang 'I Pagliacci' in Rome, and gave a concert in aid of the Partisans. In August I visited Sardinia for the first time, and sang 'La Bohème' in Cagliari.

The Teatro Bellini in Catania is, in my opinion, the most beautiful and acoustically the most perfect opera house in the world, acoustically more perfect even than the San Carlo, more beautiful even than the Fenice. Its colours and proportions are blended in a harmony that I could never tire of contemplating. To walk on to its stage was an experience that invariably filled me with delight.

I had already given a few performances there in April 1945, and I returned in the autumn, to make my début on November 8th as Pollione in Bellini's masterpiece 'Norma'. The rôle did not suit me very well, but for once I scarcely minded, and I cheerfully relinquished the greater part of the laurels to Maria Caniglia. To be singing a Bellini opera in Bellini's native city and, what was more, in my favourite of all opera houses—this alone was enough to make me happy. The past was past. The war was over. I felt at peace with myself and with the world.

The war was over and the world, it seemed, had not forgotten me. Frontiers were opening, and invitations to sing were pouring in from almost everywhere. I longed to meet my old audiences again, but as things turned out, my first post-war travels took me to a country that was completely new to me: Portugal. I spent the month of May 1946 in Lisbon, singing at the San Carlos and Rivoli theatres in 'La Forza del Destino', 'L'Amico Fritz', 'Norma' and 'Manon Lescaut'. After a few performances in Madrid, I then went to Switzerland for a month of concerts and opera.

I managed to find a little time that summer for Recanati. The war had spared my house, but there had been a constant stream of well-behaved visitors in my absence—Allied troops, who apparently considered it a kind of tourist curiosity.

I had planned a complete rest during my holiday, with no concerts anywhere but in Recanati itself. One invitation, however, I found myself unable to refuse. It was from Macerata, from the same Teatro Lauri Rossi which, forty-one years previously, had given me my first experience of the stage and the footlights, my

No! It is only mineral water—as my faithful friend and valet gives my hair a final brushing before I walk into the vastness of the Albert Hall

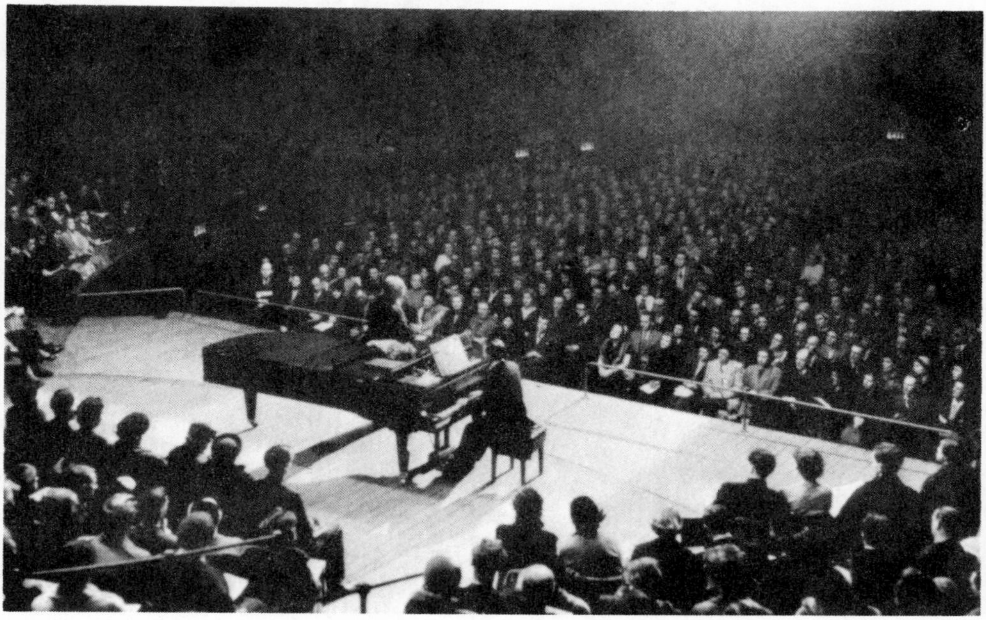

Back where I began, in my own Recanati, where I can play a peaceful game of bowls with my old friends . . .
. . . and relax

first audience, my first applause—the theatre in which I had sung Angelica.

The end of August saw me back in Spain. Apart from my brief visit to Madrid earlier that year, I had not faced Spanish audiences since my first tour abroad, in 1917. They were less critical of me this time; indeed, they unleashed such overwhelming enthusiasm on me that I almost felt as though I were a *torero* in the bull-ring. I did try to give some return for this enthusiasm; in fact, it was during this Spanish tour that I first achieved a feat of which I was rather proud. In Bilbao, in Barcelona and again in Madrid, I sang both 'Cavalleria Rusticana' and 'I Pagliacci' on the same evening. These two operas are of course often double-billed, so much so that in Italian they are familiarly known as '*Birra e gazzosa*', beer and soda-pop, which in Italy somehow go together (and in England as 'Cav Pag'), but I think it had been previously unheard-of for the same tenor to sing, on the same evening, in both. Managers and impresarios were rather pleased with this innovation of mine. It saved them money, because I sang two operas for the price of one.

After nine weeks in Spain, I went to England at the beginning of November 1946. With my daughter Rina, I sang 'La Bohème' at Covent Garden. Then I set off on a long, happy tour —the Midlands, Manchester, Scotland, Dublin, and three concerts at the Albert Hall, the last on December 15th. I found my old audiences and my old friends. I was fêted and applauded with wonderful generosity, and never the slightest reference to a war lost or won. If there could be a consolation for growing old, I thought, it was this—to have so many old friends.

CHAPTER XVII

AND SO, FAREWELL!

The year 1946 had ended happily with my return to the Albert Hall and Covent Garden; 1947 began auspiciously with my return to the Scala—now risen phoenix-like from its ashes—in 'Andrea Chénier' and 'Lucia di Lammermoor'.

I was almost fifty-seven, but I still felt myself to be at the summit of my powers, and was confident that I could remain there for several years to come. At the first sign of strain or fatigue, however, I would say good-bye; I was determined that there should be no decline. I wanted my audiences to remember me as I had endeavoured that they should always know me—at my best. My longevity as a tenor was already something of a phenomenon, but the combination of luck and prudence on which it was founded could not, I knew, prevail in the end against the inexorable laws of physiology. I had as yet no thoughts of retirement, but I had to face the fact that it lay ahead, and that I had now entered on the last lap of my career.

Communion with my audience —this was undoubtedly the most precious experience that I had found in my life as a singer. I decided that, in the active years remaining to me, it was this above all that I would seek. I decided not to learn any more new rôles—not more than one, anyhow; that would bring my repertory of operas, masses and oratorios up to an even sixty. I would concentrate on perfecting the rôles I knew already—nothing is ever perfect—and singing them as often as I could, to old audiences and new ones. I wanted as many people as possible to hear me and remember me.

I travelled so much during the next eight and a half years that any account of them will necessarily sound like a railway time-table; but since there may be some readers who like railway time-tables, I shall try to recapitulate them very briefly.

In mid-February 1947 I went to Lisbon, for a fortnight of

opera at the Teatro Coliseo—'La Gioconda', 'Manon', 'Aida', 'Cavalleria Rusticana' and 'I Pagliacci'. I gave a concert in Oporto, and then went to Spain for a month—'Manon', 'La Bohème' and 'Lucia di Lammermoor' in Seville and Madrid, concerts in Gibraltar and Cadiz.

In mid-April I went to Switzerland for a fortnight of concerts all over the country, and immediately afterwards left for a five-months' tour in South America, where I had not been since before the war. At the Colón in Buenos Aires, in Rosario, in Rio de Janeiro at the Municipal, in São Paulo, I found old audiences, old friends, the memory of old times; but I also went further afield, in search of new audiences, to La Plata in the Argentine, to Porto Alegre in Brazil, and to Montevideo. During this tour I sang in 'Aida', 'Tosca', 'Andrea Chénier', 'Cavalleria Rusticana' and 'La Forza del Destino'. I also gave four broadcast recitals, and many concerts.

The long return voyage served me in lieu of a holiday, and by the middle of November, 1947, I was off again: a six weeks' concert tour of England and Scotland, recitals in Paris, Brussels and Antwerp, a fortnight's tour of Switzerland—not even for the benefit of railway time-table enthusiasts can I bring myself to record all the towns in which I sang. Nor would there be any point in recording encores and ovations which readers who have followed me this far will be able to imagine. I will only say that I always got them. Sometimes I would wonder, a little anxiously, if my audiences were beginning to tire of me. Would there be any trace of *diminuendo* in the volume of applause? There never was.

I managed to give a few benefit concerts in Rome and a performance of 'Tosca' at the San Carlo while preparing for my next tour. I opened the season in Lisbon with 'Manon' on February 19th, 1948, and closed it with 'L'Elisir d'Amore' on May 6th. In Lisbon and Oporto, during those ten weeks, I sang in fifteen different operas.

Then came yet another Atlantic crossing, and on May 19th I was back at the Colón, beginning yet another five-month tour of South America with 'Adriana Lecouvreur'. As always, my itinerary was chiefly based on Buenos Aires, Rio de Janeiro and São Paulo; but this time again there were welcome innovations. I was grateful for the opportunity afforded me to sing in opera before the audiences in La Plata and Montevideo with which, the previous year, I had made contact only through concerts; and I was delighted to acquire an entirely new audience, at Santiago in Chile. Here, at the Teatro Municipal, I sang six operas during a three weeks' season which I gave in September.

Sad duties awaited me on my return to Rome, after nine months' absence, in November, 1948. Two dear, illustrious friends had recently died, and all that I could do was pay them my last tribute. The memorial concert for Umberto Giordano was held at the Accademia di Santa Cecilia on December 14th; I sang the '*Improvviso*' from 'Andrea Chénier', his opera that I had loved so much. Pietro Mascagni was commemorated on December 28th at the Hotel Plaza, where he had spent his last years; the Carabinieri band played the overtures to all his operas, and I sang the beautiful song '*Come col capo sotto l'ala bianca*', Flammen's aria '*Ah! ritrovarla nella sua capanna*' from 'Lodoletta', and '*Addio alla madre*' from 'Cavalleria Rusticana'.

The year 1949 began for me with 'Manon Lescaut' at the San Carlo. Then came a fortnight's tour of Switzerland and another fortnight in Belgium and Holland. After that I toured England and Scotland for almost two months, gave two recitals in Paris at the Théâtre de Chaillot, went south to sing at Marseilles and Monte Carlo, and then took a long rest—in a sleeping-car bound for Stockholm. I spent ten days in Scandinavia, giving concerts in Stockholm, Gothenburg, Oslo, Aarhus, Odense and Copenhagen; and with that my audience-hunger was, for the time being, sated. I went back to Recanati to do some sailing.

On August 10th, 1949 I sang 'Cavalleria Rusticana' and 'I Pagliacci' at the Baths of Caracalla—ten years, almost to the day, since I had last sung there in August, 1939. Nothing seemed to have changed; it was all as I remembered it—the oleanders, the endless sea of faces, the sweet-scented summer night. A war had come and gone, but the enchantment of Caracalla had not been lost.

September and October, 1949, were devoted to another extensive tour of the British Isles. I also gave one radio and one television concert for the BBC—my first television appearance. In November I went to Sicily for concerts and opera; then, for once, I spent a quiet Christmas with my grandchildren.

The New Year brought me a new continent—Africa. A traveller perforce, I was by inclination no tourist; all the same, I was glad to see the Pyramids. I spent February and half of

March, 1950, in Cairo and Alexandria, singing in concerts and opera—'Lucia' and 'Elisir' but not 'Aida'!

On leaving Egypt I plunged straight into a recital tour that began in Zurich, forced me to celebrate my sixtieth birthday in a train somewhere in Germany, and continued through Denmark, Sweden, Norway and Holland, ending on April 15th, 1950, in Berlin.

I had not seen Berlin for eight years, and I was somewhat apprehensive of returning. It had always given me such wonderful audiences; I feared the shock of seeing the great city that I had known so well reduced almost to a rubble-heap. Street after deserted street of gutted, crumbling houses—it was indeed awesome, a vision of the Apocalypse. Yet I came away from Berlin feeling, not depressed, but encouraged. The destruction of the buildings had amazed me less than the buoyant gaiety and tough courage of the Berliners. Burned-out, shattered, tragically split in two though it might be, Berlin was no rubble-heap. It was still a great city, because it still had citizens.

My doctor was beginning to remonstrate with me about my non-stop touring. At sixty, he said, I must resign myself to taking it easy now and then. So I made no other foreign engagements for the time being, and settled down to a long, not unduly busy summer in Italy. I sang in Rome, in Verdi's 'Requiem' and 'La Traviata'; and in Florence in 'L'Elisir d'Amore' at the 'Maggio Fiorentino'. I got my 'musical summer' organized again in Recanati, taking part in it myself with four open-air performances of 'Elisir'. And in August, 1950, for the first time since before the war, I sang in the open-air season at the Arena in Verona; the opera in which I appeared was 'La Forza del Destino'.

Of the English tour which I had arranged for the autumn, I was able to give only one concert—at Blackpool on October 1st. The rest of the tour had to be cancelled because I developed a serious inflammatory throat complaint. I came back to Italy at once, and was unable to sing for two months. Nothing of the kind had ever happened to me before, and I felt very upset and depressed.

By the end of November 1950 I was singing again—'Manon' and 'Elisir' in Palermo. I gave several performances of these two operas during January, 1951, in Parma, Milan and Como; I also sang Verdi's 'Requiem' again in Rome.

In February I was booked for a long engagement at the San Carlo in Naples; and from there, as soon as it ended, I was to sail for Cape Town. My first South African tour was to open at the end of March, and I had decided to make the journey by sea. Although I had flown four or five times before, I had never regarded flying as a pleasant mode of travel and I did not intend to change my opinion now.

On February 9th I collapsed while singing in 'L'Amico Fritz' at the San Carlo. I had tried to carry on in spite of a sudden attack of almost paralysing pain, but in the end I fainted. I was rushed to hospital for an operation, which proved successful; but I was not allowed to move for six weeks. During this time, the impresario of my South African tour became a familiar figure at the hospital, haunting its corridors in tragi-comic despair. At last the doctors pronounced me ready to leave.

'Thank God!' said the impresario. 'By plane, we can just make it!'

'By *plane*?' I asked in terror. Was it for this that the surgeons had saved me from death?

The impresario proceeded to draw on reserves of creative fantasy with which I had not previously credited him, to convince me of the terrible things that would happen in South Africa if I cancelled my tour.

It was not his eloquence, however, as much as my own reluctance to cause all the trouble and disappointment of a cancellation, that finally induced me to overcome my terrors and take to the air. Accompanied by the impresario and by my doctor, I accordingly reached Johannesburg in time to give my scheduled opening concert on March 29th.

This was followed by performances of 'Tosca' and 'La Traviata' at His Majesty's Theatre. A fortnight's recital tour took me to Cape Town, Pretoria and Durban; and I then returned to Johannesburg for a final fortnight of 'La Traviata' and 'La Bohème'. I greatly enjoyed this South African trip, and felt very pleased with myself for having once more scraped up the courage to fly.

'No,' said the doctor, when I got back to Italy, 'I can see no reason why you should not go ahead with your plans. You have made a complete recovery.'

'Will four months in South America be all right?' I asked.

'Well,' he smiled, 'what would you do if I said "No"?'

I reached Buenos Aires on July 1st, 1950. After a series of ten concerts there, and a few performances of 'Andrea Chénier' in Montevideo, I went to Brazil, where on this tour I was to spend most of my time. I gave a month's season at the Municipal in Rio —'La Forza del Destino', 'Fedora', 'Manon Lescaut', 'Cavalleria Rusticana' and 'I Pagliacci' together. This was followed by almost six weeks in São Paulo, during which I sang 'Adriana Lecouvreur', 'Tosca' and 'Andrea Chénier', as well as the double 'Cav Pag' programme. These weeks of opera were interspersed with many concerts, not only in Rio and São Paulo, but also in cities that were new to me—Santos, Curitiba, Belo Horizonte.

When on October 29th I sailed out of the beautiful harbour of Rio, I remember that I stood on deck for a long time, looking back. I wondered vaguely why I felt so sad. Perhaps something told me that I had sung to my South American audiences for the last time.

I got off the boat from South America just in time to catch a train for Munich, where I opened my first post-war German recital tour on November 15th, 1951. Apart from my visit to Berlin the previous year, and from fleeting glimpses through the window of a car or railway carriage, I had as yet seen nothing of the new Germany. My tour took me to Stuttgart, Heidelberg, Karlsruhe, Hamburg, to Berlin again, to Kiel, Hanover, Frankfurt, Münster, and finally to Innsbruck. In the midst of my bewilderment at all the changes I found, one thing consoled and reassured me: the affection and enthusiasm with which my audiences welcomed me back.

After a quiet family Christmas and a short season at the San Carlo, I set off again on my travels. There was so little time left, and so much that I still wanted to do. I would have liked, had it been possible, to sing in New Zealand, Mexico, Japan; indeed, I would have liked to sing for the Dyaks, the Berbers, the Eskimos. I had received this wonderful gift, this voice, and soon it would no longer be possible to share it.

On January 27th, 1952, I was in Amsterdam. For three weeks I toured Belgium, Denmark, Sweden and Western Germany, and on February 25th I opened a nine-weeks' tour of England and Scotland with a concert at the Albert Hall. At the end of May I sailed for Canada, giving concerts all over the country throughout June and July. After my return I spent six quiet weeks in Rome and Recanati, during which I gave only a few charity performances. On October 1st, in Munich, I began another month-long tour of Germany.

I made a special journey to London, to take part in the Royal Variety Performance at the Palladium Theatre on November 3rd, 1952. Afterwards I was presented to the Queen; she shook my hand and gave me a beautiful smile. At the end of February, 1953, I returned to England for a more extended visit, which lasted until April 13th.

The number of works in my repertory still stood at fifty-nine; I finally brought it up to sixty by singing 'Ezechia', a historically important oratorio by the seventeenth-century Italian composer Carissimi. This performance took place at the Oratorio del Santissimo Crocefisso in Rome, on April 25th, 1953.

I gave a short opera season in Wiesbaden and Stuttgart towards the end of May, and some open-air performances of 'Cavalleria Rusticana' and 'I Pagliacci' at the Castello Sforzesco in Milan. The older I got, the more I enjoyed astonishing audiences by my *bravura* in this double programme. It was, I confess, largely the desire to show off that made me choose it so often.

That summer I stayed at home, but I gave many charity concerts in my own province of Marche. By mid-October, I had set off on a two-months' tour of Germany and Austria, visiting Salzburg and Vienna for the first time since the war.

Throughout January and into February 1954, I continued to 'show off' in 'Cavalleria' and 'I Pagliacci': at La Spezia, Carrara, Mestre, and for a short season in Venice. But I had to confess to myself that it was a strain. I hoped that no trace of it showed in my singing, but I felt very tired afterwards.

I gave a recital in Paris, at the Théâtre de Chaillot, on February 16th, and on the 20th I was back at the Albert Hall. There followed yet another long tour of England, Scotland and Ireland —including, for the first time, Cork. After two months in the British Isles, I spent four weeks in Belgium, Western Germany and Switzerland before returning to Rome towards the end of September.

The signs were unmistakable. I was constantly, increasingly

tired. Now, if I wanted to end my career with dignity, I would have to keep my promise to myself; I would have to retire.

It was an agonizing decision to make; but when I finally made it, in the summer of 1954, I felt better, and began to plan. I took my farewell of opera that same summer. Most of those final performances had for background the familiar landscape of the Marche. I sang 'La Forza del Destino' in Pesaro, Ancona and Fermo; and on August 15th, last of all, I sang 'Cavalleria Rusticana' and 'I Pagliacci'—I could still do it!—in the Arena Beniamino Gigli at Porta Recanati. This was not really good-bye, I told myself. It was here, in this beloved countryside between the Apennines and Adriatic, that I was going to spend the rest of my days. Clutching this thought, I managed to take my last curtain call without tears.

That was only the beginning. There were still all the other farewells to be made—the farewells to my audiences. In London, Lisbon, Berlin, Copenhagen, I would not be able to find consolation by saying to myself, 'After all, I shall be coming back.' Well, I had had more than my share of satisfactions and triumphs; the months of heart-wrenching that lay ahead were part of the price I had to pay.

Short visits to Germany and to London (for two performances of Verdi's 'Requiem' and a concert at the Albert Hall) had already been planned for the early autumn; these, I decided, could not be counted as farewells. Both my English and my German audiences mattered too much to me. I would return to them later, to say good-bye properly.

My first single farewell concert was at Amsterdam, in October, 1954; my first farewell tour was of Scandinavia, in November. I sang in Stockholm, Gothenburg, Oslo, Copenhagen, and Aarlborg. Even in my melancholy, I could not resist the opportunity of acquiring a new audience; I went to Finland and sang in Helsinki for the first and, alas, the last time.

At the end of November came Paris, Brussels, Antwerp—all good-byes.

I returned home for Christmas, but on New Year's Day 1955 I was already in the train. My farewell tour of Germany and Austria opened in Freiburg on January 3rd, reached Berlin on February 5th, and ended in Vienna on February 19th.

I find I cannot bring myself to describe this time in any detail.

It is still too painfully recent. The reader who has accompanied me this far can imagine what I felt.

My last tour of Great Britain opened on February 25th, 1955, under the auspices of my old friend S. A. Gorlinsky, at the Albert Hall; I sang in Glasgow, Newcastle, Blackburn, Liverpool, Leicester, and Stockton, ending in Manchester on March 20th. My London farewell took place on March 6th, in a second concert at the Albert Hall.

From England I went to Lisbon, which I had come to know so well in recent years, for two good-bye concerts at the end of March.

The condemned man is allowed a last wish. I had not been to the United States for over sixteen years. So many people must have forgotten me, in that country where yesterday belongs to the garbage can, that a good-bye scarcely seemed necessary. But I had not forgotten the Americans. I wanted very much to sing for them once again. I wanted to hear myself called, one last time, 'Mr. Giggly.' I wanted to take one last look at the Metropolitan.

It was not easy to arrange an American tour at short notice, but Gorlinsky came to my rescue and shouldered the ungrateful task with his usual dynamic efficiency. I gladly accepted his offer to accompany me on the trip; his help and support were invaluable throughout, and enabled me to save all my energies for my recitals.

And so, on April 17th, 1955, I was back singing at Carnegie Hall, only a few steps away from the apartment on West 57th Street which had been my home for twelve years. How New York had changed! I felt like Rip Van Winkle. My friends were amused; I did nothing but exclaim.

I gave two more concerts at Carnegie Hall, on April 20th and 24th. In the programme of this last concert, my farewell to New York, I included '*O Paradiso*' from 'L'Africana', which perhaps some members of my audience could recall having heard me sing at the Metropolitan; '*Dalla sua pace*' from 'Don Giovanni'; and the '*Lamento di Federico*'. The whole concert—singing, clapping, shouting, coughing and all—was registered on an LP record, and I often play it over to myself now.

It would have been good to see San Francisco once again, to make one last sweeping coast-to-coast tour, as in the old days;

but I feared that I might not be able to give of my best to audiences after travelling such great distances. So I decided on a tour of more relatively modest proportions.

From New York I went to Hartford, Connecticut, and then to Philadelphia, Toronto, Chicago, Montreal, Ottawa, Quebec, Cleveland and Washington. My concert in Washington, on May 25th, 1955, was my final farewell, the last occasion on which I ever sang in public.

From Rovigo to Washington, my career had come full circle. I had been singing on stage and platform for forty-one years.

ENVOI

I HAVE tried to relate, as honestly as I could, my story as a singer. I have not told everything about myself. To do so would have been indiscreet, irrelevant and above all tedious; for as I have already said, apart from my voice I am a very ordinary person.

I have dwelt at some length on my early years because my formation as a singer was inseparably bound up with them; if in the later part of the book there are fewer personal allusions, this is because my personal life, what little there was of it, no longer had any bearing on my career.

I have written these pages in a haphazard sort of way, recording the dates and details of some performances in case they might be of use to students of opera, but including also odd scraps of operatic information for the benefit of the general reader. I make no apologies, for I am not a writer.

I would like to take this last opportunity of thanking all my audiences. Anyone who reads this book will realize, I hope, what their support has meant to me—in a sense, everything. I might, no doubt, have sung in the wilderness, as one sings in the bath—for fun; but it was only through my audiences that this exercise of lungs, diaphragm and vocal cords became transmuted for me into a profound spiritual experience. Like a squirrel counting his hoard of nuts in the winter, I treasure their applause in my memory.

I hope that some young singers may find encouragement in my story. I would not wish anyone as hard an apprenticeship as I had, but at least I think it proves that one does not need money or influence to succeed, provided one has perseverance—and provided, of course, that one has a voice. I have said nothing about methods of voice-training because I hold with none in particular; each voice, it seems to me, has its own special requirements. Some things cannot be taught; for example, the instinctive timing of a musical phrase. If that capacity is not inborn, it is useless to waste time trying to become a singer.

It is true that, although I had no money, I was greatly helped in my early years by the kindness of other people. I do not think that this should be entirely ascribed to luck. People helped me because they liked not only my voice but also my determination, and my willingness to work my passage. The world is full of kind people, and I think that no young singer need despair of finding help, provided he is ready to help himself.

In one thing I was truly fortunate: Recanati. I wonder what would have become of me if, like Caruso, I had been born in a city slum; for I did not have the gifts of personality that enabled Caruso to create life and warmth around him wherever he went. I am writing these lines in my tower, the high room from which I can look out over the Cathedral, the 'Hill of the Infinite', the vineyards, the Adriatic. My roots have always been here, in this serene landscape. When I lived in the world beyond the Apennines, it gave me strength; now that I have come back, it gives me peace.

APPENDIXES

I

THE OPERA REPERTORY OF BENIAMINO GIGLI

	Composer	*Opera*	*Town*	*Theatre*	*Date of Début*	
1	Ponchielli	La Gioconda	Rovigo	Sociale	October 15	1914
2	Massenet	Manon	Genoa	Carlo Felice	December 26	1914
3	Puccini	Tosca	Palermo	Massimo	February	1915
4	Boito	Mefistofele	Bologna	Corso	October	1915
5	Mascagni	Cavalleria Rusticana	Naples	San Carlo	December	1915
6	Donizetti	La Favorita	Naples	Bellini	January	1916
7	Donizetti	Lucia di Lammermoor	Verona	Ristori	October 5	1916
8	Mascagni	Iris	Turin	Chiarella	April	1917
9	Mascagni	Lodoletta	Leghorn	Politeama	August	1917
10	Puccini	Rondine	Rome	Costanzi	February	1918
11	Cilea	Adriana Lecouvreur	Rome	Costanzi	April	1918
12	Giordano	Fedora	Naples	San Carlo	February	1919
13	Puccini	La Bohème	Monte Carlo	Casino	March	1919
14	Verdi	La Traviata	Monte Carlo	Casino	March	1919
15	Donizetti	Lucrezia Borgia	Buenos Aires	Colón	September	1919
16	Wagner	Lohengrin	Rio de Janeiro	Municipal	June 28	1920
17	Catalani	Loreley	Rio de Janeiro	Municipal	July 6	1920
18	Zandonai	Francesca da Rimini	São Paulo	Municipal	August 18	1920
19	Puccini	Madama Butterfly	Buenos Aires	Coliseo	September 26	1920
20	Montemezzi	L'Amore dei Tre Re	New York	Metropolitan	January 1	1921
21	Verdi	Rigoletto	Brooklyn, N.Y.	Academy of Music	January 11	1921
22	Giordano	Andrea Chenier	New York	Metropolitan	March 7	1921
23	Mascagni	Piccolo Marat	Buenos Aires	Coliseo	September	1921
24	Lalo	Le Roi d'Ys	New York	Metropolitan	January 5	1922
25	Puccini	Manon Lescaut	New York	Metropolitan	March 18	1922
26	Gounod	Roméo et Juliette	New York	Metropolitan	November 24	1922
27	Meyerbeer	L'Africana	New York	Metropolitan	March 21	1923
28	Flotow	Marta	New York	Metropolitan	December 14	1923

29	Riccitelli	I Compagnacci	New York	Metropolitan	January	1924
30	Puccini	Gianni Schicchi	New York	Metropolitan	March	1924
31	Verdi	Falstaff	New York	Metropolitan	January 2	1925
32	Verdi	Requiem Mass	New York	Metropolitan	February	1925
33	Giordano	La Cena delle Beffe	Buenos Aires	Colón	August 31	1925
34	Thomas	Mignon	New York	Metropolitan	March 10	1927
35	Verdi	Un Ballo in Maschera	Buenos Aires	Colón	July 20	1928
36	Donizetti	L'Elisir d'Amore	Buenos Aires	Colón	August 11	1928
37	Mozart	Don Giovanni	New York	Metropolitan	November 29	1929
38	Bellini	La Sonnambula	New York	Metropolitan	March 16	1932
39	Marcacci	Evangeline	Philadelphia	Academy	May	1932
40	Verdi	La Forza del Destino	Buenos Aires	Colón	July 5	1933
41	Bellini	Il Pirata	Rome	Reale dell' Opera	January 1	1935
42	Gounod	Faust	Rio de Janeiro	Municipal	August	1935
43	Pergolesi	La Serva Padrona	Jesi (Marche)		September 25	1936
44	Verdi	Aida	Rome	Reale dell' Opera	March 28	1937
45	Gomez	Guarany	Rome	Reale dell' Opera	April 15	1937
46	Mascagni	L'Amico Fritz	Rome	Reale dell' Opera	December 23	1937
47	Cilea	La Gloria	Rome	Reale dell' Opera	January 15	1938
48	Verdi	Il Trovatore	Rome	Reale dell' Opera	December 9	1939
49	Leoncavallo	Zaza	Milan	Scala	April 25	1940
50	Pietri	Maristella	Milan	Scala	April 26	1940
51	Donizetti	Poliuto	Milan	Scala	December 26	1940
52	Cilea	L'Arlesiana	Rome	Reale dell' Opera	February 3	1941
53	Alfano	Don Juan de Manara	Florence	Comunale	May 28	1941
54	Mozart	Requiem Mass	Rome	Basilica di Santa Maria degli Angeli	December 3	1941
55	Bizet	Carmen	Rome	Reale dell' Opera	December 23	1941
56	Leoncavallo	I Pagliacci	Rome	Reale dell' Opera	April 7	1942
57	Rossini	Messa Solenne	Florence	Comunale	May 7	1942
58	Rossini	Stabat Mater	Rome	Accademia di Santa Cecilia	May 10	1945
59	Bellini	Norma	Catania	Massimo Bellini	November 8	1945
60	Carissimi	Ezechia (Oratorio)	Rome	Oratorio del Santissimo Crocefisso	April 25	1953

II

A DISCOGRAPHY

by

Mark Ricaldone

Beniamino Gigli made his first recording in Milan during October, 1918; his last known recording session was at the Kingsway Hall, London towards the end of March, 1955. Between these dates he made over 360 recordings, as well as eight complete operas and the Verdi 'Requiem Mass'. At the time of writing (February, 1957) 38 known recordings are still unpublished, 33 of which are post-war. It might be of interest to know that the Italian Radio Company holds 'tapes' of Gigli operatic concerts which have been broadcast from time to time during the past few years. In addition to these Concerts there also exists in tape form the complete recording of Puccini's 'Manon Lescaut' with Gigli, Guerrini, Boriello and the Italian Radio Orchestra conducted by Maestro Simonetto; this was recorded in 1950 for broadcasting later in that year. During the 1950 Florence May Festival Gigli and Margherita Carosio sang together in 'L'Elisir D'Amore'; this opera was 'taped' during the actual public performance and was broadcast by the B.B.C. in 1951. It is to be hoped that one day His Master's Voice will arrange for these operas to be transferred to commercial records. The last known 'tapes' in existence were made during the three Farewell Performances Gigli gave at the Carnegie Hall, New York, on the 17th, 20th and 24th April, 1955. Excerpts from these concerts have been issued on a Long Play record published by RCA Victor and His Master's Voice.

The records in this discography are listed chronologically. It was the custom to repeat the same matrix number when the title was re-recorded, and this system was in operation until the 1929–30 period. This accounts for the inconsistencies of matrix numbers with recording dates which occasionally occured.

All the Milan 1918–19 series and most of the New York 1920–24 series were originally issued on single-sided discs. (In the discography the prefix SS indicates single-side, DS double-side.) The majority of these were later coupled and issued with the DA and DB series catalogue numbers; bracketed numbers indicate that the recordings were never issued on single-sided discs, although in fact catalogue numbers had been prepared.

I would have liked to include the matrix numbers of the unpublished 1953, 1954 and 1955 recordings, but regret that His Master's Voice found themselves unable to provide the necessary information.

Gigli recorded exclusively for His Master's Voice and RCA Victor, and the following is an explanatory list of catalogue number categories:

78 r.p.m.

7–	10-inch single-sided Red Label	His Master's Voice
2–	12-inch single-sided Red Label	His Master's Voice
DA	10-inch Red Label	His Master's Voice
DB	12-inch Red Label	His Master's Voice
DM	12-inch Light Green	La Voce del Padrone
DQ	12-inch White Label	His Master's Voice
VB	12-inch White Label 'Archive Series'	His Master's Voice
AGSB	12-inch Mauve and Gold Label	American Gramophone Society (Limited Edition)
B–	12-inch 'Red Seal Label'	RCA Victor (Brazil only)

45 r.p.m. (7-inch Normal Play)

7R	Red Label	His Master's Voice
7RQ, 7RF,	Red Label	La Voce del Padrone

45 r.p.m. (7-inch Extended Play)

7ER	Red Label	His Master's Voice
7EB	Black Label	His Master's Voice
7ERQ	Red Label	La Voce del Padrone
ERA	'Red Seal Label'	RCA Victor
ERAT, WCT	'Red Seal Label' 'Collectors Series'	RCA Victor

33⅓ r.p.m.

ALP	12-inch Red Label	His Master's Voice
QALP	12-inch Red Label	La Voce del Padrone
FALP	12-inch Red Label	La Voix de Son Maitre
CSLP	12-inch White Label 'Collectors Series'	His Master's Voice
QJLP	12-inch Gold Label 'Collectors Series'	La Voce del Padrone

FJLP	12-inch Red Label 'Collectors Series'	La Voix de Son Maitre
LM	12-inch 'Red Seal Label'	RCA Victor
LCT	12-inch 'Red Seal Label' 'Collectors Series'	RCA Victor
BLP	10-inch Red Label	His Master's Voice
QBLP	10-inch Red Label	La Voce del Padrone

Finally, I would like to express my gratitude for the help given me over the past few years to Signora Barbara Grossi, Maestro Enrico Sivieri, Dr. Gustave Cronstrom and the Record Division of His Master's Voice, without whom the complete compilation of this discography would not have been possible.

M. R.

PART I

RECORDINGS IN CHRONOLOGICAL ORDER

Date	Title	Composer	Matrix Number	Speed	Catalogue Numbers HMV	Catalogue Numbers RCA Victor
MILAN, 1918–1919 (Acoustic Recordings)						
10/18	Mefistofele: *Dai campi, dai prati*	Boito	20253b	78	SS 7–52110	
10/18	La Tosca: *Recondita armonia*	Puccini	20255b	78	SS 7–52114	SS 64881
10/18	La Tosca: *E lucevan le stelle*	Puccini	20256b	78	SS 7–52115	SS 64855
10/18	Mefistofele: *Se tu mi doni un'ora di riposa* (With Carlo Scattola—Bass)	Boito	20257b	78	SS 7–52111 DS DA223	SS 64882 DS 926
10/18	Mefistofele: *Lontano, lontano, lontano* (With G. Bosini—Soprano)	Boito	3310c	78	SS 2–054086 DS DB271	
10/18	La Favorita: *Addio, fuggir mi lascia* (With G. Casazza—Mezzo-soprano)	Donizetti	3314c	78	SS 2–054083 DS DB269	SS 74614 DS 6381
10/18	La Gioconda: *Laggiù nelle nebbie* (With G. Casazza—Mezzo-soprano)	Ponchielli	3316c	78	SS 2–054085 DS DB267	SS 74619 DS 6381
11/18	*O surdato 'nnammurato*	Cannio	20265b	78	SS 7–52113 DS DA224	SS 64868
11/18	Iris: *Apri la tua finestra*	Mascagni	20270b	78	SS 7–52109	SS–64867
11/18	Mefistofele: *Giunto sul passo estremo*	Boito	20275b	78	SS 7–52112	SS 64854
11/18	Lodoletta: *Ah, ritrovarla nella sua capanna*	Mascagni	3323c	78	SS 2–052143 DS DB270	SS 74615 DS 6382
11/18	La Gioconda: *Cielo e mar*	Ponchielli	3324c	78	SS 2–052142	
11/18	La Favorita: *Spirto gentil*	Donizetti	3325c	78	SS 2–052141	SS 74620
11/18	La Gioconda: *Enzo Grimaldo* (With D. Zani—Baritone)	Ponchielli	3331c	78	SS 2–054084 DS DB267	SS 74606 DS 6382

11/18	Faust: *Salve dimora casta e pura*	Gounod	3332c	78	SS 2–052140	SS 74605
12/19	Fedora: *Amor ti vieta*	Giordano	4233ah	78	SS 7–52150 DS DA225	
12/19	Fedora: *Vedi io piango*	Giordano	4234ah	78	SS 7–52151 DS DA225	
12/19	Faust: *Dammi ancor* (With Maria Zamboni—Soprano)	Gounod	1046aj	78	SS 2–054105 DS DB268	
12/19	La Bohème: *O soave Fanciulla* (With Maria Zamboni—Soprano)	Puccini	1048aj	78	SS 2–054106 DS DB271	
12/19	Cavalleria Rusticana: *Mamma quel vino*	Mascagni	1049aj	78	SS 2–052175 DS DB270	
12/19	L'Amico Fritz: *Suzel buon di* (With Nerina Baldiserri—Soprano)	Mascagni	1051aj	78	SS 2–054107 DS VB46	
12/19	L'Amico Fritz: *Tutto tace* (With Nerina Baldiserri—Soprano)	Mascagni	1052aj	78	SS 2–054108 DS VB46	
12/19	Faust: *Sempre amar* (With Maria Zamboni—Soprano)	Gounod	1053aj	78	SS 2–054114 DS DB268	
12/19	I Pescatori di Perle: *Del tempio al limitar* (With Adolfo Pacini—Baritone)	Bizet	1055aj	78	SS 2–054109 DS DB269	

NEW YORK, 1920–1924 (Acoustic Recordings)

1/21	Mefistofele: *Dai campi, dai prati*	Boito	B24782	78	SS 7–52170 DS DA222	SS 64933 DS 644
1/21	La Tosca: *Recondita armonia*	Puccini	B24919	78	SS 7–52176 DS DA221	SS 64944 DS 646
2/21	Mefistofele: *Giunto sul passo estremo*	Boito	B24783	78	SS 7–52200 DS DA222	SS 64942 DS 644
2/21	La Tosca: *E lucevan le stelle*	Puccini	B24920	78	SS 7–52180 DS DA223	SS 64943 DS 926, 942

Date	Title	Composer	Matrix Number	Speed	Catalogue Numbers HMV	RCA Victor
NEW YORK, 1920–1924 (Acoustic Recordings)—*continued*						
2/21	La Gioconda: *Cielo e mar*	Ponchielli	B24922	78	SS 7–52171 DS DA220	SS 64938 DS 643
3/21	La Favorita: *Spirto gentil*	Donizetti	C24921	78	SS 2–052197 DS DB273	SS 74688 DS 6139
3/21	*Santa Lucia luntana*	Mario	B24990		Unpublished	
3/21	Faust: *Salve dimora casta e pura*	Gounod	C25109	78	SS 2–052214 DS DB273	SS 74687 DS 6138
3/21	Iris: *Apri la tua finestra*	Mascagni	B25110	78	SS 7–52198 DS DA221	SS 64959 DS 646
4/21	*Tu sola*	De Curtis	B25141	78	SS 7–52201 DS DA224	SS 66010 DS 906
4/21	*Santa Lucia luntana*	Mario	B25017	78	SS 7–52195 DS DA572	SS 64975 DS 645
1/22	*Notturno d'amore*	Drigo	C26061		Unpublished	
3/22	*Notturno d'amore*	Drigo	C26061	78	SS 2–052219 DS DB670	SS 74742 DS 6446
3/22	Le Roi d'Ys: *Vainement ma bien aimée*	Lalo	B26191	78	SS 7–32073 DS DA556	SS 66070 DS 906
3/22	I Pagliacci: *Vesti la giubba*	Leoncavallo	B26192	78	SS 7–52219 DS DA220	SS 66095 DS 643
9/22	*Serenata*	Toselli	B26795	78	SS 7–52220 DS DA572	SS 66102 DS 945
10/22	Andrea Chénier: *Come un bel dì di Maggio*	Giordano	B27009	78	SS 7–52222 DS DA556	SS (66208) DS 975
10/22	La Tosca: *O dolci mani*	Puccini	B27010	78	SS 7–52223 DS DA586	SS 66170 DS 942

5/10/22	Andrea Chénier: *Un di all'azzurro spazio*	Giordano	C27011	78	SS 2–052233 DS DB670 DB2234	SS 74793 DS 6139
				33	CSLP502	
2/23	L'Africana: *O paradiso*	Meyerbeer	C27531	78	SS 2–052235 DS DB109	SS 74804 DS 6138
2/23	Roméo et Juliette: *Ah, léve toi soleil*	Gounod	C27532		Unpublished	
2/23	Loreley: *Nel verde Maggio*	Catalani	B27533	78	SS 7–52257 DS DA586	SS (66207) DS 975
3/23	Roméo et Juliette: *Ange adorable* (With Lucrezia Bori—Soprano)	Gounod	C27714	78	SS (2–034033)	DS AGSB58
3/23	Roméo et Juliette: *Ah, nefuis pas encore* (With Lucrezia Bori—Soprano)	Gounod	B27715	78	SS 7–34006 DS DA381	SS 87581 DS 3027
5/23	*Il canto del cigno*	Saint-Saens	B28018	78		SS (66274) DS 1025
5/23	*Maria, Mari*	Di Capua	C28019		Unpublished	
6/23	Marta: *M'appari tutto amor*	Flotow	C27995	78	SS 2–052244 DS DB109	SS 74876 DS 6446
10/23	*Paquita*	Buzzi-Peccia	B27996	78	SS	SS (66275) DS 1025
10/23	*Mandulinata a Napule*	Tagliaferri	C28815		Unpublished	
11/24	*Funiculi funicula*	Denza	B31457	78	SS (7–52286) DS DA713	DS 1064
11/24	*Povero pulcinella*	Buzzi-Peccia	B31477	78	SS (7–52287) DS DA713	DS 1064

NEW YORK, 1925–1930 (Electric Recordings*)

4/25	*Sentinella*	De Curtis	BVE32142	78	DA730	1084
4/25	*Sto 'penzanno a Maria*	De Curtis	BVE32143	78	DA730	1084

*All subsequent entries are electric recordings

Date	Title	Composer	Matrix Number	Speed	Catalogue Numbers HMV	RCA Victor
NEW YORK, 1925–30 (Electric Recordings*)—*continued*						
4/25	*Mandulinata a Napule*	Tagliaferri	BVE28815	78	DA797	1157
4/25	*Come love with me*	Carnevali	BVE32148	78	DA732	1096
4/25	*Good-bye Mari*	De Curtis	BVE32149	78	DA732	1096
4/25	L'Elisir D'Amore: *Quanto e bella*	Donizetti	BVE32500	78	DA797	1157
4/25	Lucia di Lammermoor: *Tombe degl'avi*	Donizetti	CVE32501	78	DB870	6511
4/25	Lucia di Lammermoor: *Tu che a Dio*	Donizetti	CVE32502	78	DB870	6511
11/25	*Maria, Mari*	Di Capua	BVE28019	78	DA763	1134
11/25	*Quanno a femmena vo*	De Crescenzo	BVE33882	78	DA763	1134
10/26	La Tosca : *Recondita armonia*	Puccini	BVE24919	78	DA856	1213
				45		ERA181
10/26	*Notturno d'amore*	Drigo	CVE26061	78	DB1002	6610
10/26	*Serenata*	Toselli	CVE26795	78	DB1002	6610
10/26	Manon Lescaut: *Donna non vidi mai*	Puccini	BVE36741	78	DA856	1213
12/26	*Santa Lucia luntana*	Mario	CVE25017	78	DB1296	6925
12/26	*Rondine al nido*	De Crescenzo	BVE36928	78	DA899	1243
12/26	*Torna amore*	Buzzi-Peccia	BVE37117	78	DA899	1243
12/26	*Stornelli marini*	Mascagni	BVE37118	78	DA1052	1403
12/26	La Forza del Destino: *Solenne in quest'ora* (With Titta Ruffo—Baritone)	Verdi	CVE37319	78		AGSB49
12/26	La Bohème: *O Mimi tu più non torni* (With Titta Ruffo—Baritone)	Puccini	CVE37320	78		AGSB56
12/26	La Gioconda: *Enzo Grimaldo* (With Titta Ruffo—Baritone)	Ponchielli	CVE37321	78		AGSB49
				45		17–0028
				33	QJLP101 FJLP5010	LCT1004

2/27	Mefistofele: *Dai campi, dai prati*	Boito	BVE24782	78	DA883	1239
2/27	Mefistofele: *Giunto sul passo estremo*	Boito	BVE24783	78	DA883	1239
2/27	*Addio a Napoli*	Cottrau	BVE37835	78 33 	DA941 DA2000 BLP1034 QBLP5014	1292
2/27	La Bohème: *O Mimi tu più non torni* (With Giuseppe De Luca—Baritone)	Puccini	CVE37836	78 45	DB1050	8069 ERAT10
2/27	La Forza del Destino: *Solenne in quest'ora* (With Giuseppe De Luca—Baritone)	Verdi	CVE37837	78	DB1050	8069
10/27	*O bei nidi d'amore*	Donaudy	BVE36927	78	DA941	1292
10/27	Marta: *M'appari tutto amor*	Flotow	CVE27995	78		6446
11/27	I Pescatori di Perle: *Del tempio al limitar* (With Giuseppe de Luca—Baritone)	Bizet	CVE41071	78 45	DB1150	8084 ERAT10
11/27	La Gioconda: *Enzo Grimaldo* (With Giuseppe De Luca—Baritone)	Ponchielli	CVE 41072	78 45	DB1150 DB2235 	8084 ERAT10
1212/27	Lucia di Lammermoor: *Giusto cielo* (With Ezio Pinza—Bass)	Donizetti	CVE41225	78 45 33	DB1229 CSLP518	8096 17–0355 17–0357 LCT1037
1212/27	Lucia di Lammermoor: *Tu che a Dio* (With Ezio Pinza—Bass)	Donizetti	CVE41226	78 45 33	DB1229 CSLP518	8096 17–0355 17–0357 LCT1037
1212/27	Lucia di Lammermoor: *Tombe degl'avi*	Donizetti	CVE41227	78	DB1222 DB2235	6876
12/27	Lucia di Lammermoor: *Chi mi frena* (With Galli-Curci, Homer, De Luca, Pinza, Bada)	Donizetti	CVE41232	78	DQ102	10012

* All subsequent entries are electric recordings

Date	Title	Composer	Matrix Number	Speed	Catalogue Numbers HMV	RCA Victor
NEW YORK, 1925–1930 (Electric Recordings*)—*continued*						
12/27	Rigoletto: *Bella figlia dell'amore* (With Galli-Curci, Homer, De Luca)	Verdi	CVE41233	78	DQ102	10012
1/28	Cavalleria Rusticana: *Viva il vino*	Mascagni	CVE41298	78	DB1499	8222, 13902
5/28	La Traviata: *De miei bollenti spiriti*	Verdi	CVE45120	78	DB1222	6876
11/28	Mignon: *Addio, Mignon*	Thomas	CVE45119	78	DB1270	6905
11/28	Mignon: *Ah non credevi tu*	Thomas	CVE45121	78	DB1270	6905
12/28	L'Africana: *O paradiso*	Meyerbeer	CVE27531	78	DB1382	7109
				45		ERAT12
				33		LCT6010
12/28	*Voce e notte*	De Curtis	CVE49149	78	DB1296 DB3907	6925
				45	7ERQ121	
12/28	*Canta pe' me*	De Curtis	BVE49150	78	DA1052 DA1278 DA5401	1403
1/29	Marta: *M'appari tutto amor*	Flotow	CVE27995	78	DB1382 DB4592 DB5385	7109
				33		LCT6010
1/29	*Notte lunare*	Doda	CVE49049	78	DB1454	7261
12/29	La Gioconda: *Cielo e mar*	Ponchielli	CVE58118	78	DB1499 DB2234	7194
				45		ERAT12
				33		LCT6010
12/29	I Pescatori di Perle: *Mi par d'udir ancora*	Bizet	CVE58119	78		AGSB56
12/29	L'Elisir D'Amore: *Una furtiva lagrima*	Donizetti	CVE58123	78		7194

12/29	*Se*	Denza	CVE58125	78	DB1454	7261
12/30	*Musica proibita*	Castaldon	CVE64390	78	DB1585	7400
12/30	*Carmela*	De Curtis	BVE64391	78	DA1195	1575
					DA5401	1973
				33	BLP1034	
					QBLP5014	
12/30	*Mamma mia che vo sape*	Nutile	CVE58124	78	DB1585	7400
12/30	*Vecchio ritornello*	Kreisler	BVE67704	78	DA1195	1575
12/30	*Occhi turchini*	Denza	CVE67705	78	DB1903	8222
						15187
12/30	I Lombardi: *Qual volutta trascorrere* (With Rethberg and Pinza)	Verdi	CVE67748	78	DB1506	8194
12/30	Attila: *Te sol quest'anima* (With Rethberg and Pinza)	Verdi	CVE67749	78	DB1506	8194

* All subsequent entries are electric recordings

LONDON, 1931

6/31	*Good-bye*	Tosti	2B1401	78	DB1526	8767
						14359
6/31	Manon: O *dolce incanto*	Massenet	0B1402	78	DA1216	1656
				33	QALP10132	
					QALP10133	
6/31	*The lost chord*	Sullivan	2B1403	78	DB1526	8767
						14359
7/31	La Bohème: *Che gelida manina*	Puccini	2B1411	78	DB1538	8769
7/31	Faust: *Salve dimora casta e pura*	Gounod	2B1412	78	DB1538	8769
					DB3906	
				33	QALP10132	
7/31	I Pescatori di Perle: *Mi par d'udir ancora*	Bizet	0B1413	78	DA1216	1656
				33	QALP10145	

Date	Title	Composer	Matrix Number	Speed	Catalogue Numbers HMV	RCA Victor
NEW YORK, 1932						
5/32	*Marta*	Simons	BSHQ72534	78	DA1278	1570
5/32	*Quisiera olvidar tus ojos*	Alberniz	BSHQ72535	78	DA1295	1646
						1830
5/32	*Eres tu*	Sandoval	BSHQ72536	78	DA1295	1646
						1830
5/32	*Triste Maggio*	De Crescenzo	BSHQ72831	78	DA1307	1973
5/32	Sadko: *Chanson Hindoue*	Rimsky-Korsakov	BSHQ72832	78	DA1307	1570
MILAN, 1932						
9/32	Cavalleria Rusticana: *Tu qui Santuzza* (With Dusolina Giannini—Soprano)	Mascagni	2M804	78	DB1790	8559
						17697
				33		LCT6010
9/32	Cavalleria Rusticana: *No, no Turiddù* (With Dusolina Giannini—Soprano)	Mascagni	2M805	78	DB1790	8559
						17697
				33		LCT6010
10/32	*Serenata*	Schubert	2M836	78	DB1903	
10/32	*Pieta Signore*	Stradella	2M837	78	DB1831	8768
				45	7ERQ134	
10/32	Stabat Mater: *Cujus Animam*	Rossini	2M838	78	DB1831	8768
10/32	*Lucia, Luci*	De Curtis	0M844	78	DA1292	1640
				33	BLP1034	
					QBLP5014	
10/32	*'A canzone a Napule*	De Curtis	0M845	78	DA1292	1640
				33	BLP1034	
					QBLP5014	

MILAN, 1933

3/33	Andrea Chénier: *Se fui soldato*	Giordano	0M1168	78	DA1312	1833
3/33	Cavalleria Rusticana: *Mamma quel vino*	Mascagni	2M1169	78	DB1902	11-9676
					DB3905	

LONDON, 1933

3/33	Serse: *Ombra mai fu*	Handel	2B3505	78	DB1901	
3/33	I Pagliacci: *No, Pagliaccio non son*	Leoncavallo	0B3506	78	DA1312	1833
3/33	*Santa Lucia*	Cottrau	2B3507	78	DB1902	15348
					DB3907	
3/33	L'Elisir D'Amore: *Una furtiva lagrima*	Donizetti	2B3508	78	DB1901	
					DB3906	
					DB4592	
				33	QALP10120	

MILAN, 1934

3/34	La Tosca: *E lucevan le stelle*	Puccini	OW2403	78	DA1372	1704
3/34	Rigoletto: *La donna è mobile*	Verdi	OW2404	78	DA1372	1704
				33	QALP10120	
3/34	*O sole mio*	Di Capua	OW2405	78	DA1373	1678
				45	7ERQ121	
				33	BLP1034	
					QBLP5014	
4/34	*Addio bel sogno*	De Curtis	OW2430	78	DA1374	1686
					DA1451	1783
					DA1459	
4/34	*Solo per te Lucia*	Bixio	OW2431	78	DA1374	1686
					DA4409	
4/34	*Senza nisciuno*	De Curtis	OW2432	78	DA1373	1678
				33	BLP1034	
					QBLP5014	

Date	Title	Composer	Matrix Number	Speed	Catalogue Numbers HMV	RCA Victor
MILAN, 1934—*continued*						
7/34	I Pagliacci (Complete recording) See Part 2 for further details	Leoncavallo				
7/34	I Pagliacci: *Vesti la giubba* (from the complete recording)	Leoncavallo	2W2598	78	DB3158	14423
					DB6307	
				45	7R152	
					7RQ3019	
				33	QALP10132	
7/34	I Pagliacci: *O Colombina* (With Iva Pacetti—Soprano)	Leoncavallo	2W2599	78	DB3158	14423
				45	7R152	
					7RQ3019	
MILAN, 1935						
4/35	Carmen: *Il fior che avevi a me*	Bizet	2BA563	78	DB2531	13902
					DB6307	14030
4/35	*Mattinata*	Leoncavallo	0BA564	78	DA1454	1784
					DA1713	26574
				45	7EB6003	
					7ERQ108	
4/35	*Torna a Surriento*	De Curtis	0BA565	78	DA1454	1784
					DA2000	26574
				33	BLP1034	
					QBLP5014	
4/35	*Plaisir d'amour*	Martini	2BA566	78	DB2530	15348
4/35	Paride ed Elena: O *del mio dolce ardor*	Gluck	2BA567	78	DB2531	14030
4/35	*Elegie*	Massenet	2BA568	78	DB2530	15187

BERLIN, 1935						
10/35	*Mille cherubini in coro*	Schubert	0RA839	78	DA1447	1782
					DA1458	1842
10/35	*Non ti scordar di me*	De Curtis	0RA840	78	DA1447	1782
					DA1458	1842
10/35	*Serenata Veneziana*	Melichar	0RA841	78	DA1451	1783
					DA1459	
					DA4409	
BERLIN, 1936						
5/36	*Soltanto tu, Maria*	De Curtis	0RA1307	78	DA1487	1785
5/36	*Anima mia*	Melichar	0RA1308	78	DA1487	1785
5/36	*Ave Maria*	Bach—Gounod	0RA1309	78	DA1488	1786
				45	7EB6013	
					7ERQ134	
					7ERQ145	
5/36	*Agnus Dei*	Bizet	0RA1310	78	DA1488	1786
				45	7EB6013	
					7ERQ134	
					7ERQ145	
6/36	*Panis Angelicus*	Franck	2RA1334	78	DB2914	14312
6/36	*Il fior di loto*	Schumann	0RA1335	78	DA1504	1831
6/36	*Un rêve*	Grieg	0RA1336	78	DA1504	1831
6/36	L'Arlesiana: *E la solita storia*	Cilea	2RA1337	78	DB2914	14312
					DB3905	
				45		ERAT12
				33	QALP10120	
8/36	*Tu sei la vita mia*	Becce	0RA1406	78	DA1511	1808
					DA1535	1811
8/36	*Notte a Venezia*	Curci	0RA1407	78	DA1511	1808
					DA1535	1811

Date	Title	Composer	Matrix Number	Speed	Catalogue Numbers HMV	RCA Victor
MILAN, 1937						
3/37	*Giovinezza*	Blanc	2BA1777	78	DB3128	15188
3/37	*Inno a Roma*	Puccini	2BA1778	78	DB3128	15188
LONDON, 1937						
5/37	Aida: *Celeste Aida*	Verdi	2EA5255	78	DB3225	14746
						14872
						18221
				33	QALP10132	
5/37	La Bohème: *O soave fanciulla* (With Maria Caniglia—Soprano)	Puccini	2EA5256	78	DB3225	14746
						14872
MILAN, 1938						
2/38	*Ninna nanna della vita*	Bixio	oBA2346	78	DA1608	2134
2/38	*Serenata*	Tosti	oBA2347	78	DA1618	
					DA1713	
				45	7EB6003	
					7ERQ108	
2/38	*Mattinata Veneziana*	Cinque	oBA2350	78	DA1618	
2/38	*Ti voglio tanto bene*	De Curtis	oBA2351	78	DA1608	2134
5/38	La Bohème (Complete Recording) See Part 2 for further details	Puccini				
LONDON, 1938						
4/6/38	*L'Ultima canzone*	Tosti	2EA6349	78	DB3551	15201
4/6/38	*Marechiare*	Tosti	oEA6350	78	DA1650	1941

					DA1654	2181
				45	7EB6003	
					7ERQ108	
					7ERQ121	
4/6/38	*Occhi di fata*	Denza	2EA6351	78	DB3551	15201
4/6/38	*La Danza*	Rossini	oEA6352	78	DA1650	1941
						2181
				45	7EB6003	
					7ERQ108	

ROME, 1938

9/38	La Tosca (Complete Recording) See Part 2 for further details	Puccini				

MILAN, 1938

8/9/38	*Standchen*	Schubert	oBA2746	78	DA1657	1916
					DA1658	
				45	7EB6013	
					7ERQ145	
8/9/38	*Desiderio*	Bixio	oBA2747	78	DA1654	
8/9/38	*Nur dir gehort mein hertz*	Bixio	oBA2748	78	DA1658	
8/9/38	*Wiegenlied*	Brahms	oBA2749	78	DA1657	1916
				45	7EB6013	
					7ERQ145	

LONDON, 1939

5/39	*Amarilli*	Caccini	2EA7749	78	DB3895	17557
					DB6313	
5/39	Don Giovanni: *Dalla sua pace*	Mozart	2EA7750	78	DB3809	15601
5/39	*Notte d'amore*	De Crescenzo	2EA7901	78	DB3815	15609
5/39	*Aprile*	Tosti	2EA7902	78	DB3815	15609

Date	Title	Composer	Matrix Number	Speed	Catalogue Numbers HMV	Catalogue Numbers RCA Victor
LONDON, 1939—*continued*						
6/39	La Traviata: *Parigi, o cara*	Verdi	2EA7907	78	DB3811	15602
	(With Maria Caniglia—Soprano)			33	QALP10132	
6/39	La Traviata: *Un dì felice*	Verdi	2EA7908	78	DB3811	15602
	(With Maria Caniglia—Soprano)			33	QALP10132	
6/39	Don Giovanni: *Il mio tesoro*	Mozart	2EA7909	78	DB3809	15601
6/39	*La Spagnola*	Di Chiara	oEA7910	78	DA1711	2129
ROME, 1939						
8/39	Messa da Requiem (Complete Recording) See Part 2 for further details	Verdi				
8/39	Madama Butterfly (Complete Recording) See Part 2 for further details	Puccini				
MILAN, 1939						
7/39	*La Paloma*	Yradier	oBA3334	78	DA1711	2129
7/39	*O del mio amato ben*	Donaudy	2BA3335	78	DB3895	17557
					DB6313	
MILAN, 1940						
1/40	*Maria, tu sei per me la vita*	De Curtis	oBA3647	78	DA5376	2098
1/40	*Lolita*	Buzzi-Peccia	oBA3648	78	DA1722	2098
					DA5376	2128
1/40	Maristella: *Io conosco un giardino*	Pietri	oBA3649	78	DA5377	10–1229
23/1/40	Il Trovatore: *Ai nostri monti*	Verdi	2BA3650	78	DB5385	12–0767
	(With Cloe Elmo—Mezzo-soprano)			33	CSLP504	

1/40	Fedora: *Amor ti vieta*	Giordano	0BA3651	78	DA1722	2128
					DA5377	10–1229
						10–1475
				45		49–0436
				33	QALP10132	
4/40	Cavalleria Rusticana (Complete Recording) See Part 2 for further details	Mascagni				
11/40	*Mamma*	Bixio	0BA4186	78	DA5397	10–1334
						10–1339
				45	7RQ154	49–0573
11/40	*Se vuoi goder la vita*	Bixio	0BA4187	78	DA5397	10–1334
						10–1339
				45	7RQ154	49–0573
11/40	Manon Lescaut: *No, pazzo son guardate*	Puccini	0BA4189	78	DA5398	
					DA5411	
				33	QALP10120	
11/40	Il Trovatore: *Di quella pira*	Verdi	0BA4190	78	DA5398	10–1475
				45		49–0436
						49–3663
				33	QALP10120	LM1202

MILAN, 1941

6/41	L'Arlesiana: *E la solita storia*	Cilea	2BA4478	78	DB5406	
6/41	Manon Lescaut: *Ah, Manon mi tradisce*	Puccini	0BA4479	78	DA5411	
6/41	Lodoletta: *Ah ritrovarla nelle sua capanna*	Mascagni	2BA4480	78	DB5408	
6/41	Andrea Chénier: *Un dì all'azzurro spazio*	Giordano	2BA4483	78	DB5406	
				33	QALP10132	
6/41	Isabeau: *Non colombelle*	Mascagni	2BA4484	78	DB5407	
					DB5408	
6/41	Isabeau: *E passera la viva creatura*	Mascagni	2BA4485	78	DB5407	
6/41	La Forza del Destino: *La vita è inferno*	Verdi	0BA4487	78	DA5410	
				33	QALP10120	

Date	Title	Composer	Matrix Number	Speed	Catalogue Numbers HMV	RCA Victor
MILAN, 1941—*continued*						
6/41	La Forza del Destino: *O tu che in seno*	Verdi	0BA4488	78 33	DA5410 QALP10132	
11/41	Andrea Chénier (Complete Recording) See Part 2 for further details	Giordano				
11/41	*Ninna nanna grigio verde*	Militello	0BA4813	78	DA5414 DA5500	
11/41	*Tenerezza*	Militello	0BA4814	78	DA5414 DA5500	
MILAN, 1942						
2/42	*Passione*	Valente	0BA4918	78	DA5418	
2/42	*Tre rose*	Cioffi	0BA4919	78	DA5417	
2/42	Carmen: *Ah, mi parla di lei* (With Rina Gigli—Soprano)	Bizet	0BA4920	78	DA5416	
2/42	Carmen: *Mia madre vegge ancor* (With Rina Gigli—Soprano)	Bizet	0BA4921	78	DA5416	
2/42	*Surdate*	Nardella	0BA4925	78	DA5419	
2/42	*'Na sera a Maggio*	Cioffi	0BA4926	78	DA5417	
2/42	*Troppo 'nnammurato*	Valente	0BA4929	78	DA5418	
2/42	*Son poche rose*	Olivieri	0BA4930	78	DA5419	
BERLIN, 1943						
27/4/43	I Pagliacci: *Si può* (*Prologue*)	Leoncavallo	2RA5608	78	DB05353 DB7623	

27/4/43	*Valzer della felicita*	Millocher	2RA5609	78	DB05353 DB7623	

ROME, 1943

6/43	*Cinefollià*	Bixio	0BA5485	78	DA5443	
6/43	*Dimmi tu primavera*	Bixio	0BA5486	78	DA5443	
7/43	Un Ballo in Maschera (Complete Recording) See Part 2 for further details	Verdi				

ROME, 1946

7/46	Aida (Complete Recording) See Part 2 for further details	Verdi				

LONDON, 1946

12/46	La Juive: *Rachel, quand du Seigneur*	Halevy	2EA11482	78	DB6366	
12/46	Le Roi d'Ys: *Vainement ma bien aimée*	Lalo	2EA11483	78	DB6366	12–0767
12/46	*Parted*	Tosti	0EA11484	78	DA1870	
12/46	*I'll Walk beside you*	Murray	0EA11485	78	DA1870	
12/46	*Core 'ngrato*	Cardillo	2EA11510	78 45	DB6436 7R105 7RQ3016	12–0398
12/46	Manon: *Ah, dispar vision*	Massenet	2EA11511	78	DB6346	12–0403
12/46	Werther: *Ah, non mi ridestar*	Massenet	2EA11512	78 33	DB6346 QALP10132	12–0403
12/46	*Dicitencello vuje*	Falvo	2EA11513	78 45	DB6436 7R105 7RQ3016	12–0398

Date	Title	Composer	Matrix Number	Speed	Catalogue Numbers HMV	RCA Victor
LONDON, 1947						
11/47	*Adeste fideles*	Traditional	0EA12477	78	DA1874	10–1440
				45	7ERQ134	
11/47	*Silent night, holy night*	Gruber	0EA12478	78	DA1874	10–1440
11/47	*Ave Maria*	Schubert	2EA10684	78	DB6619	12–0400
11/47	Cavalleria Rusticana: *O lola* (This recording was issued with the complete set [See Part 2] to replace the original, it has never been published as a separate recording)	Mascagni	2EA10685			
11/47	*Reviens mon amour*	Chopin	0EA10686	78	DA1892	
11/47	*Ninna nanna*	Cittadini	0EA10687	78	DA1892	
11/47	*Segreto*	Tosti	2EA10688	78	DB6705	
11/47	*Nostalgia d amore*	Cittadini	2EA10689	78	DB6705	
11/47	*Vidalita*	Williams	0EA12595	78	DA1891	
11/47	*Cancion del carretero*	Buchardo	0EA12596	78	DA1891	
11/47	*Bless this house*	Brahe	0EA12597	78	DA1894	
				45	7R118	
11/47	*Smilin' through*	Penn	0EA12598	78	DA1894	
				45	7R118	
12/47	*La Violetta* (K. 476)	Mozart	0EA12623	78	DA1895	
12/47	Jocelyn: *Caches dans cet asile*	Godard	2EA12624	78	DB6619	12–0400
12/47	Naughty Marietta: *Ah sweet mystery of life*	Herbert	0EA12625	78	DA1979	
12/47	*Song of Songs*	Moya	0EA12626	78	DA1979	
12/47	*Come raggio di sol*	Caldara	0EA12644	78	DA1895	
12/47	*Selve amiche ombrose piante*	Caldara	0EA12645	78	DA1896	

				33	ALP1174 QALP10073	
12/47	*Vergin, tutto amor*	Durante	0EA12646	78	DA1896	
				33	ALP1174 QALP10073	
12/47	*Intorno all'idol mio*	Cesti	0EA12647	78	DA1906	
				33	ALP1174 QALP10073	
12/47	*Mattinata Siciliana*	Mazziotti	0EA12656	78	DA1912	
12/47	Arianna: *Lasciatemi morire*	Monteverdi	0EA12657	78	DA1955	
				45	7RF266	
				33	ALP1174 QALP10073	
12/47	*Caro mio ben*	Giordani	0EA12658	78	DA1955	
				45	7RF266	
				33	ALP1174 QALP10073	

LONDON, 1948

1/48	Orontea: *O cessate di piagarm*	Scarlatti	0EA12663	78	DA1906	
				33	ALP1174 QALP10073	
1/48	Don Juan de Manara: *Tu vedi in bel ciel*	Alfano	0EA12664	78	DA1937	
1/48	*Ritorno*	Mazziotti	0EA12666		Unpublished	
1/48	L'Amico Fritz: *O amore o bella luce*	Mascagni	0EA12667	78	DA1937	
				45		ERAT26

LONDON, 1949

2/49	*Quando l'amore nasce*	Cittadini	0EA13602	78	DA1916
2/49	*Alla danza*	Cittadini	0EA13603	78	DA1916

Date	Title	Composer	Matrix Number	Speed	Catalogue Numbers HMV	RCA Victor
LONDON, 1949—*continued*						
2/49	*Serenata malinconica*	Giordano	oEA13604	78	DA1925	
3/49	*Sona chitarra*	De Curtis	oEA13680	78	DA1917	
3/49	*Paese che 'ncatena*	De Curtis	oEA13681	78	DA1917	
3/49	*Ave Maria*	Carnevali	oEA13682	78	DA1918	
3/49	Atlanata: *Care selve*	Handel	oEA13683	78	DA1918	
					DA1956	
				33	ALP1174	
					QALP10073	
3/49	Griselda: *Per la gloria d'adoravi*	Bononcini	2EA13688*	78	DA1956	B5023
				33	ALP1174	
					QALP10073	
3/49	*Tu mancavi a tormentarmi*	Cesti	2EA13689	78		B5023
3/49	*Già il sole del Gange*	Scarlatti	oEA13690	78	DA1934	
				33	ALP1174	
					QALP10073	
3/49	*Cangia, cangia tue voglie*	Fasolo	oEA13691	78	DA1934	
				33	ALP1174	
					QALP10073	
3/49	*Sebben crudele*	Caldara	2EA13734	78	DB6995	
3/49	*Quella fiamma che m'accende*	Marcello	2EA13735	78	DB6995	
3/49	*Vittoria, vittoria*	Carissimi	oEA13736	78	DA1927	
				33	ALP1174	
					QALP10073	
3/49	*Ah, se tu dormi ancora: Posate, dormite*	Bassani	oEA13737	78	DA1927	
				33	ALP1174	QALP10073
					QALP10073	

4/49	*Casarella*	Di Veroli	0EA13752	78	DA1924	
4/49	*Varcarola triste*	Cecconi	0EA13753	78	DA1963	
				45	7R135	
					7RQ3003	
4/49	Marcella: *Non conosciuto voi con gli amici*	Giordano	0EA13754	78	DA1925	
4/49	*Cancion Moresca*	Piccinelli	0EA13755	78	DA1924	
5/49	*Carrettieri*	Gibilaro	0EA13605	78	DA1912	
10/49	L'Elisir D'Amore: *Quanto è bella*	Donizetti	2EA14230	78	DB21138	
				45	7R127	
					7RQ114	
10/49	*Omaggio a Bellini*	Chopin	2EA14321		Unpublished	
10/49	Turandot: *Nessun dorma*	Puccini	2EA14232	78	DB21138	10-3761
				45	7R127	49-3761
					7RQ114	ERAT12
10/49	*Inno alla Patria*	Chopin	2EA14233		Unpublished	
10/49	*Santa Lucia*	Cottrau	0EA14262	78	DA1963	10-3761
				45	7R135	49-3761
					7RQ3003	
				33	BLP1034	
					QBLP5014	
10/49	*Funiculi funicula*	Denza	0EA14263	78	DA2044	
				45	7ERQ121	
10/49	*Alba e tramonto*	Gibilaro	2EA14264	78	DB21096	
10/49	*Che 'sso turnato a fa?*	Di Veroli	2EA14265	78	DB21096	

MILAN, 1950

30/7/50	*Con la pioggia o con la luna*	Caslar	0BA7430	78	DA11324
30/7/50	*Città silente*	Caslar	0BA7431	78	DA11324

* When this recording was transferred to a 10-inch matrix the number 0EA14970 was allocated

Date	Title	Composer	Matrix Number	Speed	Catalogue Numbers HMV	Catalogue Numbers RCA Victor
MILAN, 1950—*continued*						
30/7/50	*Luntananza*	Campanino	0BA7432	78	DA11325	
30/7/50	*Senza più serenate*	Bixio	0BA7433	78	DA11325	
MILAN, 1951						
18/1/51	L'Elisir D'Amore: *Chiedi al rio* (With Rina Gigli—Soprano)	Donizetti	2BA7578	78	DB11347	
18/1/51	Otello: *Già nella notte densa* (With Rina Gigli—Soprano)	Verdi	2BA7579	78	DB11345	
18/1/51	Otello: *Ed io vedea fra le tue tempie* (With Rina Gigli—Soprano)	Verdi	2BA7580	78	DB11345	
18/1/51	L'Amico Fritz: *Ah, ditela per me* (With Rina Gigli—Soprano)	Mascagni	2BA7581	78 33	DB11342 QALP10132	
18/1/51	Mefistofele: *Lontano, lontano, lontano* (With Rina Gigli—Soprano)	Boito	2BA7582	78	DB11342	
18/1/51	I Pescatori di Perle: *Non hai compreso* (With Rina Gigli—Soprano)	Bizet	2BA7583	78	DB11347	
RIO DE JANEIRO, 1951						
10/51	Lo Schiavo: *Quando nacesti tu*	Gomez	SO93089	78		B5042
10/51	Il Guarany: *Vanto io pur*	Gomez	SO93090	78		B5042
10/51	*Mimosa*	Froes	SO93091	78		B5043
10/51	*A casinha pequenina*	Traditional	SO93092	78		B5043
LONDON, 1952						
3/52	*Ninna Nanna*	Fedri	0EA16386	78	DA2003	

3/52	*Anima e core*	d'Esposito	0EA16387	78	DA2007
3/52	*Madrigale villereccio*	Gibilaro	0EA16396	78	DA2003
4/52	*Amicu ventu*	Gibilaro	0EA16464	78	DA2015
4/52	*Canzone senza parole*	Cittadini	0EA16465	Unpublished	
4/52	*Suonno*	Di Veroli	0EA16466	78	DA2044
4/52	*Nustalgia ricordo*	Cittadini	0EA16467	78	DA2027
4/52	*Notte a mare*	Bonessi	0EA16468	78	DA2027
4/52	*Nostalgia*	Selvaggi	0EA16469	78	DA2015
4/52	*Serenata Espanola*	Cittadini	0EA16470	78	DA2012
4/52	*Stornellata*	Selvaggi	0EA16471	78	DA2012
5/52	*Ave Maria*	Khan	2EA16540	78	DB21524
5/52	*O Grande Sommo Iddio*	Di Veroli	2EA16541	78	DB21524
6/52	*Ritorna amore*	Di Veroli	0EA16539	78	DA2007

LONDON 1953

4/53	*Chesta Canzone*	Piccinelli	Unpublished		
4/53	*Tre Parole*	Cecconi	Unpublished		
4/53	*Canario Cantatore*	Campese	Unpublished		
4/53	*Ninna Nanna*	Ricci	Unpublished		
4/53	*Ninna Nanna*	Menotti	Unpublished		
4/53	*Ave Maria*	Cecconi	Unpublished		
4/53	*Varca Lucente*	Mangieri	Unpublished		
4/53	*Luna Nova*	Costa	Unpublished		
4/53	*E' sempre notte*	Cittadini	Unpublished		
4/53	*Bambina bruna*	Fedri	0EA17299	78	DA2055
4/53	*Doie stelle*	Selvaggi	0EA17300	78	DA2055
4/53	*Notte d'o core*	Campanino	0EA17306	78	DA2060

Date	Title	Composer	Matrix Number	Speed	Catalogue Numbers HMV	RCA Victor
LONDON, 1953—*continued*						
4/53	Maristella: *Io conosco un giardino*	Pietri	Unpublished			
4/53	*Ave Maria*	Gibilaro	2EA17314	78	DB21597	
4/53	*Pecche' Mari*	Di Veroli	Unpublished			
4/53	*Nuttata*	Rendine	Unpublished			
4/53	*Autunno*	De Curtis	2EA17318	78	DB21597	
4/53	*Senza te*	Silveri	0EA17319	78	DA2060	
4/53	*Papaveri e Papere*	Mascheroni	0EA17340	78	DA2038	
4/53	*Havaiana*	De Veroli	0EA17341	78	DA2038	
LONDON, 1954						
3/54	*Wiegenlied*	Brahms	Unpublished			
3/54	*Ave Maria*	Raffa	Unpublished			
3/54	*Ninna Nanna*	Piccinelli	0EA17869	78	DA2076	
3/54	*Ave Maria*	Liviabella	Unpublished			
3/54	*Marion*	Cecconi	Unpublished			
3/54	*Tutti i miei sogni*	Sardi	0EA17887	78	DA2076	
3/54	*Canzone a stornello*	Volonnino	0EA17888	78	DA2081	
3/54	*Dolce crepuscolo*	Vanuzzi	0EA17889	78	DA2081	
3/54	*Terra straniera*	Marletta	0EA17893	78	DA2069	
3/54	*Nisciuno*	Cittadini	0EA17894	78	DA2069	
3/54	*Ritornerò stasera*	Di Veroli	0EA17895	78	DA2067	
3/54	*Surriento*	Tufano	0EA17896	78	DA2067	
4/54	*Tango notturno*	Gibilaro	Unpublished			

4/54	*Io t'ho cercato*	Fedri	Unpublished		
4/54	Maggiolata Veneziana: *Maggio, sereno il cor*	Selvaggi	Unpublished		
13/4/54	*Mother Machree*	Young	0EA17930	45	7EB6019
13/4/54	The Bohemian Girl: *When other lips*	Balfe	0EA17931	45	7EB6019
13/4/54	*The Rosary*	Nevin	0EA17932	45	7EB6019
13/4/54	*Love stay with me*	De Veroli	0EA17933	45	7EB6019
16/10/54	*Rosi, Rosi*	Chipolloni	0EA18131	78	DA2077
16/10/54	*Notte sul mare*	Di Veroli	0EA18132	45	7EB6016 7ERQ153
16/10/54	*Ultima speme*	De Curtis	Unpublished		
16/10/54	Maggiolata Veneziana: *Ballata*	Selvaggi	Unpublished		
16/10/54	*Ninna nanna Ninna oh*	Carabella	0EA18145	45	7EB6016 7ERQ153
16/10/54	*Parla*	Rosati	0EA18146	45	7EB6016 7ERQ153
16/10/54	*O pittore e tutto 'o munno*	Garrone	0EA18147	78	DA2077
16/10/54	*Serenata amara*	Gibilaro	0EA18148	45	7EB6016 7ERQ153

LONDON, 1955

3/55	*Donna Milena*	Fedri	Unpublished
3/55	*Senz'amore*	Fedri	Unpublished
3/55	*Questo foulard*	Carabella	Unpublished
3/55	*Ritorna ancor*	Di Veroli	Unpublished
3/55	*Luntano, luntano*	Volonnino	Unpublished
3/55	*L'eterna canzone*	Visco	Unpublished
3/55	*Ave Maria*	Isidoro	Unpublished
3/55	*Valzer cammagnolo*	Fedri	Unpublished

Date	Title	Composer	Matrix Number	Speed	Catalogue Numbers HMV	Catalogue Numbers RCA Victor
NEW YORK, 1955 (Farewell Concerts)						
17/4/55	Manon: *O dolce incanto*	Massenet				
17/4/55	*Notte a venezia**	Curci				
20/4/55	Serse: *Ombra mai fu*	Handel				
20/4/55	Lohengrin: *Merce, merce cigno gentil*	Wagner				
20/4/55	*Un Rêve*	Grieg				
20/4/55	*Reviens mon amour*	Chopin				
20/4/55	*Begere légère*	Weckerlin				
20/4/55	*Come love with me*	Carnevali				
20/4/55	*Addio bel sogno*	De Curtis				
20/4/55	*Ritorna amore*	Di Veroli				
24/4/55	L'Africana: *O paradiso*	Meyerbeer		33	ALP1329 QALP10150	LM1972
24/4/55	*Amarilli*	Caccini				
24/4/55	*O del mio amato ben*	Donaudy				
24/4/55	Werther: *Ah non mi ridestar*	Massenet				
24/4/55	Lo schiavo: *Quando nacesti tu*	Gomez				
24/4/55	Tosca: *E lucevn le stellea*	Puccini				
24/4/55	*Life*	Curran				
24/4/55	*Rondine al nido*	De Crescenzo				
24/4/55	*Mamma*	Bixio				
24/4/55	*O sole mio*	Di Capua				
24/4/55	La Fanciulla del West: *Ch'ella mi creda*	Puccini				
24/4/55	Don Giovanni: *Dalla sua pace*	Mozart				

*Wrongly named ou the label, sleeve and catalogues as '*Vidalita*', by Williams.

PART 2

THE COMPLETE OPERAS

Title	Composer	Date	Matrix Number	Speed	Catalogue Numbers HMV	RCA Victor
I PAGLIACCI	Leoncavallo	July, 1934	2W2582/98 & W2600	78	DB2299/2307 DB7760/7768 (Auto)	M249 8524/8532
				33	QALP10119/20 FJLP5038/9	LCT6010
				45		WCT6010 (449–0136/0144) ERAT16 (Excerpts)
LA BOHEME	Puccini	May, 1938	2BA2362/2387	78	DB3448/3460 DB8452/8464 (Auto)	M518 M12385/12397 M519 AM12398/12410 DM12727/12739 M980 11–8684/8688 (Excerpts) DM980 11–8689/8693 (Excerpts)
				33	QALP10077/8 FJLP5027/8	
				45	7ERQ146/147 (Excerpts)	

S

Title	Composer	Date	Matrix Number	Speed	Catalogue Numbers HMV	Catalogue Numbers RCA Victor
LA TOSCA	Puccini	Sept., 1938	2BA2590/2617	78	DB3562/3575	M539 M15611/15624
					DB8530/8543 (Auto)	M540 AM15625/15638
						DM16092/16105
				33	ALP1020/1	LCT6004
					QALP10004/5	LCT1102 (Excerpts)
					FJLP5011/12	
				45	7ER5037 (Excerpts)	WCT82 (17–0434/0442)
					7ERQ122 (Excerpts)	WCT1102 (Excerpts)
						ERAT13 (Excerpts)
MESSA DA REQUIEM	Verdi	Aug., 1939	2BA3251/3270	78	DB3875/3884	M734 M17580/17589
					DB6210/6219	AM17590/17599
					DB8754/8763 (Auto)	DM17600/17709
					DB8984/8993 (Auto)	
				33	QALP10016/7	LCT6003
					FJLP5002/3	
				45		WCT78 (17–0406/0415)
						ERAT27 (Excerpts)
MADAMA BUTTERFLY	Puccini	Aug., 1939	2BA3271/3300	78	DB3859/3874	M700 17357/17372
			2BA3314/3315		DB8717/8732 (Auto)	M701 AM17373/17388
						DM17389/17404
				33	QALP10048/9	LCT6006
					FJLP5020/1	
				45	7ERQ155/156 (Excerpts)	WCT6006 (449–0086/0094)
					7RQ3053 (Excerpts)	

<table>
<tr><td>CAVALLERIA
RUSTICANA</td><td>Mascagni</td><td>April, 1940</td><td>2BA3811/3830
2BA3837/3838</td><td>78 DB3960/3970
DB8791/8801 (Auto)

33 QALP108/9
FALP108/9
45 7ERQ149/52 (Excerpts)</td><td>M1139 11–8089/8099
DM1139 11–8078/8088
DM1139 11–9655/9565
LCT6000

WCT33 (17–0134/0144)
ERAT16 (Excerpts)</td></tr>
<tr><td>ANDREA
CHENIER</td><td>Giordano</td><td>Nov., 1942</td><td>2BA4787/4812</td><td>78 DB5423/5435
DB9050/9062 (Auto)

33 QALP10069/70
FJLP5040/41</td><td>M1265 12–0599/0605
M1266 12–0613/0618
DM1265 12–0606/0612
DM1266 12–0619/0624
LCT6014</td></tr>
<tr><td>UN BALLO IN
MASCHERA</td><td>Verdi</td><td>July, 1943</td><td>2BA5487/5496
2BA5500/5505
2BA5508/5518
2BA5525/5529</td><td>78 DM0100/0116
DB9075/9091 (Auto)
33 QALP10057/8
FJLP5033/4
45</td><td>

LCT6007

WCT6007 (499–0095/0103)</td></tr>
<tr><td>AIDA</td><td>Verdi</td><td>July, 1946</td><td>2BA5951/5990</td><td>78 DB6392/6411
DB9131/9150 (Auto)

33 QALP10010/13
FJLP5005/8

45 7ER5037 (Excerpts)
7ERQ122 (Excerpts)</td><td>M1174 11–9911/20
M1175 11–9931/9940
DM1174 11–9921/9930
DM1175 11–9941/9950
LCT6400
LCT1101 (Excerpts)
LCT1035 (Excerpts)
WCT31/2 (17–0145/0164)
WCT1101 (Excerpts)
WCT51 17–0340 (Excerpts)</td></tr>
</table>

PART 3

LIST OF RECORDED TITLES

(The numbers following each entry indicate the pages on which the details of the various recordings can be found.)

INDEX

Opera Biographies

An Arno Press Collection

Albani, Emma. **Forty Years of Song.** With a Discography by W. R. Moran. [1911]

Biancolli, Louis. **The Flagstad Manuscript.** 1952

Bispham, David. **A Quaker Singer's Recollections.** 1921

Callas, Evangelia and Lawrence Blochman. **My Daughter Maria Callas.** 1960

Calvé, Emma. **My Life.** With a Discography by W. R. Moran. 1922

Corsi, Mario. **Tamagno, Il Più Grande Fenomeno Canoro Dell'Ottocento.** With a Discography by W. R. Moran. 1937

Cushing, Mary Watkins. **The Rainbow Bridge.** With a Discography by W. R. Moran. 1954

Eames, Emma. **Some Memories and Reflections.** With a Discography by W. R. Moran. 1927

Gaisberg, F[rederick] W[illiam]. **The Music Goes Round.** 1942

Gigli, Beniamino. **The Memoirs of Beniamino Gigli.** 1957

Hauk, Minnie. **Memories of a Singer.** 1925

Henschel, Horst and Ehrhard Friedrich. **Elisabeth Rethberg:** Ihr Leben und Künstlertum. 1928

Hernandez Girbal, F. **Julian Gayarre:** El Tenor de la Voz de Angel. 1955

Heylbut, Rose and Aimé Gerber. **Backstage at the Metropolitan Opera** (Originally published as **Backstage at the Opera**). 1937

Jeritza, Maria. **Sunlight and Song:** A Singer's Life. 1929

Klein, Herman. **The Reign of Patti.** With a Discography by W. R. Moran. 1920

Lawton, Mary. **Schumann-Heink:** The Last of the Titans. With a Discography by W. R. Moran. 1928

Lehmann, Lilli. **My Path Through Life.** 1914

Litvinne, Félia. **Ma Vie et Mon Art:** Souvenirs. 1933

Marchesi, Blanche. **Singer's Pilgrimage.** With a Discography by W. R. Moran. 1923

Martens, Frederick H. **The Art of the Prima Donna and Concert Singer.** 1923

Maude, [Jenny Maria Catherine Goldschmidt]. **The Life of Jenny Lind.** 1926

Maurel, Victor. **Dix Ans de Carrière, 1887-1897.** 1897

Mingotti, Antonio. **Maria Cebotari,** Das Leben Einer Sangerin. [1950]

Moore, Edward C. **Forty Years of Opera in Chicago.** 1930

Moore, Grace. **You're Only Human Once.** 1944

Moses, Montrose J. **The Life of Heinrich Conried.** 1916

Palmegiani, Francesco. **Mattia Battistini:** Il Re Dei Baritoni. With a Discography by W. R. Moran. [1949]

Pearse, [Cecilia Maria de Candia] and Frank Hird. **The Romance of a Great Singer.** A Memoir of Mario. 1910

Pinza, Ezio and Robert Magidoff. **Ezio Pinza:** An Autobiography. 1946

Rogers, Francis. **Some Famous Singers of the 19th Century.** 1914

Rosenthal, Harold [D.] **Great Singers of Today.** 1966

Ruffo, Titta. **La Mia Parabola:** Memorie. With a Discography by W. R. Moran. 1937

Santley, Charles. **Reminiscences of My Life.** With a Discography by W. R. Moran. 1909

Slezak, Leo. **Song of Motley:** Being the Reminiscences of a Hungry Tenor. 1938

Stagno Bellincioni, Bianca. **Roberto Stagno e Gemma Bellincioni Intimi** *and* Bellincioni, Gemma, **Io e il Palcoscenico:** Trenta e un anno di vita artistica. With a Discography by W. R. Moran. 1943/1920. Two vols. in one.

Tetrazzini, [Luisa]. **My Life of Song.** 1921

Teyte, Maggie. **Star on the Door.** 1958

Tibbett, Lawrence. **The Glory Road.** With a Discography by W. R. Moran. 1933

Traubel, Helen and Richard G. Hubler. **St. Louis Woman.** 1959

Van Vechten, Carl. **Interpreters.** 1920

Wagner, Charles L. **Seeing Stars.** 1940